Trade, Debt and Growth in Latin America

Pergamon Titles of Related Interest

Agarwala THE NEW INTERNATIONAL ECONOMIC ORDER: An Overview
Jorge FOREIGN DEBT AND LATIN AMERICAN ECONOMIC DEVELOPMENT
Klein PRICES, WAGES AND BUSINESS CYCLES: A Dynamic Theory
Puyana de Palacios ECONOMIC INTEGRATION AMONG UNEQUAL PARTNERS: The Case of the Andean Group
Seiber INTERNATIONAL BORROWING BY DEVELOPING COUNTRIES

Related Journals*

ECONOMIC BULLETIN FOR EUROPE
LONG RANGE PLANNING
SOCIO-ECONOMIC PLANNING SCIENCES
WORLD DEVELOPMENT

***Free specimen copies available upon request**

Trade, Debt and Growth in Latin America

ANTONIO JORGE & JORGE SALAZAR CARRILLO
Florida International University
ENRIQUE P. SANCHEZ
Wharton Econometrics

PERGAMON PRESS
New York Oxford Toronto Sydney Paris Frankfurt

Pergamon Press Offices:

U.S.A.	Pergamon Press Inc., Maxwell House, Fairview Park, Elmsford, New York 10523, U.S.A.
U.K.	Pergamon Press Ltd., Headington Hill Hall, Oxford OX3 0BW, England
CANADA	Pergamon Press Canada Ltd., Suite 104, 150 Consumers Road, Willowdale, Ontario M2J 1P9, Canada
AUSTRALIA	Pergamon Press (Aust.) Pty. Ltd., P.O. Box 544, Potts Point, NSW 2011, Australia
FRANCE	Pergamon Press SARL, 24 rue des Ecoles, 75240 Paris, Cedex 05, France
FEDERAL REPUBLIC OF GERMANY	Pergamon Press GmbH, Hammerweg 6, D-6242 Kronberg-Taunus, Federal Republic of Germany

Library of Congress Cataloging in Publication Data

Main entry under title:

Trade, debt, and growth in Latin America.

Proceedings of the Conference on Latin American Trade and Economic Growth, sponsored by the Department of Economics at Florida International University and Wharton Econometrics Forecasting Associates; held in Miami, Florida, on March 7th and 8th, 1983.
1. Latin America--Commerce--Congresses. 2. Latin America--Foreign economic relations--Congresses.
3. Latin America--Economic conditions--1945- --Congresses. I. Jorge, Antonio, 1931- . II. Salazar-Carrillo, Jorge. III. Sanchez, Enrique P.
IV. Conference on Latin American Trade and Economic Growth (1983: Miami, Fla.) V. Florida International University. Dept. of Economics. VI. Wharton Econometrics Forecasting Associates.
HF3230.5.A46T72 1984 337.8 83-25116
ISBN 0-08-030981-X

Printed in the United States of America

TABLE OF CONTENTS

CONTRIBUTORS

F. Gerard Adams
Director of Economic Research Unit
Department of Economics
Univerity of Pennsylvania

Irma Tirado de Alonso
Associate Professor
Department of Economics
Florida International University

Donald E. Baer, Economist
Latin American and the Caribbean
The Royal Bank of Canada

Roger C. Bird
Vice President
World Economic Service
Wharton Econometrics

Compton Bourne, Professor
Department of Economics
University of the West Indies
St. Augustine, Trinidad-Tobago

Colin I. Bradford, Jr.
Associate Professor
Concilium on International Area Studies
Director, International Relations Program
Yale University

Eduardo R. Conesa, Director
Institute for the Integration
of Latin America
Inter-American Development Bank

Rober David Cruz
Assitant Professor
Department of Economics
Florida International University

Amitiva Dutt
Assistant Professor
Department of Economics
Florida International University

Juan Jose Echavarria,
Senior Researcher
Fedesarrollo
Colombia

Contributors (continued)

Roberto Fendt
Superintendente de Estudos e Pesquisas
FUNCEX

Manuel Gollas
Professor of Economics
El Colegio de Mexico

Francisco de Paula Gutierrez
Economist, DIEMEX
Wharton Econometrics

Mostafa F. Hassan
Courtesy Professor
Department of Economics
Florida International University

Hugo M. Herivtz
Assistant Professor
Department of Economics
Barry University

Wallace Joefield-Napier
Professor, Department of Economics
University of the West Indies
St. Augustine, Trinidad-Tobago

Antonio Jorge
Professor of Political Economy
Florida International University

Juan Lara
Economist, DIEMEX
Wharton Econometrics

Mickey D. Levy
Senior Vice-president and Chief Economist
Fidelity Bank of Philadelphia

J. Kenneth Lipner
Assistant Professor
Department of Economics
Florida International University

Lionel H. Olmer
Under Secretary for International Trade
United States Department of Commerce

Jorge Salazar-Carrillo,
Chairman and Professor
Department of Economics
Florida International University
Non-resident Staff Member
Brookings Institution

Edward K. Smith
Former Director,
International Banking Center
Florida International University

Enrique P. Sanchez
Director, Latin American Service
Wharton Econometrics

J. Antonio Villamil
Vice President and International Economist
Southeast Bank, N.A.

TRADE, DEBT AND GROWTH IN LATIN AMERICA

by

Antonio Jorge
Jorge Salazar-Carrillo
Enrique P. Sanchez

PREFACE

The present book consists of the proceedings of the Conference on Latin American Trade and Economic Growth, sponsored by the Department of Economics at Florida International University and Wharton Econometrics Forecasting Associates. The event took place in the City of Miami, Florida, on March 7th and 8th 1983.

This work could be considered a sequel to the publication of the proceedings of a previous conference, sponsored by Florida International University's Department of Economics and the International Banking Center, on the closely related topic of the foreign debt and economic development of Latin America. In that book our main purpose was the examination of the external debt problem as it affected the region as a whole and certain individual countries in particular. What we now seek to accomplish is to explore the inter-relations of the foreign debt with the international trade of the area and its prospects for economic development.

It is becoming increasingly evident that the issues in question cannot be productively or realistically contemplated in isolation and much less resolved independently of one another. The interdependence of these variables has by now become inextricable and its consequent reverberations will decisively affect the working of the world economy. Now more than ever it is clear that the economic integration of the international trade, financial and monetary systems, is a reality. The well-being of developed and developing nations are dependent upon the outcome of their mutual interactions and the coordination of their policies.

In light of the above, it is highly important to emphasize the need of a vigorous recovery in the developed nations as a necessary condition for a resurgence of economic growth in the developing countries. Stimulating the linkages between both groups of countries is essential for the restoration of world trade and the health of the global economy. In turn, this conditions must be fulfilled in order to resume the orderly transfer of resources from debtor to creditor countries and thus satisfy outstanding debt obligations.

Recent events in the world economy may well be seen at a future point in time as a watershed. Structural changes in the international world system will concomitantly require new perceptions and more flexible and accomodative behavior by all parties involved. The increasing complexity of the system poses both grave risks of world disequilibria and also the opportunity to creatively resolve the manifold challenges confronting all nations.

Both the conference and the book have been made possible by the enthusiastic support and participation of the local and international banking and business communities. In a special manner, the editors would like to express their gratitude to Angel Fernandez Varela, Chairman of the Board of Consolidated Bank of Miami and Carlos Arboleya, Vice-Chairman of Barnett Bank of South Florida, for their financial generosity and personal support. We take this opportunity to recognize once again the persevering efforts of Robert Schwarzreich, a graduate student of economics at F.I.U., and Pat Egner, of Wharton Econometrics, who were an essential element in the editing of this manuscript. Finally, our special recognition of Lourdes Gonzalez-Novo, who, not only was a key support in the organization of the conference, but also went through many hours of patient typing to get this book to press.

BY WAY OF A BRIEF OVERVIEW

Antonio Jorge

There has been a stagnation in the volume of world trade evident during the course of this decade, while the growth of world production for the same period has also closely resembled the performance of trade. The declining trend in volume of world trade is clearly signified by the decrease in the average annual rate of advance of the volume of world exports between 1963-73 and 1973-81. While for the former periods it was 8.5 percent, for the latter it had been reduced to a much lower 3.5 percent.

In terms of value, world trade experienced a 1 percent contraction in 1981 relative to the preceding year, representing a total of $2,000 billion. Likewise, 1982 was similarly disappointing in performance. The eighties have thus sharply contrasted with the buoyant seventies, characterized by a yearly average rate of growth of 20percent. These recent changes, it should be noted, mainly reflected the decline in unit values expressed in dollars. These had diminished by about 1 percent in 1981, while they had increased by 14percent annual average for the decennium of the seventies. As we know, previous to the present difficulties of the world economy, the tempo of world trade growth amply surpassed that of the global expansion in output, as has been the case for the last two and a half decades.

As for the distribution of trade between developed market economies and the group of less developed countries, a rough division of their relative shares in terms of world exports would assign from slightly over three-fifths to less than two-thirds of the total to the former and about 27 percent to the latter. Of this last figure, approximately 14 percent would correspond to oil-exporting developing countries, with the other developing countries accounting for the balance of 13 percent. It is also worth noting that although there has been a decrease in the eighties relative to the preceding decade in the intradeveloped countries' market for exports, it still absorbs about 70 percent of the total exports of these countries. In a related context, it should be pointed out that more than two-thirds of the developing countries' exports are destined to the markets of developed nations, with only a little above one-quarter of their total exports constituting trade among themselves.

Concerning the composition of world exports, it is of great importance to remember that, as of the end of the decade of the seventies, the proportion of manufactured products in the exports of developed countries was about 3/4 of the total. By contrast, primary products represented about the same proportion of the total exports of developing market economies. Nonetheless, developing countries have succeeded in expanding their participation in the market for manufactured goods imported by developed nations from 7 percent in 1970 to 13 percent in 1980. This advance has taken place while the imports of manufactures as a fraction of GNP in these nations increased from about 6 percent in 1970 to more than 9 percent in 1980. For such progress to take place, the less developed countries had to mount a sustained effort to increase their exports of manufactures goodd among themselves), expanded at an annual average rate of 12 percent for the 1960s and 1970s. Still, the total value of this category of exports by developing nations amounted to approximately only 1.3 percent of the industrial countries GDP. Given that the rate of growth of market penetration by less developed countries of the markets for industrial goods of the developed nations advanced at an annual rate of 8 percent for the 1970's, in contrast to a mere 5 percent import penetration rate for all sources, there remains hope of a gradually improving position for less developed countries in these markets.

However, price developments have not, on an overall basis, favored developing countries. The prices of manufactured goods exported by developed countries went up from an index value of 100 in the base year 1975 to 150 in 1981. During the same period, the export prices of primary commodities (with the exception of crude petroleum) advanced from 100 to 147. It should be pointed out that for the entire category of food commodities, the terminal value was only 139. Figures for 1982 seem to indicate that the performance of the overall index of prices for primary commodities may be still weaker for this period than it was in 1981, when it had already fallen 15 percent from its 1980 level. Most of the low income and many of the middle-income less developed countries were, and still are, affected by these price changes. Given the 325 percent price increase in crude petroleum from 1975 to 1981, the impact on the non-oil exporting developing countries has been a very severe one. Compounding the problems of the low-income members of the group of less developed countries is the fact that they account for only 2 percent of world exports.

As for Latin America, a brief review of some telling data will suffice to highlight some elements of its trade panorama. The tempo of the area's exports began to accelerate towards the middle of the 1960s. In fact, between 1970 and 1981, the value of exported goods increased at an average annual rate of 19 percent. It should be noted that due to a decline in the unit value of exports, there was a value decline in exports of 10 percent in 1982. These developments were accompanied by a process of export diversification. Sales of industrial goods have represented for certain years about 20 percent of the total value of exports. Also, the range of agricultural and other primary goods exported has widened considerably during this period.

There has been a concomitant evolution in the trend of Latin America's imports. Since the late sixties they have been expanding vigorously as the area's economies have become more open. In contrast to the strategy of the fifties and early sixties, the Latin nations are now striking a more balanced position between an inward-looking, import-substitution approach to development, and an outward-directed, international trade-static comparative-advantage-guided, growth pattern.

Just as in the case of exports, the value of imports for the area decreased by 19 percent in 1982. However, the main cause for this contraction stood in opposition to the origin of the decline in foreign sales. It was due in the main to a decrease of 16 percent in the quantum of imported goods. It should be kept in mind that this decline has adverse implications for the growth of the area, given the high proportion of intermediate and capital goods, as well as of fuel, in the total of imported goods.

As for the terms of trade relationship, it experienced a new deterioration of 6 percent in 1982, after the 7 percent loss suffered in 1981. In general, for those countries other than the exporters of oil, after a brief improvement of the terms of trade in 1972-73, these registered a level for the rest of the decade of the seventies much like that prevailing in the sixties, which in turn was itself lower than the corresponding relation during the decennium of the fifties.

Undoubtedly, Latin America's increasing participation in the international trade system has been marked by success. The figures amply demonstrate that the region has been able to establish itself in the world system and expand its level of involvement at a rapid pace. While this will greatly enhance the growth prospects of the area, facilitating its occurrence through the acquisition of international resources, it will also make Latin America more vulnerable to the fluctuations of the world economy. As a matter of fact, the unfavorable behavior of the economy in 1981 and 1982 is very much linked to developments in the international situation. This is not to deny that internal factors, especially in relation to fiscal and exchange rate policy were not of major importance in some countries, as political ones were of decisive influence in others. It only asserts that as the network of global interrelations becomes more intrecate, exogenous variables will increasingly determine the constraints and upper limits to growth open to the region.

On the average, and abstracting from the sharp fluctuations in growth experienced by the area during the seventies and up to 1980, the GNP of Latin America expanded at an acceptable rate. On the average, the annual rate of growth of this indicator was 6 percent for the period in question, as was almost the case during the preceding decade of the sixties. In 1981 the rate of advance has decreased to 1.5 percent and during 1982 a negative rate of growth close to 1 percent was registered. In general, the growth history of the area has been a fairly good one and compares favorably with the records of developing countries and other developing areas.

Meanwhile, the pace at which the region integrated with the international economy has been a rapid one indeed. As is well known, world trade has grown faster than world output. The former advanced at an annual rate of 5.1 percent from 1955 to 1980, and at an even faster tempo of 6.9 percent from 1965 to 1980. Latin America has moved to open its economy at a pace above that of the global economy.

The commerce of Central and South America with the world expanded by more than tenfold between 1963 and 1981. Latin America's trade with the developed countries accounts for two-thirds of its total international trade. Specifically, Central and South America's trade with North America increased by about tenfold for the previously cited period of 1963-81. Concurrently, intra-regional trade was augmented by fifteenfold. It is also of considerable interest to note that the trade of the area with developing countries, including its own intra-regional commerce, grew by more than seventeenfold for the indicated period.

In order for self-sustained development to continue to take place at rates comparable to those of the decades of the sixties and seventies, and for the area to meet its external debt obligations in an orderly fashion, Latin America's external trade must keep on growing at a good pace, intra-regional economic cooperation has to be reinvigorated, and an adequate flow and composition of financial resources has to be made available to the region.

Latin America's external debt has been accumulating at a 29 percent annual rate since 1977 and until 1981. Last year there was a drastic slowing of the growth pace to a modest 7 percent and the total figure for the debt reached $274 billion. Meanwhile, the ratio of external debt service to the value of exports climbed from 20 percent in 1977 to almost 30 percent in 1981, and will certainly be still higher in 1982. During the last year, interest remittances absorbed 50 percent of the export earnings of Argentina, Brazil and Chile, and 44 percent of those of Mexico. Worse yet, the relation between debt service payments and new credits to the area, which was 48 percent in 1976, has ascended to 80 percent for 1980 and 1981. The meaning of this, of course, is that the flow of financial capital to the area has diminished considerably.

As an ever larger portion of the external debt has become short term (constituting approximately 80 percent of the total outstanding by 1981), and as it has grown increasingly concentrated in the hands of private banking institutions extending it on purely commercial terms, and which by their very nature are unable under the present circumstances to sustain the momentum of the lending spiral they helped to generate back in 1974-75, the Latin American debt situation has progressively turned bleaker. If we add to this the exceptionally high level of real interest holding at present, the unfavorable portfolio position of banks, the high risks and poor immediate prospects of debtor countries, the limited capability of international institutions to extend concessional credits in the amount (or for the purpose and time required), and last, but certainly not least in importance, both as direct cause and contributing condition to this scenario, the deep and prolonged world recession, we begin to fathom the gravity of the predicament in which the world system as a whole and the individual economies of developed and developing nations find themselves enmeshed.

The interesting, yet fearful aspect of the panorama facing developed and less developed, public as well as private institutions is that a positive sum gam kind of solution is the only viable one. That is, either all parties to this situation cooperate in solving it, in which case all will benefit individually, or the outcome will not be favorable to any of the participants.

Clearly, Latin America needs both the access to the markets and the financial resources of developed countries which will enable it to maintain the developmental pace of the last two decades. Only under such conditions could the area hope to honor its debt obligations to the rest of the world. The world economy has become too interdependent for any other formula to work.

The circumstances prevailing towards the middle of the seventies, when commercial banks were willing and able to help finance the deficit on the current account of the balance of payments of Latin American countries, have radically changed at present. An illustration of the situation now facing the area is given by the fact that during 1982 there was a 35 percent decrease in the net flow of capital resources accruing to the non oil-exporting countries of the area.

The double danger of protectionism gaining the upper hand in the international economy, and of the external flow of resources drying up, thus forcing a reduction in the high rates of capital formation typical of the area in the past, are very serious possibilities whose ominous consequences are obvious. Again, there is scant comfort in imagining that partial approaches to these multifaceted problems are possible. Only a profound rethinking of the global strategies, criteria and policies in the relations of developed and developing nations, as they operate in the context of both domestic and international, private and public institutions, offers any hope for the resolution of the world economy's crisis.

In the particular case of Latin America, continued access to the markets of developed countries, particularly those for manufactured goods, and renewed efforts to stengthen intra-regional trade are necessary conditions for the reestablishment of the economic health of the area. Concomitantly, the external flow of private and public funds to the area must be resumed if the wherewithal for these efforts is to be found at all.

It is now clear that export expansion, especially of manufactured goods, will prove vital to the continued development of the area. Parallel to this and in a complementary policy move, a much higher degree of regional cooperation and trade will also contribute to the expansion of markets and the rationalization of the resource allocation process, as well as enhance the efficiency of the area's national economies. In an expanding world economy, there is no reason for the share of exports of developing countries, among them the Latin American nations, not to continue expanding as it did during the last decade. The same applies to the proportion exported by developing countries of the manufactured goods consumed by developed nations, particularly when, as in the case of Latin America, the market penetration rate for these goods just remained stable during the seventies.

It would seem justified to conclude these notes by quoting, perhaps rather extensively, from some observations by this author and his colleague Jorge Salazar-Carillo, in a book recently edited by them in conjunction with Rene P. Higonnet.

> There is enough reason to worry about the course of events in the short and medium run, considering the more than eightfold growth in Latin America's total public debt outstanding over the decade of the seventies. The fact should be kept in mind that the area contributes slightly more than half the total of service payments made on the developing countries' debt, while it holds about 35 percent of the total, of which more than 57 percent is held by private banks. Nonetheless, our final assessment should be an optimistic one, due to the simple reason that the area's developmental potential would amply justify it. In dealing with developmental processes one must keep in mind that they normally do not proceed along a smooth and perfectly divisible ascending path. Intelligent policy, even intelligent private decision making, has to take into account the discontinuities and indivisibilities which typify the evolution of development at various stages. What is of decisive importance is to realize that, in accordance with every reasonable estimate, the potential for continued growth exists and it is highly probable that it will historically materialize.

A renewed effort to increase the volume of exports should no doubt have a high priority in the policy package of Latin American nations. In this context, it is interesting to note that the annual rate of increase in this area's export of manufactures has been very high, at times greater than that of any other region, since the early seventies onwards. In spite of this observed growth, while Latin America accounts for half the industrial output of the developing countries, it contributes only a fifth of the exports of manufactures originating in these countries. The policy of export promotion requires urgent attention because of another factor which greatly influences the external accounts of the area. Preliminary data for 1980 seem to indicate that about 30 percent of the foreign exchange earning of oil-importing countries went to pay for their oil imports. As recently as 1978 the corresponding figure was only 21 percent.

Latin America is not only the most economically developed region of the Third World, but also the one with the brightest prospects in the short and medium term for high and sustained growth. Under the most reasonable alternative scenarios that could be postulated at the time of this printing as a basis for forecasting the evolution of the area's economy, one would be led to conclude that both its potential and the probabilities for its realization are highly favorable, in absolute terms and also in terms relative to the prospects of other regions.

In the subject of our concern, and given the present specific traits of the debt situation, in the less developed countries in general and Latin America in particular, expectations and misperceptions have a greater weight than usual in molding future realities. As a result, we may also quite insensibly fall prey to the famous fallacy well known to all beginners in the field of economics: Post Hoc, Ergo Propter Hoc. If the flow of resources or its accompanying conditions are such as to curtail or hinder the normal servicing of the debt and the developmental process itself, this will tend to bring about the very results which are often feared by the more pessimistic observers. In that case, their inclination will be to attribute the experienced reality to the operation of some inevitable forces that predetermined the outcome itself rather than to the very same policies which are adopted in order to forestall its occurrence.[1]

[1] Foreign Debt and Latin American Economic Development, (New York: Pergamon Press, 1982), pp. 19, 29.

REFERENCES

CEPAL, "America Latina en la Nueva Estrategia Internacional de Desarrollo," Nos. 311/313, febrero-marzo 1980.

CEPAL, "Balance Preliminar de la Economia Latino Americana en 1982," No. 373, enero, 1983.

CEPAL, "La Evolucion Economica de America Latina en 1981," No. 355/356, enero, 1982.

Chenery, Hollis B., "Interaction between Industrialization and Exports," World Bank Reprint Series: Number 150, 1980.

General Agreement on Tariffs and Trade, International Trade 1981-82, Geneva, 1982.

Hughes H. and Waelbroeck J., "Can Developing-Country Exports Keep Growing in the 1980s," World Bank Reprint Series: Number 194, 1981.

Inter-American Development Bank, Economic and Social Progress in Latin America, 1982 Report, Washington, DC 1982.

International Monetary Fund, World Economic Outlook, Washington, DC 1982.

Jorge, Antonio, Jorge Salazar-Carrillo, and Rene P. Higonnet, Foreign Debt and Latin American Economic Development (New York: Pergamon Press, 1982).

Overseas Development Council, U.S. Foreign Policy and the Third World, Agenda 1982 (New York: Praeger Publishers, 1982).

World Bank, World Development Report, 1982 (New York: Oxford University Press, 1982).

PERSPECTIVES ON LATIN AMERICA AND THE WORLD ECONOMIC OUTLOOK*

by F. Gerard Adams

Developments in 1982 have been disappointing to the many who expected that the world economy would pull out of stagnation. While on a worldwide basis recovery is not yet a reality, in the United State an economic turnaround is under way, and the other industrial countries should show some improvement as the year progresses. Prospects are still deteriorating in some developing countries, particularly in Latin America, where the burden of huge debts and debt service are impacting on economic and social development. But we are hopeful that recovery in the industrial world will serve to get the world economy through its current period of crisis.

More than ever the world's economic blocks are interrelated. The industrial economies, with the United States in the lead, are pulling themselves up by their own bootstraps. The developing economies are greatly dependent on the economic recovery of the industrial world as a market for their primary products and for their burgeoning manufacturing output. In turn the industrial countries rely heavily on markets in the LDCs, as is amply demonstrated by the relationship between the United States and Latin America or by the connection between Japan and the Pacific Basin.

The situation of the world economy is greatly complicated at this point by past and present movements of petroleum prices and by the overwhelming burden of debt which some countries have accumulated. Consequently, in addition to an appraisal of the "most probable" path of economic developments, it is important to consider the risks associated with world financial problems. It goes almost without saying that these risks are particularly associated with the situation in Latin America, and the threatened world financial crisis.

World Economic Situation

From a worldwide perspective, 1982 was a year of growth recession. Growth declined to 0.3 percent worldwide and for the industrial countries it averaged near zero. This meant sharp declines for some countries, the United States for example, and stagnation or only very modest growth for others like Japan, Germany, and the United Kingdom. In the less developed countries, growth also slowed radically with significant declines in both the oil-exporting and the oil-importing LDCs. The centrally planned block also showed a slowdown to less than half its desired growth rate.

The recession has resulted in the most serious buildup of unemployment since the Great Depression, with unemployment rates in excess of 10 percent in the United States and the United Kingdom and with total OECD unemployment now above the 30 million mark. But there has been some positive payoff, though at high cost. Inflation rates are down worldwide, except in Latin America, to more bearable level. Equally significant is the substantial decline in interest rates as a result of change of monetary policy in the United States. The impact is not only on the domestic economy through improvement in prospects for investment, particularly in housing, but there is also significant international impact. There has been some easing of the over valuation of the U.S. dollar and some relief for the interest burden of the debtor countries. Prospects for 1983 and beyond are somewhat more optimistic.

Though signs of improvement are still very modest, recovery appears to be on the

* This paper is based on forecasts prepared by the World Economic Service and the Latin American Service of Wharton Econometrics, Philadelphia, Pa. Wharton Econometrics has just completed extensive studies of a world financial crisis.

horizon at last. In the United States strength in housing and autos and the end of a huge inventory rundown have set the stage for recovery. The United States alone cannot act as the "locomotive" for the world economy, but with lower interest rates and falling petroleum prices other industrial countries should soon also show some gains. Wharton Econometrics forecasts a gradual turnaround of the world economy with modest growth in 1983 and beyond. The recovery will be sluggish at an annual rate of 2-3 percent for the world as a whole—lower than the 4 percent per year of the recovery of the mid-1970s. The growth of world markets for primary products and manufactures should provide a welcome boost for the LDCs as well in 1983 and 1984.

A brief tour through the major world regions will highlight the prospects for 1983 and beyond.

Industrial Countries

The industrial countries continue to suffer from unemployment and stagnant demand. The easing of inflation has made it possible to lower interest rates and to turn policies somewhat more in the direction of international stimulus. The United States is on the threshold of an economic turnaround. The inventory cycle appears to be reaching its end. Consumer purchases of automobiles and other goods have begun to pick up. Housing is making a much improved showing, with housing starts of 1.7 million in January. While the financial community is still concerned about the potential impact of large continued deficits on financial markets, the fundamental policy problem of the Reagan Administration appears to be somewhat closer to resolution. On one hand, the supply-siders have pushed for the large income tax cuts which account in part for the deficits in the $200 billion range. On the other side were the monetarists, who had sought to reduce inflation through control of the money supply. It has been six months now since the Federal Reserve signaled an easing of its tight monetary guidelines. Interest rates have dropped sharply, but have not declined further recently in view of fears that the Federal Reserve will be forced to reassert its control over the money supply as deficits increase. Much depends consequently on a willingness of the Congress to compromise by going at least part way toward improved budgetary balance. If that occurs, further easing of interest rates, particularly on the long end of the yield curve, is likely. In any case, substantial improvement in economic activity is expected, with GNP in 1983 2.4 percent higher than the comparable 1982 figure.

Other industrial countries are behind in the cycle. Some recovery is expected in Japan and Canada, and the Western European recovery is likely to come later. Germany has produced a discouraging pessimistic forecast of growth of less than 1 percent, after three years of slump. France, which has had to rein in its economy after excessive expansion in the first years of the socialist government, is likely to show no growth at all in 1983 and only modest expansion thereafter. Italy, too, will show unfavorable results in 1983. The United Kingdom, on the other hand, will show a slight pickup this year and next, some 1.7 percent, but the upturn will not be enough to bring down the record unemployment near 11 percent. Japan's growth rate will continue in the 2.5-3 percent level for the next couple of years, well below its average rate of the 1970s. And that assumes that exports, which are slumping, will not be affected too much more by slowing world demand and by rising protectionist barriers. All in all, the situation of the industrial economies remains stagnant, though a recovery in the United States, lower worldwide interest rates and inflation, and perhaps a gradual decline in oil prices may provide an upward boost later in 1983 and on into 1984.

Non-Oil-Exporting Developing Countries

The situation of the LDCs, particularly the non-oil-exporting developing countries, continues to be threatened by the prolonged recession in the industrial world. With export receipts growing slowly and high service payments on foreign debt, many developing countries have been forced to reassess their growth prospects. We will be discussing the situation of the Latin American countries at this conference. They are, of course, the outstanding example of difficulties, though they are not the only example. In Africa conditions have long been disastrous. Even the new industrial countries of the Pacific Basin, which heretofore appeared to be immune to the world slowdown, are being affected.

The heavy debt burdens are having serious repercussions. The hope that some of these problems would be eased through rapid increases in exports has faded as markets in the industrial world are closing because of economic stagnation or because of protectionism, and other developing countries simply lack the financial resources to increase their purchases. To deal with debt obligations, we will see Latin American growth being cut back to negative figures. But the imbalances on current account are so large that even heroic actions on trade will not offset them. Debt restructuring just barely accomplished in Mexico is becoming necessary in almost all Latin America.

The Oil Producers

The decline in energy demand as a result of the economic slowdown and as a result of conservation has had particular impact on the oil producers. As these pages are being written we are at a decision point in the controversy within OPEC with respect to the price of oil. Excess supply is forcing a downward erosion of prices, though it is not yet clear how far the adjustment will be allowed to go. In any case the surplus of available crude supply suggests that even with some recovery of the world economy and an end to inventory decumulation, crude oil price will not strengthen significantly for some time. The oil-producing countries are coming into a slowdown associated with weakness in the sales of their principal export, and some of them are having severe difficulties. Many producers—Nigeria, Indonesia, Libya, Venezuela—have seen their earnings diminish to the point where they can no longer meet their external obligations and carry on their development plans.

Centrally Planned Economies

In the centrally planned economies the sources of the difficulty are somewhat different, though the slowdown is nonetheless just as real. Production targets in industry and agriculture have not been met. The policy situation is only the most glaring example. Declines in oil export volumes, declines in export prices, insufficient short-term credits, and debt service burdens, in some cases, combine to force a reduction in imports of capital goods. This lowers chances for gains in productivity and, with slow labor force growth, reduces already sluggish prospects for growth.

World Financial Crisis

The risks to the world economy are almost as serious and immediate today as at any time in the postwar period. The events observed in world financial markets since mid-1982 correspond closely to what we have seen in our simulation studies as a "crunch" case. The picture can be summarized as follows: Many major borrowing countries have encountered balance of payments and debt servicing problems. The commercial bank lenders have sought to reduce their exposure in international debt markets. Numerous countries, among them the major debtor countries in Latin America, have asked for rescheduling and IMF lending facilities. With the help of the IMF, the BIS, and the central banks of the industrial countries, outright defaults have been avoided. Indeed, the IMF has been able to persuade the commercial banks to continue to extend loans to the debtor countries and to smooth rescheduling more effectively than had been anticipated. This process has been carried on repeatedly during the past few months with most countries of Latin America and others in Eastern Europe and Africa being covered. On one hand, the process has been remarkably successful, and the extension of the IMF credit base makes it possible to continue for some further period. On the other hand, each one of the rescheduling agreements has been supported by a detailed IMF prescription to cut back imports and, where possible, to expand exports. Some economists have argued that the fault does not lie with the IMF since similar steps would be required in any case. But the effect is the same: a huge simultaneous reduction in imports by a large part of the world. The feedback impact on the industrial countries is illustrated by the sharp reduction of U.S. exports last summer when Mexico stopped its imports.

The question, then, is whether the world economy can continue to recover in the face of significant cutbacks in world trade.

What are the prospects that the crisis can be weathered? Assuming that defaults can be avoided and that the world banking system can continue to operate without significant interruption, prospects hang greatly on a recovery of the world's industrial economies. If the U.S. recovery proceeds and if the other industrial countries gradually join in the recovery in 1984, a resurgence of world export markets for primary commodities and for manufactures can help the debtor countries. Improvement in primary commodity prices and some decline in petroleum prices would help, though the latter would cause additional difficulties for oil-producing countries like Mexico and Venezuela. While debt restructuring appears so far to have been successful, the resulting adjustments in economic activity and imports in Latin American and in other debtor countries impose a heavy burden on the world economy.

The debtor countries will not be a good market for the products of the industrial world for many years to come. The IMF restructuring efforts are thus largely a "band aid" meant to tide the debtors over until better times. There is need to consider more fundamental solutions. One way would be a systematic effort to wipe out or neutralize some of the excess debt overhang, estimated by some to be near $100 billion. A variety of proposals along these lines are being floated. They would involve refinancing some of the outstanding debt into long-term low interest rate loans from public institutions. Perhaps the commercial banks might also be persuaded to wipe out some of the problem loans. Such a proposal encounters great political and institutional difficulties, but it would go a long way toward easing the impact of the debt burden on the world economy, to the benefit of debtor and creditor countries alike.

LATIN AMERICAN OUTLOOK UNDER IMF CONDITIONALITY

Enrique P. Sanchez

Background

There is little doubt that 1982 was a year of crisis for Latin America. It was the first year to register a decline in GDP since the U.N.'s Economic Commission for Latin America (ECLA) began to keep comparable, reliable records in 1945. Practically all the large countries (with the exception of Colombia) were forced to go through major foreign and domestic adjustments. Table 1 summarizes the financial events leading to what could easily be called the Latin American financial crisis. This table shows how all the Latin American countries, caught by what Pedro Pablo Kuczynski calls the "scissors effect"[1] (sharp drops in commodity prices and rapid increases in interest rates), dried up their reserves, suffered serious capital outflows, were forced to implement import and exchange controls, experienced massive devaluations and finally had to resort to the International Monetary Fund, requesting, in most cases, a renegotiation of their debt.

This table is helpful in establishing a pattern of measures, adopted by government officials when a country faces simultaneously a depletion of reserves and a cutback in foreign financing.[2] This "pattern" of response includes the following measures, most often—but not always—in this order:

1. Increases in domestic interest rates.

2. Implementation (or intensification) of import controls (through licenses, bans, effective delays, etc.) and tariff increases.

3. Exchange controls and devaluations (often including a multiple-tier exchange rate system).

4. Gradual unification of the multiple-tier exchange rate system into a single exchange rate.

5. Simultaneous request for IMF intervention and debt renegotiation, including a temporary cessation of amortization payments (usually for around 90 days).

6. After all these shock, measures the domestic financial system is destabilized and the government either nationalizes the banking system (as in Mexico) or takes over some private banks (as in Brazil, Chile, Venezuela), absorbing, consequently, part of the private foreign debt into the public debt.

Despite the early warnings of the first half of 1982, the response to the Latin American crisis did not come until the fourth quarter of the year, when the situation had reached a stage where bridge loans to avoid default had to be arranged in 24 hours. The response to the crisis came in three interlinked ways: emergency loans, stand-by loans combined with those and from the compensatory fund for losses in export revenues, and commercial bank loans (as an IMF requirement to pull these countries out).

The IMF Conditions

The bail-out did not come without strings, however. It came tied, as usual, to the IMF's conditions of tight monetary restrictions and strict fiscal constraint. These conditions also follow a clear pattern: the public deficit as a percentage of GDP should be reduced to about half of what it had been before the intervention, imports must be constrained (by exchange-rate measures) in the coming year; export subsidies must be lifted, exchange rates must be unified and floating (keeping a "real effective exchange rate"), domestic real interest rates must not be negative, and wage increases must be minimized. Table 2 summarizes the assumptions of economic policies suggested by the IMF. It must be noted here that this table was constructed with secondary information, since neither the IMF nor the countries' authorities have made public all the conditions to which they agreed.

Table 2
IMF Assumptions of Economic Policies

Policy	Exchange Rate	Exports	Imports
Argentina	Unified rate floating	increase	restrain
Brazil	acceleration of mini-dev.*	increase	restrain
Chile	unified rate floating	increase	decline
Mexico	unified rate floating	increase	restrain
Peru	floating	increase	restrain

*The recent 30 percent devaluation was not considered during the official IMF talks.

In the past, such policies of constraint and austerity have been quite successful in stabilizing any particular country in which they were inplemented. The most recent example in a large Latin American country is that of Mexico in 1976-77, just before the oil boom. In that case, as in others, stability was returned to the country, but not to the target level established at the beginning of the program and with the social cost of, what was considered then, a steep deceleration of the economy (Mexico's growth decelerated from 5.6 percent in 1976 to 4.2 percent in 1977).[3] It must be remembered, too, that in 1978 Mexico discontinued its 1976 IMF-stabilization plan (responding to the social and oil-boom pressures) and as a result no further improvements were made in controlling inflation.

It was also observed that in some cases (such as Argentina from 1978 to 1981, and Chile from 1978 to 1982) a quick liberalization of the economy created such external competitiveness that domestic industries could not survive (partly because the competitors were the aggressive Asian NICs). Nevertheless, it must be recognized that in Argentina and Chile a policy of currency overvaluation was one of the instruments used to reduce inflation. If a "real effective exchange-rate" policy is applied now, as specified in the IMF requirements, then the competition might be "fairer" and domestic industry might not suffer as much as in the prior cases of Argentina and Chile. But, on the other hand, until full domestic adjustment is achieved, a "real effective exchange-rate" policy will create additional inflationary pressures in countries where inflation is already quite high.

It is argued that these inflationary pressures will be compensated by monetary or fiscal measures, such as the reduction of the fiscal deficit (as a proportion of GDP). The IMF requirements clearly specify that such a reduction is to be obtained by reducing current expenses and/or increasing tax revenues. Applying the former will dismantle the unemployment "safety net" which in these countries is the public sector (usually there is no unemployment compensation system as in the United States and certain European countries), thus reducing personal income. The latter measure, tax increases, will also reduce personal income and/or create inflationary pressures (unless the tax changes imply a major income distribution, an unlikely probability). Such a reduction in personal income will certainly contract domestic demand, at a time when international demand is expected to be relatively weak.

Latin American Outlook

The most disturbing point is that these policies (though successful when applied to any one individual country when others are in an "upturn"), will contribute, in combination with a weak recovery in the industrialized countries, to the continuation of the global Latin American recession. Under these conditions, our estimates for Latin American regional growth in 1983 show another 1.4 percent decline, with the two largest economies (Brazil and Mexico) each falling almost 3.0 percent and the next two largest economies (Argentina and Chile) showing very slight positive growth—only because their respective gross domestic products have already fallen more than 10 percent in the last year or two. Table 3 summarizes our growth estimates for the major countries in the region. In short, the adjustments will continue this year, and 1982-83 will be the first two consecutive years with negative rates of growth in regional GDP.

Table 3
Latin America: GDP
(percent change)

	1980	1981	1982	1983	1984
Argentina	1.4	-6.1	-4.0	2.5	4.2
Brazil	8.0	-1.9	.5	-2.9	2.6
Chile	7.5	5.3	-14.1	2.5	.0
Colombia	4.2	2.5	1.5	2.0	3.5
Mexico	8.3	8.1	-.5	-3.2	3.5
Peru	3.1	4.0	1.0	1.0	2.5
Venezuela	-1.1	.6	-2.8	-.9	1.9
Latin America	5.9	1.5	-1.2	-1.4	2.9

With this historical background and institutional setting, it is necessary to recognize that even in the best of cases the Latin American outlook for 1983 regarding growth is very gloomy—that indeed, Latin America is in crisis. The question at this point is, how much worse can this become and can it develop into a depression as it extends through 1984 and beyond? Or, what are the probabilities and conditions for a recovery?

Those countries which did not complete the necessary adjustments in 1982 will do so in 1983. The recent Brazilian and Venezuelan devaluations are the first signs in this direction.[4] Argentina, pressed by high inflation, the need to keep imports down, and a high speculative parallel market, will accelerate the official rate of mini-devaluations. Again, Colombia will most likely remain as the exception to these exchange rate adjustments.

The recent drop in oil prices, however, will undoubtedly ease the problem in the oil importers of the region. In Brazil, for example, a $6.00 decline in oil prices would bring about a $1.5 billion savings in imports.[5] But in the oil exporters (Ecuador, Mexico and Venezuela), the situation will not be easy at all. For each $1.00 decline in the price of crude oil (sustained throughout the whole year), Mexico would lose $580 million, Venezuela $570 million, and Ecuador, $36 million, annually. These prospects may force these countries to adopt any or several of the following measures:

- to cut back imports even further, in which case the rest of the region and the United States would also be affected, through the trade links (please see Appendix);

- to cut back or delay unilaterally interest payments—an unlikely probability, as it would threaten the already weak relations with the financial community and make furture lending extremely difficult;

- to request a new renegotiation of the debt or a capitalization of interest payments, until six months from now, when lower interest rates resulting from lower oil prices and a recovery in the industrialized countries reduce their financial constraint;

- to obtain advance payment for future deliveries of oil—though it could result in an extension of the oil glut; and

- to increase barter agreements and bilateral credit lines, in lieu of lack of financing.

Table 4 summarizes the current account deficits for the major Latin American countries, excluding the effects of the possible "responsive measures" outlined above. However, it must be noted here that the largest improvement in the current account balance will result from a further decline in interest rates. For example, for any one-percentage-point variation in interest rates, the debt service varies annually by $500 million in Brazil, by $500 million in Mexico, and by $300 million in Argentina.

Table 4
Current Account Balance
(in bill. US$)

	1979	1980	1981	1982	1983	1984
Argentina	-.550	-4.767	-4.057	-2.263	-1.956	-2.602
Brazil	-10.470	-12.900	-11.739	-12.982	-7.900	-7.301
Chile	-1.189	-1.971	-4.869	-2.540	-3.138	-3.192
Colombia	.490	-.121	-1.969	-2.400	-1.413	-1.410
Mexico	-4.876	-6.761	-12.997	-3.526	-3.733	-4.364
Peru	.729	-0.25	-1.680	-1.675	-1.600	-1.500
Venezuela	.350	4.728	4.045	-2.325	-1.957	-.758
Latin America	-17.249	-24.241	-38.122	-33.045	-24.108	-23.474

On the inflation front, the improvements will not be so great, as each country absorbs the effects of the numerous devaluations (which most times are followed by major wage adjustments) and the cutbacks in subsidies (which are immediately passed on to prices, though they help to balance the public deficits). Table 5 summarizes the inflationary outlook for the major Latin American countries.

Table 5
Inflation
Consumer Price Index-Annual Average (percent)

	1979	1980	1981	1982	1983	1984
Argentina	159.5	100.8	104.5	164.8	385.5	245.2
Brazil	54.1	115.3	114.3	98.0	96.3	89.7
Chile	33.4	35.1	19.7	10.0	46.0	22.0
Colombia	24.6	26.5	26.7	24.6	25.5	25.0
Mexico	18.2	26.3	27.9	58.9	97.0	41.3
Peru	66.7	59.2	75.7	75.0	65.0	55.0
Venezuela	12.3	21.6	16.2	9.9	9.7	9.1
Latin America	55.4	74.7	74.7	82.2	122.1	85.8

What would facilitate the recovery in the Latin American countries? The quickest and soundest way would be for the world economy to recover to a good pace of growth with high commodity prices. This would mean, on the one hand, expanded markets for the manufactured products of countries like Brazil and Mexico (assuming, of course, that renewed economic expansion in the industrial world would come without recourse to additional protectionism). Equally positive would be a substantial increase in the prices of primary commodities like copper, coffee, cocoa and tin. This would provide a basis for additional trade and perhaps for capital flows associated with foreign investment in resource development as well. The impact would be in part real, through faster domestic growth and exports, and in part psychological through the demonstration that the debts are soundly backed.

The other solution would be a better mechanism to reschedule the debt at a much longer period, say 10 to 15 years, in such a way that the renegotiated portion would be more "spread out" into the future, instead of concentrated in four years after 1986. In any case, the outlook for 1983 and 1984 is not necessarily very optimistic.

As difficult as it is to be realistic (without being alarmist) in analyzing the present unprecedented stormy times in Latin America, it is also difficult to be realistic (without being overoptimistic) in analyzing "the end of the storm." Even with a recovery in the industrialized nations at the end of 1983 and in 1984, with net foreign lending growing around 6-8 percent annually, in nominal terms, Latin America should not be expected to grow more than 2.9 percent in 1984. Growth for the region should remain around 4.4 percent at an annual average from 1985 to 1987.

Appendix

The effects of changes in trade were analyzed using a 1981 trade matrix including the six major Latin American countries (Argentina, Brazil, Chile, Colombia, Mexico and Venezuela), the United States and the rest of the world. This matrix was constructed using the IMF's Direction of Trade and statistics published by INTAL. Not surprisingly, the largest weights fall in the U.S./Latin American relationships.

By applying directly the 1981 trade structure to the 1982 estimates of imports and to Wharton's 1983 and 1984 base projections, we are assuming the continuation, during those years, of the same trade structure as in 1981. It must be noted that in 1982 there have been changes in trade flows as a result of at least two factors: a) the synchronized recession in the continent (for example, Brazilian exports to Argentina and Chile were substantially less than in 1981); and b) import cutbacks from oil-exporting countries (like Nigeria and Iran, again affecting Brazil). Nevertheless, as the trade structure among the major trade partners was quite similar to that of 1978, we decided it would be a good, simple approximation to estimate trade multipliers.

Three simulations were prepared and were titled Base Case, Case I and Case II.

Table A-1 includes the results from the Base Case, while Tables A-2 and A-3 show the results obtained from different levels of import cutbacks, starting from the Base Case. These results indicate how the United States and the rest of the world have relatively larger losses in export revenues than the six Latin American countries which would, for one reason or another, cut back imports in the beginning.

Table A-1
Base Case Projections

	1983	1984
Six major Latin American Countries:*		
Exports (in bill. $)	75.2	87.6
%	(6.7)	(16.5)
Imports (in bill. $)	59.4	69.8
%	(0.8)	(17.6)
U.S. Exports (in bill. $)	231.6	262.7
%	(5.3)	(13.4)
Row** Exports (in bill. $)	277.5	313.8
%	(9.1)	(13.1)

*Argentina, Brazil, Chile, Colombia, Mexico, Venezuela
**Rest of the World (includes other Latin American countries)

Table A-2
Effects of a 10 percent decline in Latin American Imports

	1983	1984
1. A cutback in imports* of (in bill. $)	6.2	11.3
(% of imports from Base Case)	(10.4)	(16.2)
Will produce a decline in exports amounting to:		
2. In the same six countries*	0.7	1.1
(% of exports in Base Case)	(0.9)	(1.3)
3. In the U.S.	2.8	5.2
(% of exports in Base Case)	(1.2)	(2.0)
4. In the rest of the world	2.7	5.0
(% of exports in Base Case)	(1.0)	(1.6)

*Six largest Latin American economies: Argentina, Brazil, Chile, Colombia, Mexico and Venezuela.

Table A-3
Effects of a 27 percent Decline in Imports

	1983	1984
1. A cutback in imports* of (bill. $)	15.9	21.2
(% of imports from Base Case)	(26.8)	(30.4)
Will produce a decline in exports amounting to:		
2. In the same six countries*	1.7	2.2
(% of exports in Base Case)	(2.3)	(2.5)
3. In the U.S.	6.8	9.3
(% of exports in Base Case)	(3.2)	(3.5)
4. In the rest of the world	7.4	9.7
(% of exports in Base Case)	(2.7)	(3.1)

*Six largest Latin American economies: Argentina, Brazil, Chile, Colombia, Mexico and Venezuela.

FOOTNOTES

[1]Pedro Pablo Kuczynski, Latin American Debt, Foreign Affairs, Winter 1982-83.

[2]From 1979 to 1981 the six major countries in Latin America (Argentina, Brazil, Chile, Colombia, Mexico and Venezuela) required increases in gross financial requirements amounting to 28 percent per year. Nevertheless, until 1981, even the first quarter of 1982 (coinciding with the South Atlantic crisis), the world financing system appeared to be able and willing to extend such loans, and led to the assumption that the debt burden could be handled without Draconian measures.

[3]This is according to the new National Income Accounts produced by the Secretaria de Programacion y Presupuesto. The old system of National Accounts (produced then by the Banco de Mexico) showed a GDP deceleration from 4.1 percent in 1976 to 2.1 percent in 1977. In early 1978, when this figure was published, there was a consensus that 1977 had carried a serious recession "because the growth of the economy was lower than the population growth."

[4]For an accurate forecast (amount and timing) and further analysis of the Brazilian devaluation, please see Wharton's Brazilian Eonomic Outlook, October 1982. For the Venezuelan events, please see Wharton's Exchange Rate monthly report, the Fall 1982 Latin American Outlook and updates in the weekly News Perspectives, triggered by the acceleration of events in the oil market.

[5]Nevertheless, it remains to be seen how much Brazilian exports will be affected by cutbacks in imports from the oil exporters (like Nigeria, Iran, Mexico and Venezuela). Please see Appendix.

THE ECONOMIC OUTLOOK FOR LATIN AMERICA AND THE IMF

Raul Moncarz

The economic prospects for Latin America under the new IMF supervision in the 1980s are as varied as the countries themselves that make up the region. There are not only obvious differences among the countries in terms of size and population, natural and human resources, development levels, and political and economic systems, but there are also differences in economic opportunities as 1983 begins.

The situation of external indebtedness in the different Latin American countries is usually examined only as it relates to the short-term aspects and to those having a monetary, exchange or financial connotation. This type of approach is inappropriate and partial in nature, since it leaves out the factors that are vitally important to look at, such as the feasibility and effectiveness of growth paths, social imbalances, production, employment and the general well-being of the total population. Only when we look at these variables, and their rate of change through time, can we talk about the debt and its implications for the present and future of the area. There is a need to maintain a monetary, exchange and financial balance, both at the national and international level, and this should be related to the structural and long-term problems of the area.

Recent and Long-Term Achievements by Latin America

The average annual growth of real GNP per capita for the oil importing economies of the region improved from 2.7 percent in the 1960's to 3.5 percent in the 1970's. The only other region of oil importing developing countries with a better record was East Asia and the Pacific, where growth accelerated during the same periods from 4.9 percent to 5.6 percent. In the sixties, average annual growth in real per capita GNP in Latin America was only 2.7 percent, compared with 3.9 percent in the industrialized, high-income countries. However, in the seventies, average growth in Latin America of 3.5 percent per year surpassed the increase of 2.4 percent for industrialized countries. If we included the region's two major oil producers, Venezuela and Mexico, Latin America's average growth would improve slightly.

With regard to both the growth of domestic capital markets and the rise in total levels of savings and investments, again the region also experienced considerable improvement. In 1960, total average domestic savings in the area amounted to 19 percent of GDP, while total investments stood at 21 percent in 1970. These ratios rose to 20 percent and 32 percent respectively, and in 1978, despite an adverse economic cycle, they had risen further to 22 percent and 25 percent. The difference between these two ratios has been the external financing of investment. As can be seen, the major development effort is increasingly being made by the countries themselves, even though external financing remains an essential complement. There have also been significant increases in human capital formation in every country in the region, and exports have also increased continuously in the period 1960-78. Efforts to increase and diversify exports were strengthened significantly in almost every country starting in 1966. What seems to account for the superior economic and social progress of Latin America in the 1970s are improved economic management in the region, sustained direct investment, and the willingness by international banks to lend a substantial share of the deposited financial surpluses of the rich OPEC members to Latin America, and specifically to Argentina, Brazil, Mexico, and Chile.

Changing World Conditions Regarding Foreign Indebtedness

The largest portion of external financing has changed significantly in the last 20 years. Funds from private sources increased their share of the total, going from an average of 34.5 percent in 1961-65, to 51 percent in 1971-75, and to 68.7 percent between 1976 and 1980. The largest portions of the change have come from private banks.

What this means for Latin America is that the ratio between external finance received and the GNP of the area went from an annual average of 1.9 percent in 1961-69 to 5 percent in 1976-79. The share in the composition of the debt by private sources became markedly significant, while official, bilateral, and multilateral aid, though increasing in absolute terms, showed a relative decrease. It went from 60 percent of the total in 1961-65 to 26.8 percent in 1970-75 and to only 12 percent in 1975-78, On the other hand, the share of multilateral agency financing in that total decreased from 16.6 percent in 1961-65 to 7.3 percent in 1976-78.

As for private banking, its share of the financing expanded as Latin America increasingly used private capital markets. Its absolute value augmented from 500 million in 1970 to $4.8 billion in 1974 and to $12.4 billion in 1978. As a result of that increase, this portion of the total external flow to Latin America rose from 14.7 percent in 1970 to 56.7 percent in 1978.

Over these years, those funds were substantially denominated in Eurocredits. Although statistics on such operations are incomplete, the contracted amounts went from $4.45 billion in 1974 to $17.8 billion in 1978 and, finally, to $22.6 billion in 1979. Between 1974 and 1979, four countries accounted on the average for somewhat more than 83 percent of that total, the countries being Argentina, Brazil, Mexico, and Venezuela. Regarding direct private investment, while growing in absolute terms, it decreased in relative terms from 34 percent of the net total flow in 1966-70 to 21 percent between 1976 and 1978.

International Banks and the IMF

The traditional criteria of the early 1970s that had been established by the international private banks and the IMF have lost much of their potency. The paradigm which advocates changes in relative prices in order to benefit export prices, the reduction of government expenditures, with the slowdown of the money supply growth and the decline of local demand, has been proven ideologically inconsistent with the Latin American experience, and specifically with that of Argentina, Brazil, Chile, and Peru in the last 20 years. In the 1980s, assuming that the IMF and the international banks have not learned from their mistakes, the same causes would inhibit the success of the traditional policies just cited. Reinforcing the above conditions is the difficulty that any devaluation of the different national currencies will increase exports while the terms of trade are decreasing for commodities, and also when countries do not possess export experience. Logically, we cannot ask all countries simultaneously to tighten their belts, cut back imports and increase exports. That would cause a drastic reduction in world trade, and the projected trade figures would not add up. In a way, the developing countries are now in a position similar to that of Germany after World War I. As a result, it seems that countries are not prepared to tolerate continuous Brazilian trade surpluses. If so, Brazil and Mexico could find themselves unable to meet these debt repayments and, therefore, would lose their creditworthiness.

The drop in exports by the OECD members to the weaker countries has also affected employment in the healthy ones. More and more countries are trying to export more and are subsidizing their exports. Since markets are like parachutes--they only work when open—many countries are getting poorer and their prospects are not much better for the immediate future.

History proves that things can happen, not that they must. Compared to previous IMF interventions, the institutions's current role is very different from preceding ones, because of the growth and development that the countries in question have experienced. Nations like Brazil and Mexico have reached or are reaching a sufficient level of industrialization to enable them to protect their self-interest and the gains in production, employment and well-being achieved during the 1970s. A good example of Mexico's willingness to maintain its gains is the decision of the government to nationalize the private banking system, thereby changing the rules of the game when deemed necessary. What, then, is to be done? We should, of course, acknowledge the realities of international trade. But world competitors are not necessarily free marketeers in the classical mold. It is absurd to let foreign mercantilist enterprises overrrun Mexican, Brazilian, and as a matter of fact any other countries' industries, in the name of free trade. The alternative is not jingoist protectionism. It is managed trade, on the model of the Multi-Fiber arrangement. If domestic industries are assured some limits to import growth, then it becomes rational for them to keep retooling and modernizing. Bertrand Russell's humorous maxim—that you should never make the same mistake twice in life when there are so many to choose from—has today to be taken seriously.

Raw Materials and Agricultural Commodities

Governments cannot afford to neglect the decline in raw material prices and agricultural commodities. This is one of the main causes of the current economic difficulties in a number of developing countries. These difficulties would be considerably alleviated if there were to exist a worldwide system to stabilize export earning along the lines of the Stabex system which the EEC has agreed to with a number of developing countries in Africa, the Caribbean and the Pacific. With an assured base of export earning, many countries would have a better opportunity to plan and modify their economies according to their needs. This arrangement would also stabilize the exports of OECD countries to the developing nations.

As the Spanish poet Antonio Machado said: "Caminante no hay camino, se hace camino al andar." Latin America is heavily indebted with external borrowing and financial pressure. But this to some extent reflects the more advanced phase of its development and the increasing sophistication of economic management. If the world oil prices and interest rates stabilize, this in turn will give policy makers in the world, both at the private and public levels, an opportunity to restructure their economies, and to establish cooperation for economic and social growth and development at a global level.

ECONOMIC GROWTH AND INTERNATIONAL TRADE IN THE CARIBBEAN BASIN

Irma Tirado de Alonso

The use of the term Caribbean Basin has emerged as a unified concept only in the last couple of years. Much of the credit is due to the Caribbean Basin Initiative (CBI) sponsored preeminently by the United States. Fundamentally, the CBI consists of a package of (1) a one time $350 million emergency aid fund for the Caribbean Basin countries; (2) duty-free access to the U.S. market for 12 years for many Central American and Caribbean products; and (3) a five-year investment tax credit for Americans who invest in the region. According to President Reagan, this plan will foster stability in the region. So far only the first part of the CBI has been approved, because of opposition by the Congress.

The Caribbean Basin countries comprise a heterogenous set of economies, cultures, languages and political systems. Yet they are all tied by their proximity and the commonality of sharing the Basin's resource pools, historical experiences and geopolitical dimensions.

The interest of the U.S. in the Caribbean Basin is not casual. The countries of the Basin possess unsuspected strength. Without including South Florida, its richest member, they represent: over one hundred and fifty million people with an income of $1,500 per capita; a gross domestic product (GDP) close to $300 billion a year; a rate of growth of real income in the range of 5-6 percent yearly in the last decade; and a population growing at annual rates of 2-3 percent. These statistics show that the Caribbean Basin is already a very important geoeconomic area, and one that can be expected to expand vigorously into the next century. With such incentives it is no wonder that the U.S. is exploring new ways of relating to these countries and that the nations belonging to the region are themselves actively exploring their economic interconnections, and continuously developing new trade, financial and other ties among themselves. Although a treaty spelling in a formal way the common interests of the member countries may not be forthcoming for a while, informal cooperation certainly appears to be headed upwards in the Caribbean Basin. One such cooperation effort is exemplified by IESCARIBE (Institutes of Economic and Social Research of the Caribbean Basin).

IESCARIBE is an organization comprised of the main research institutes of the Caribbean Basin. It includes representatives from the universities, central banks, and the government sectors of most of the countries in the Basin. Although the prospects for many other studies are excellent, at present the members of IESCARIBE are studying the relationship between industrialization and trade among their countries. They want to determine the possibilities of internalizing trade within the region. With this purpose in mind they want to study both the intra-regional and the extra-regional trade, so as to consider the available alternatives for industrializing in those areas of trade that can be shifted from extra-zone to intra-zone trade. The objective of our presentation is to make a first attempt at evaluating this possibility.

For our purposes, we are utilizing statistics from the Inter-American Development Bank. Basing our discussion in this information, it is found that the Caribbean Basin is a composite entity within which several homogenous and heterogenous zones are easily distinguished. There are two formal integration schemes: the Central American Common Market (CACOM) and the Caribbean Common Market (CARICOM). Another group is composed of the continental nations that are inserted in the Basin, including Mexico, Colombia and Venezuela. The rest of the Caribbean Basin comprises mostly small countries, which are either islands or continental nations. Included in this group are the islands of the Bahamas, the Dominican Republic and Haiti. Also part of the Caribbean Basin, but excluded from our statistical analysis, are the Netherlands Antilles, Surinam, Martinique, Guadeloupe, Puerto Rico, South Florida in the U.S., the Virgin Islands, many other English-speaking islands, and Cuba.

Table 1 provides information on total population and gross domestic product. Taking GDP per capita as an indicator of the degree of advancement, at one extreme we find the group of "other nations" with Haiti at the lower end and Bahamas at the upper end. CACOM appears next, as the other poor segment of the Basin. CARICOM is substantially ahead of these two groupings. At the same time it should be noted that the CARICOM countries are not far behind the set of more advanced countries.

Table 2 provides information about the value added by manufacturing. Taking this as an indicator of industrial development, it is found that only the Mexican industrial sector has evolved to the point of achieving close to a 25 percent industrial share in gross domestic product, which is common in developed countries. It is CARICOM which has the weakest manufacturing strength. CACOM attained a level of industrial vitality similar to that of Colombia and Venezuela, due in large measure to the surge in industrial trade among its members in the last two decades.

Looking at Table 3 it is found that most of the countries have tied their industrial development to food and agriculture, except in the case of Venezuela, Trinidad-Tobago and Mexico, whose industrial development is related to petroleum.

The importance of the external sector can be measured by the ratio of exports and imports to gross domestic product. Taking into account the trade of merchandise (Table 4) it can be mentioned that the CARICOM countries are extremely dependent on the external sector, while the CACOM nations are relatively less dependent on the external sector. The continental and other nations are moderately less dependent, with the exceptions of Venezuela, the Bahamas and Panama. In general terms, the larger the domestic market, the smaller the importance of the external sector.

The economic growth of the Caribbean Basin countries is strongly fostered by exports. The rates of growth of exports are higher than those recorded by other components of the GDP. This shows an interdependence between these countries and the industrialized world, the latter being the most important markets for those exports.

By the end of the 1970s, the most important trading partners for both exports and imports were the United States, the European Economic Community, Canada and Japan. These nations accounted for two-thirds of the trade. However, from 1974 onward the growth of trade among the developing countries accelerated, and this is shown in Table 5 in terms of the intra-regional trade among them. But in order for these countris to expand their intra-regional trade, they have to be more than mere exporters of primary products and natural resource type services (like tourism). Seldom do we find in history that close economic relations develop among countries, unless they are predicted on the basis of an exchange of industrial products. Thus, in the Basin the road to industrialization will probably lead to increased intra-regional commerce and further economic integration.

The principal export items of the countries of the region have traditionally been foodstuffs and raw materials, fuels and manufactures. Their main import category was manufactured goods. These have become an important component of the region's merchandise exports, although not all the countries reflect the same performance (Table 6).

Areas of new exported strength are revealed analyzing the growth of manufactured exports. Table 7 shows manufactured exports per capita and also in relation to total merchandise exports, GDP, and manufactured value added, as well as their percentage increases from 1970 to 1978. It is found that all the Caribbean Basin nations have expanded their exports of manufactures, in particular in the cases of Colombia, Haiti and Venezuela. As mentioned, the share of manufactures in total exports reflects considerable differences in performance. Panama, Guyana, Colombia and El Salvador showed the highest percentage increases. The CARICOM countries have a higher proportion of manufactured exports as a proportion of GDP than the rest of the nations of the Basin. But in percentage increases the cases of Colombia, Nicaragua,

Panama and Haiti should be signaled out. Panama, Colombia and Nicaragua also showed significant progress in their manufactured exports as a proportion of manufactured value added.

Changes in the composition of manufactued exports are reveled once the data are disaggregated. The Inter-American Development Bank, using UNIDO data, shows growth of manufactured exports other than foodstuffs and non ferrous metal products for a number of countries. Those referring to the Caribbean Basin are summarized in Table 8. These are the less traditional exports and it is significant to find that in some of the countries these categories represented more than 25 percent of their total manufactured exports. In this category the countries of the Caribbean Basin with the highest rates of growth during the 1970s were Barbados, Colombia and Nicaragua.

Many factors have been goods mentioned for the increase in the exports of manufactured goods. Among them, probably the most important are: (1) the increase in the world rates of economic growth; (2) the liberalization of trade in the developed nations; and (3) the acceptance by the developing nations that export promotion fosters economic development. Very important for the region has been the production sharing arrangements that led to significant increases in exports of metalworking, machinery and transportation parts. In addition, such arrangements underlie the growth of the offshore assembly industries, that were very important for Mexico, Haiti, the Dominican Republic, El Salvador and other Caribbean Basin countries.

However, the "new protectionism" of the developed countries, motivated by their higher unemployment rates and their stagnant domestic demand, has encouraged the intra-regional flow of trade. This experience may lead to further economic integration in the area, which requires added research on the subjects of industrialization and trade. We have to determine the most productive use of the resources of each nation; this in turn would dictate different degrees of industrialization across the Caribbean Basin. In this aspect, the IESCARIBE project will make a significant contribution.

ACKNOWLEDGEMENT

The author wishes to acknowledge the significant contribution of Dr. Jorge Salazar-Carrillo to the development of this paper.

Table 1
Total Population and Gross Domestic Product, Total and Per Capita, and their Annual Rates of Growth, by country, 1980.

COUNTRIES	Population TOTAL (thousands)	Population 1970-81	Gross Domestic Product (millions of 1980 dollars)	Gross Domestic Product Rate of Growth 1970-80	GDP Per Capita (1980 dollars)	GDP Per Capita Rate of Growth 1970-80
CARICOM:	4280	0.8*	7365.9	2.94*	1721.0	2.25*
Barbados	252	0.5	651.9	1.65	2586.8	1.07
Guyana	787	0.9	618.2	1.58	785.5	0.62
Jamaica	2174	1.1	3144.9	(-0.01)	1446.6	(-0.02)
Trinidad-Tobago	1067	0.4	2950.7	5.41	2765.5	5.01
CACOM:	20,155	2.9*	19523.8	4.51*	968.6	1.72*
Costa Rica	2218	2.8	3406.6	5.63	1535.9	2.94
El Salvador	4813	3.0	3312.3	3.11	688.4	0.09
Guatemala	6999	2.9	8434.2	5.63	1205.1	2.65
Honduras	3703	3.2	2347.8	4.27	634.0	1.06
Nicaragua	2422	2.4	2022.9	0.55	835.2	(-0.02)
CONTINENTAL NATIONS	110,016	3.0*	191801.0	6.03*	1743.0	2.40*
Colombia	26173	2.1	14126.6	5.81	921.8	3.61
Mexico	69900	3.4	130613.6	6.60	1868.6	3.10
Venezuela	13943	2.7	37060.5	4.17	2658.0	1.48
OTHER:	12642	2.1*	12110.9	5.82*	958.0	2.96*
Bahamas	224	2.4	1326.1	n.a.	5920.1	n.a
Dominican Republic	5515	2.4	5700.1	6.91	1033.6	4.38
Haiti	5008	1.7	1373.6	4.27	274.3	2.53
Panama	1895	2.4	3711.1	4.71	1958.4	2.27

Source: Inter-American Development Bank, Social and Economic Progress in Latin America, 1982 Report. (Washington, DC) Statistical Appendix, Table 1 and Table 3.

n.a. not available

*Average rates weighted by the GDP.

Table 2
Value Added by the Manufacturing Sector, Total and as a Percent of GDP by country, 1070, 1980, and 1981.

COUNTRIES	Value Added by the Manufacturing Sector (millions of 1980 dollars)			Value Added by the Manufacturing Sector (as percent of GDP)		
	1970	1980	1981**	1970	1980	1981**
CARICOM:	866.2	968.2	999.6	14.0*	13.1*	13.4*
Barbados	45.8	80.8	73.1	8.3	12.4	11.6
Guyana	54.1	11.2	123.8	12.1	18.0	19.8
Jamaica	592.4	468.8	494.0	17.6	14.9	15.9
Trinidad-Tobago	163.9	307.4	308.7	9.4	10.4	9.9
CACOM:	2219.4	3649.3	3534.9	17.4*	19.7*	18.3*
Costa Rica	366.3	749.3	741.0	18.6	22.0	22.6
El Salvador	446.7	578.2	477.7	18.3	17.4	15.9
Guatemala	769.9	1413.2	1380.8	15.8	16.8	16.2
Honduras	220.3	385.2	397.3	14.2	16.4	16.9
Nicaragua	416.2	523.4	538.1	21.7	25.8	24.4
CONTINENTAL NATIONS:	22867.0	43711.0	46039.8	21.3*	22.8*	22.6*
Colombia	2546.7	4527.0	4481.7	18.6	18.8	18.1
Mexico	16322.2	32531.9	34939.2	23.7	24.9	24.7
Venezuela	3998.1	6652.1	6618.9	16.2	17.9	17.7
OTHER:	1061.8	1774.8	1785.7	17.2*	16.5*	16.1*
Bahamas	n.a.	n.a.	n.a.	n.a.	n.a.	n.a.
Dominican Republic	541.9	1037.6	1065.3	18.5	18.2	18.1
Haiti	117.8	229.3	224.3	13.0	16.7	16.2
Panama	402.1	507.9	496.1	17.2	13.7	12.9

Source: Inter-American Developing Bank, Social and Economic Progress in Latin American, 12982 Report, (Washington, D.C), Statistical Appendix, Table 3 and Table II.

**Preliminary figures
*Average percentage weighted by the GDP.
n.a. = not available

Table 3
Percentage Distributions of Manufactured Value Added by Sector, for some Countries, 1979

COUNTRIES	Food and Agriculture	Textile and Clothing	Machinery & Transp. Equip.	Chemicals	Other
CARICOM:					
Jamaica	50	8	6	8	28
Trinidad-Tobago	13	4	10	7	66
CANCOM:					
Honduras	43	15	1	6	35
CONTINENTAL NATIONS:					
Colombia	30	17	12	12	29
Mexico	20	9	18	12	41
Venezuela	18	9	7	7	59
OTHER:					
Dominican Republic	72	4	1	5	18
Panama	52	11	2	5	20

Source: World Bank, World Development Report 1982, (Washington, DC, 1982), Table 6.

Table 4
Exports and Imports of Merchandise, Total and as Percent of the Gross Domestic Product, by country, 1980

	Exports (million of dollars)	Imports (million of dollars)	Exports as % of GDP	Imports as % of GDP
CARICOM:	4201.9	3791.3	57.0*	51.5*
Barbados	188.5	479.5	28.9	73.6
Guyana	388.9	386.3	62.9	62.5
Jamaica	1088.9	1173.0	34.6	37.3
Trinidad-Tobago	2535.6	1752.5	85.9	59.4
CACOM:	4789.9	5621.8	24.5*	38.8*
Costa Rica	1017.5	1375.3	29.9	40.4
El Salvador	968.6	971.7	29.2	40.4
Guatemala	1518.9	1471.6	18.0	17.4
Honduras	834.5	956.0	35.5	40.7
Nicaragua	450.4	874.2	22.3	41.9
CONTINENTAL NATIONS	39700.6	34186.0	20.7*	17.8*
Colombia	4112.8	3851.2	17.0	16.0
Mexico	16306.9	19016.7	12.5	14.6
Venezuela	19280.9	11318.1	52.0	30.5
OTHER:	1804.4	3881.8	14.9*	29.9*
Bahamas	200.4	784.4	15.1	59.2
Dominican Republic	961.9	1514.6	16.9	26.6
Haiti	211.1	293.8	15.4	21.4
Panama	431.0	1289.0	11.6	34.7

Source: Inter-American Development Bank, Social and economic Progress in Latin America, 1982 Report, (Washington D.C) Statistical Appendix, Table 42 and Table 2.

*Average percentages weighted by the GDP.

Table 5
Intra-regional trade: Percentage Destination of Export to and Origin of Imports from Regional Countries, various years.

COUNTRIES	Exports Average 1961-63	Exports Average 1977-79	Imports Average 1961-63	Imports Average 1977-79
I. IDB Members				
CARICOM:				
Barbados	1.2	17.5	10.4	22.9
Guyana	13.6	18.9	13.0	28.3
Jamaica	1.7	9.8	7.4	24.1
Trinidad-Tobago	5.1	8.7	26.6	6.0
CACOM:				
Costa Rica	5.4	26.7	9.0	27.3
El Salvador	15.4	26.6	21.4	38.9
Guatemala	7.5	25.1	11.2	29.4
Honduras	19.2	10.6	14.8	28.4
Nicaragua	5.3	21.7	13.2	44.2
CONTINENTAL NATIONS:				
Colombia	6.5	12.7	5.6	17.1
Mexico	4.3	9.5	1.3	6.0
Venezuela	10.1	12.5	2.6	10.0
OTHER:				
Bahamas	1.0	2.2	9.0	5.3
Dominican Republic	1.4	6.0	2.7	23.4
Haiti	1.8	2.1	2.5	4.6
Panama	5.0	17.8	12.4	34.3
	1970	1980	1970	1980
II. CACOM, Total	26.1	24.9	24.2	19.4
Costa Rica	19.9	28.1	21.7	14.4
El Salvador	32.3	29.9	28.4	32.8
Guatemala	35.3	28.6	22.8	13.6
Honduras	10.6	11.4	24.9	10.3
Nicaragua	25.8	17.3	25.2	33.9
	1967	1978	1967	1978
III. CARICOM				
Barbados	7.8	29.9	19.6	14.3
Guyana	13.1	15.2	12.6	29.0
Jamaica	2.7	6.0	2.0	5.7
Trinidad-Tobago	5.8	7.0	2.2	3.5

Sources: IDB Members: Inter-American Development Bank, op.cit., Social and Economic Progress in Latin America, 1982 Report, (Washington, D.C.), Statistical Appendix, Tables 8 and 9.

CACOM: SIEGA, VII Compendio Estadistico Centroamericano, 1981, Table 192 and Table 193.
CARICOM: G. Ranis, et. al., Production and Export Incentives in the CARICOM Region (mimeo), May 1982.

Table 6
Country Shares of Latin American Manufactured Exports, 1970 and 1978.

	1970	1978
CARICOM:		
Barbados	0.4	0.3
Guyana	0.7	0.7
Jamaica	3.2	2.1
Trinidad-Tobago	5.7	4.2
CACOM:		
Costa Rica	1.1	2.1
El Salvador	1.4	1.4
Guatemala	2.0	1.8
Honduras	0.7	0.6
Nicaragua	1.6	1.8
CONTINENTAL NATIONS:		
Colombia	1.9	2.9
Mexico	10.2	9.7
Venezuela	12.6	11.5
OTHER:		
Dominican Republic	1.8	1.3
Haiti	0.2	0.2
Panama	0.5	0.5

Source: Inter-American Development Bank, Social and Economic Progress in Latin America, 1982 Report, (Washington, D.C.), Statistical Appendix, Table 6, page 118, using UNIDO definition of manufactured exports.

Table 7
Manufactured Exports Per Capita and Manufactured Exports to Total Exports, GDP, and Manufactured Value Added, 1970 and 1978, and Percentage Increase 1970–78.

Countries	Manufactured Exports Per Capita (US Dollars)			Manufactured Exports as Proportion of Total Exports			Manufactured Exports as Proportion of GDP			Manufactured Exports as Proportion of Manufactures		
	1970	1978	% Increase	1970	1978	% Increase	1970	1978	% Increase	1970	1978	% Increase
CARICOM:												
Barbados	318	445	40	92.0	99.0	10	n.a.	n.a.	n.a.	135.0	155.7	15
Guyana	142	265	85	40.3	63.3	55	19.3	34.8	80	182.1	238.5	30
Jamaica*	211	307	45	71.6	73.4	5	14.0	20.5	45	80.2	121.6	50
Trinidad-Tobago	810	1304	60	89.0	57.0	-35	48.6	55.7	15	215.8	308.7	45
CANCOM:												
Costa Rica	93	173	85	35.5	34.0	-5	8.1	11.0	35	43.7	51.9	20
El Salvador	58	103	80	47.0	62.0	30	8.6	12.5	45	46.8	66.0	40
Guatemala	57	91	60	53.0	46.9	-10	6.2	7.8	25	39.2	47.9	20
Honduras	38	60	60	31.0	29.0	-5	6.7	9.7	45	51.8	68.1	30
Nicaragua	120	265	120	68.0	62.0	-10	12.6	25.7	105	55.3	96.1	75
CONTINENTAL NATIONS:												
Colombia	13	37	185	20.0	26.0	30	2.0	4.3	115	10.9	22.4	105
Mexico	30	49	65	64.0	43.0	-35	2.2	2.9	30	9.2	11.7	25
Venezuela	173	256	105	30.0	35.0	15	7.6	10.3	35	46.5	61.4	30
OTHER:												
Dominican Rep.*	62	75	20	56.1	55.0	0	9.2	7.6	-15	49.6	41.3	-15
Haiti*	6	16	165	41.4	40.0	0	3.5	6.1	75	26.7	36.3	35
Panama	45	85	90	31.0	52.0	70	2.9	5.6	95	16.9	35.1	110

Source: Inter-American Development Bank, Social and Economic Progress in Latin America, 1982 Report, (Washington D.C.), Statistical Appendix, Table 9, page 122.

Table 8

Growth of Manufactured Exports Other than Foodstuffs and Non-Ferrous Metal Products[1]

(Percentages)

Ranking Countries		Ranking for countries in which the categories included constituted at least 25% of total manufactured exports	
	Compounded rate of growth		Compounded rate of growth
Guyuna	26.0		
Barbados	17.9	Barbados	17.9
Colombia	16.9	Colombia	16.9
Nicaragua	15.0	Nicaragua	15.0
Mexico	12.6	Mexico	12.6
Honduras	12.2	Honduras	12.2
Trinidad-Tobago	11.8	Trinidad-Tobago	11.8
Venezuela	10.4	Venezuela	10.4
Panama	9.7	Panama	9.7
Guatemala	9.6	Guatemala	9.6
El Salvador	8.9	El Salvador	8.9
Costa Rica	6.2	Costa Rica	6.2

Source: Inter-American Development Bank, Social and Economic Progress in Latin America, 1982 Report, (Washington, D.C.) Statistical Appendix, Table 14, page 128, based on UNIDO data.

Note: [1]Compound rates of growth from 1970 through the last year available. That year varies for the different countries form 1977 through 1980.

TRADE AND DEBT IN CENTRAL AMERICA IN THE 1970s

Jorge Salazar-Carillo

The idea of a Jubilee, which has been mentioned as part of the solution of the debt dilemma, is shown to be of doubtful applicability once the situation in Central America is considered. Even within such a small region, the debt burden and the repayment pressures have been quite varied. How could a simple rule be made to encompass differing circumstances? Central America, as shall be demonstrated, has in general been relatively prudent with its external debt. Being one of the poorest regions of the world, how could less be forgiven to them than to the richer nations that have been less risk-averse? With behavior such as this, it is no wonder the Jubilee has been abandoned in ancient Israel. Only the coming of the Messiah and the reestablishment of justice was supposed to bring it back.

In the following pages the situation in Central America will be examined, and the picture that will emerge in terms of the concerns of this paper will be quite different from the one that portrays Latin America as a whole. The point that will be made is that for forecasting and decision-making, a clear distinction has to be made between Central America[1] and the rest of Latin America.

First, the economic growth record between 1970 and 1980 in Central America and Latin America as a whole will be compared.[2] As can be confirmed from the chart below, in the last decade, one of the best which developing countries ever had, gross domestic product (GDP) grew at an annual rate of 4.6 percent in the case of Central America and at a pace of 6.1 percent for Latin America. These rates are net of the effects of inflation. The rates of growth of Central America reflect some of the difficulties experienced towards the end of the 1970s.

Table 1
Annual Rates of Growth of GDP

	Central America	Latin America
1970-80	4.6%	6.1%

Actually in the 1980s the rates of growth have dropped down to zero, and into the negative numbers in 1982 and 1983 (projected) in Central America. Even in the early 1980s the performance of Latin America was much superior, with negative growth only encountered in 1982.

To understand the Central American situation, the greater degrees of openness of the economies of this region must be taken into account. Exports and imports represent a much larger share of GDP than in Latin America overall, which includes the closed economies of Brazil and Mexico. This difference became more important in the 1970s, basically resulting from the first and second oil price shocks. Particularly devoid of oil resources, the Central American countries had to open up their economies to a larger extent than the typical Latin American republics in order to earn the dollars needed for energy imports.

Although in a milder form, the Central American countries also suffered from the financial shock. This consisted of a sharp increase in the international rates of interest and the more recent restrictions in world credit availability. Additional pressures have come from the acute drop in the prices of primary commodities, even though this ultimately brought along the silver lining of decreasing oil prices. On balance, these meant increased pressures on the export sector of the Central American economies.

A less well recognized cause of increasing opening of these economies to the outside was the slowing down and finally the reversion of the Central American

Economic Integration scheme. At the beginning of the period being examined, nearly one-third of the Central American trade was being conducted within the region. This important source of foreign exchange savings has significantly diminished in importance now that intra-regional trade has dropped down to almost one-fifth of the total.

In sum, and as shown below, not only are the Central American republics more open than global Latin America, but the degree of openness has increased more during the decade in question.

Table 2
Exports plus Imports as a Share of GDP

	C.A.	L.A.
1970	46.7%	26.3%
1980	87.1%	50.0%

The terms of trade declined more rapidly, in Central America than in Latin America during the seventies, representing once more an important difference. If 1970 is taken as the base (1970=100), and considering it was rather a low point in the terms-of-trade evolution of primary producers throughout time, the value of this relative price index in 1980 was 110 for Latin America as a whole, and only 87 for Central America. This factor particularly afflicted Central America after 1978, and certainly matters have gotten worse in the early 1980s. Although a slight turnaround in commodity markets is apparent in early 1983, it has basically affected some metals that are Latin American exports, but that are not Central American ones.[3]

One point that may not be apparent in connection with the opening of the Central American economies is that of the increase in the degree of overvaluation of their currencies that occurred during the seventies. Even with the devaluations which took place within this period, and which broke the magic spell that fixed parities had cast over Central America for many decades, they could not compensate for the rapid increase in prices in the region. Consider the trajectory of the real exchange rate, defined as the par value with respect to the U.S. dollar in 1970 (as 100) multiplied by the ratio of the price change in Central America or Latin America, over this period, and adjusted for any nominal devaluation.

Table 3
Evolution of Real Exchange Rate

	C.A	L.A.
1970	100	100
1980	77	76

The process of overvaluation has been the more intense the lower the value of the real exchange rate in 1980. This has meant that inflation in Central America or Latin America was greater than in the U.S., and that the difference was not compensated by devaluation. In this case, in unison, these two regions during the 1970s were cutting their own chances of expanding their world exports, particularly of manufactured goods and services, which are more price-elastic. In fact, it is remarkable that their export performance has held up so well under such conditions.

Consider now the worrisome debt situation. It is a fact that after WW II, and up to 1970, the levels of debt absorption by developing countries had been quite low, when compared to earlier experiences in this century. Suddenly those levels increased because of the pressure originated by the quadrupling of oil prices, liquidity in the world capital markets at the petrodollar surplus provided, and the low real rates of interest relative to the resulting high rates of inflation. To better understand these changing circumstances consider the debt service payment ratios in 1970 and in 1980.

Table 4
Debt Service Over Total Exports

	C.A.	L.A.
1970	7.1%	13.3%
1980	10.4%	23.8%

It would seem apparent that Central American debt prospects are more promising than those for the rest of Latin America. Furthermore, even though the political risk may be higher at this point, the geopolitical and economic significance of Central America compensates for this fact, and provides an additional incentive for trading and lending to the area's economies.

Just consider, in addition, that in the next five years only 29 percent of the outstanding Central American debt will mature, while in the case of Latin America 50 percent of the debt will come due. Also, obligations maturing between 5 and 10 years represent 36 percent of the total in Latin America and 28 percent in Central America. Furthermore, official concessionary lending, which has a grant element included (as opposed to commercial lending) constitutes 73 percent of all Central American debt, while for Latin America the corresponding figure is only 30 percent. In addition, Central America owes to private banks less than one-quarter of its debt, while this share is over 55 percent for Latin America overall.

Finally, price and protection studies indicate that manufactured products from Central America can compete successfully with foreign imports in many industries, and may already be poised for an important export expansion into the Caribbean Basin initially, and into the U.S. market later on. If overvaluation is corrected, and the relatively unfavorable economic scenarios faced by Central America in the 1970s and early 1980s take a turn for the better, as could be expected, the increasingly open Central American economies may enjoy a solid expansion in the latter part of the decade.

FOOTNOTES

[1]Central America is defined as: Costa Rica, El Salvador, Honduras, Guatemala, Nicaragua, and Panama.

[2]Even though Central America is included in the Latin American statistics, its small weight ensures that its influence over the total is rather negligible. The availability of statistical series does not easily alllow for the presentation of the Latin American aggregate *sans* Central America.

[3]The main exports of the Central American countries are: coffee, cotton, bananas, sugar, meat and shrimp.

A COMMENT ON CENTRAL AMERICA

Francisco de Paula Gutierrez

Jorge Salazar pointed out some characteristics of the Central American economies. I want to start from these characteristics to look at the perspectives for these countries.

In general, we can say that these economies are:

- Very open
- Highly dependent on very few export commodities
- Interdependent for their manufactured output
- Dependent on oil imports

Given these facts, let us look at the recent performance of the five economies according to the preliminary figures of the tables handed out during the meeting.

As can be seen in Table 1, in 1982 all Central American countries showed negative rates of growth. As Jorge was saying, there are some economic reasons for this behavior. But there are also political factors. The economic reasons are:

- The adverse change in the terms of trade due to the second oil shock of 1979 combined with a drop in commodity prices. While the price of oil more than doubled from 1978 to 1980, the export prices of coffee and sugar declined in the world markets.
- The slowdown in the activity of the Central American Common Market (CACM), which represents about 25 percent of the total trade of the region. This slowdown started in the early seventies, but was more notorious in the last years of the decade.
- The world recession, which was deeper and lasted longer than expected, together with the high level of interest rates.

But the economic problems are not the important ones to explain why all the Central American economies showed negative rates of growth in 1982. I think that, with the exception of Costa Rica, the important facts are related to the political environment:

- In 1978 and 1979 there was the Nicaraguan revolution, which caused a drop in the country's GDP of 9 percent in 1978 and 25 percent in 1979. The revolution also divided the CACM in two blocks, with the Costa Rican market—one of the largest of the region—separated from the rest of the area.
- The Salvadorean civil war started at the end of 1979 and, according to the figures in Table 1, real GDP declined near 25 percent during the period 1979-82.
- The political unrest triggered capital outflows and caused a strong drop in private investment. In 1980, all Central American economies had negative

rates of growth of private investment, and the situation did not change in 1981 and 1982. Capital outflows, on the other hand, almost depleted the international reserve position to the point that, at the end of 1982, net international reserves were negative in all the countries but Guatemala, which had a very low positive balance.

Given these facts, we started 1983 with an economy in deep recession and without foreign exchange. And despite the low debt-service ratio of Guatemala and El Salvador, the region does not seem to be a very creditworthy area. In this sense, I expect that during 1983 private capital inflows will be practically null, and although there will be some financial assistance from institutional and multilateral organizations—IDB, World Bank, IMF, CABEI, the Caribean Basin Initiative, etc.—it is not going to be enough. As a consequence, Central America will face during 1983 a severe external constraint.

The weak foreign exchange position will imply not only an increase in the market exchange rate, but also the need to cut imports or, at least, to try to maintain them at the low level reached last year. Looking at figures for total imports, we can see that in 1981 the Central American economies imported goods for a total value of $5.3 billion. In 1982, the value of imports dropped to $4.5 billion, and given the foreign exchange constraint, it does not seem to be possible to import substantially more in 1983. In addition, prospects for Central American exports are not very encouraging. The Latin American economies—and Mexico in particular—are going through a recession period, and commodity markets for Central American crops are not strong.

In the short term an improvement of the political climate does not seem probable; therefore, I do not expect a surge in private investment or a reacceleration of the economies. I expect a stagnant economy with a rate of growth—on the average—negative and close to zero, and that is an optimistic view. However, considering the absolute level of real GDP, zero growth means that real GDP per capita in 1983 will be lower than the one we had in 1975.

I do not want to leave a totally negative image of the future. Let me point out that there are some favorable things that could help the economy of the region: one is the recovery of the world economy; the second one is the drop in interest rates, which will reduce the burden of the external debt; the last one is the fall in oil prices, given the fact that all countries are net importers of oil. This drop in the price of oil will not be fully reflected in the foreign exchange flows because of the San Jose agreement, the scheme established by Mexico and Venezuela to supply and finance the oil requirements of the area, but it will improve the trade balance and reduce the accumulation of debt.

Summarizing, I think the short-term prospects of the area are still pessimistic. Unless the political climate tends to improve dramatically, or huge transfers of official resources take place, I do not expect a reacceleration of the Central American economies in the near future, which means that—from the point of view of trade opportunities— these countries will continue to have a low demand for imports and to face problems to pay their purchases and service their debt.

Table 1
Central America
Real GDP Growth Rates

	1979	1980	1981	1982
GUATEMALA	4.7	3.5	1.0	-3.5
EL SALVADOR	-1.5	-9.6	-9.5	-4.5
HONDURAS	6.6	2.5	-0.4	-1.5
COSTA RICA	4.9	0.6	-3.6	-6.0

Table 2
Central America
GDP per Capita
(1970 Dollars)

	1970	1975	1980	1982
GUATEMALA	439	494	560	514
EL SALVADOR	422	476	428	349
HONDURAS	313	296	340	311
NICARAGUA	431	480	345	348
COSTA RICA	740	875	1001	867

SOURCE: ECLA

Table 3
Central America
Consumer Price Index
(Annual Change)

	1979	1980	1981	1982
GUATEMALA	13.7	9.1	8.7	-0.6[a]
EL SALVADOR	14.8	18.6	11.6	12.6[b]
HONDURAS	18.9	15.0	4.9	9.1[a]
NICARAGUA	70.3	24.8	23.2	26.0[c]
COSTA RICA	13.2	17.8	65.1	100.6[d]

a August 1982 - August 1981
b September 1982 - September 1981
c July 1982 - July 1981
d October 1982 - October 1981

SOURCE: ECLA

Table 4
Central America
Terms of Trade
(1970 = 100)

	1981	1982	% CHANGE
GUATEMALA	74	73	-1.4
EL SALVADOR	91	93	2.2
HONDURAS	95	96	1.1
NICARAGUA	83	79	-4.8
COSTA RICA	82	81	-1.2

SOURCE: ECLA

Table 5
Central America
Balance of Payments 1982
(Million Dollars)

	G	ES	H	N	CR
CURRENT ACCOUNT	-350	-190	-330	-395	-180
TRADE BALANCE	-90	-140	-120	-245	190
EXPORTS	1200	735	710	430	1010
IMPORTS	1290	875	830	675	820
SERVICES (NET)	-320	-105	-35	-50	-5
INTEREST PAYMENTS AND PROFITS	-90	-85	-190	-100	-395
OTHER	150	140	15	0	30
CAPITAL ACCOUNT	325	230	230	220	80
CHANGE INTL. RESERV.	-25	40	-100	-175	-100

SOURCE: ECLA

Table 6
Central America
External Debt
(Million Dollars)

	1979	1980	1981	1982
GUATEMALA	983	1120	1159	1350
EL SALVADOR	798	846	1010	1200
HONDURAS	1130	1303	1426	1650
NICARAGUA	1453	1660	2173	2400
COSTA RICA	1690	2124	2577	2600

SOURCE: ECLA

EXPORT PERFORMANCE AND PROSPECTS FOR THE COMMONWEALTH CARIBBEAN

Compton Bourne and Wallace Joefield-Napier

The economic performance of Commonwealth Caribbean countries is closely intertwined, perhaps inextricably, with that of the world economy. Movements in international commodity and capital markets significantly influence key macroeconomic variables, and these in turn determine trade performance. The sub-region performed unimpressively during the 1970s--a performance due in large measure, but not exclusively, to the impact of sharp increases in international prices of primary energy and to economic recession in the OECD countries. Import restraint policies adopted by many governments have also retarded economic growth and intra-regional trade.

Because import restraint policies have been manifestly counterproductive in developing countries, export expansion has been advocated as an appropriate alternative strategy. This prescription has gained many adherents in both academic and official circles world wide. In the Commonwealth Caribbean, the policy approach has distinctly shifted in favor of export expansion.

This paper assesses the prospects for growth of Commonwealth Caribbean exports of goods and services in the context of the current structure of the region's exports, and against a background of the importance of export performance to the balance of payments, output and prices.

Table 1:
Commonwealth Caribbean: Size, Income and Trade Ratios

Countries	Area Km^2	Population Mid-1979 (000)	1979 per Capita US$	Exports/ GDP 1978	Imports/ GDP 1978
ANTIGUA	443	74	1070	51	69
BAHAMAS	13,939	231	1780	117	96
BARBADOS	430	253	2400	69	73
BELIZE	22,965	131	1030	86	98
DOMINICA	790	79	410	52	71
GRENADA	344	108	630	56	71
GUYANA	215,000	843	570	63	63
JAMAICA	11,424	2,184	1240	40	39
MONTSERRAT	104	14	N/A	39	96
ST.KITTS-NEVIS	396	50	780	53	76
ST. LUCIA	616	122	780	56	98
ST. VINCENT	388	106	490	55	84
TRINIDAD AND TOBAGO	5,128	1,152	3390	41	37
ALL	271,967	5,347			

Source: Population and GDP: 1980 World Bank Atlas; Area and Trade Ratios: Task Force on Private Sector Activities Report to Caribbean Group for Cooperation in Economic Development (Washington, D.C., 1980).

Influence of Trade Performance on Macroeconomic Variables

The data in Table 1 describe several basic characteristics of the Commonweath Caribbean economies. First, they are small economies with narrow resource bases and small populations. The total land area is 272,000 Km^2, 79 percent of this being Guyanese. The estimated population in 1979 was 5.3 million, giving a low population density of 20 persons per Km^2. Income levels vary greatly among the countries, ranging from US$410 per capita in Dominica to US$3,390 in Trinidad and Tobago. The ratios of exports and imports to gross domestic product are quite large, ranging between 39 percent and 117 percent for exports, and 38 percent and 98 percent for imports. Such high trade to GDP ratios make the economies susceptible to pronounced changes in their external trade sectors.

Trade performance is linked to the behavior of the overall balance of payments, the growth of domestic output, and domestic prices in several ways. First, given the level of import demand, the exports level determine the trade balance. Second, private capital inflows are positively correlated with exports earnings and negatively correlated with the size of trade deficits. The purchasing power of exports, i.e. the value of exports deflated by the price of imports, influences real output and the domestic production, changes in the purchasing power of exports can result in changes in domestic output. Domestic output performance, in turn, is a critical determinant of export performance. Depending on the import-intensity of consumption (typically high) and the low elasticity of substitution between imports and domestic output, declines in the purchasing power of exports reduce the availability of final demand commodities and thereby contribute to demand inflation.

Each mechanism operated in the Commonwealth Caribbean in recent times. Current account balances, chronically negative in most countries, have tended to widen with a few exceptions (Table 2). Only Trinidad and Tobago and the Bahamas have had current account surpluses, while the Barbadian current account deficit having, declined continually between 1977 and 1980, turned into a sizable surplus in 1981. Positive net capital inflows, though moderating the impact of current account deficits on the overall balance of payments, have lost the buoyancy of previous years and in some cases have tended to stagnate or decline. The countries with the most rapidly widening current account deficits, i.e. Jamaica and Guyana, have also been those with diminishing capital inflows, a feature which emphasizes the influence of net export earnings on the supply of foreign capital. By the start of the current decade each country, except the Bahamas and Trinidad and Tobago, was experiencing difficulties with its overall balance of payments. The problems are considerably more acute in Jamaica, Guyana and Barbados. The Jamaican payments deficit rose from US$77 million (2 percent of GDP) in 1978 to US$155 million (5 percent of GDP) in 1981, and international reserves decreased from minus US$447 million to minus US$1253 million. In Guyana, the overall payments deficit increased from US$30 million (7 percent of GDP) in 1977 to US$48 percent million (14 of percent GDP) in 1980, while foreign reserves fell from US$23 million to US$13 million. The Barbadian balance of payments deficit, which had decreased from US$42 million (10 percent of GDP) in 1976 to US$10 million in 1978 and 1979, quadrupled to US$47 million (6 percent of GDP) in 1981; international reserves, however, grew slowly between 1977 and 1980, and then declined 7 percent in 1981.

The purchasing power of exports stagnated in a few countries and declined in most others. In Trinidad and Tobago, the purchasing power of exports having increased from US$928 million in 1975 to US$1,616 million in 1979, decreased to US$1,361 million in 1980 and US$1,078 million in 1981. The purchasing power of Barbadian exports rose 22 percent between 1975 and 1980, but then fell 16 percent in the next two years. Guyana's export purchasing power fell cumulatively by 38 percent between 1976 and 1981, while the purchasing power of Jamaican exports, having expanded from US$608 million to US$668 million in 1978, decreased to US$702 million in 1980.

The trend of export purchasing power is a contributory factor to the trend in real output. From Table 3, it can be seen that real gross domestic product grew uninterrupted in Trinidad and Tobago. Output grew continuously in Barbados between 1976 and 1980, but declined subsequently. The Guyanese and Jamaican economies experienced almost uninterrupted negative growth between 1977 and 1981. The smaller economies, e.g. St. Vincent, St. Lucia, and Grenada, having continued to grow throughout most of the 1970s, went into decline in 1980 and 1981. The basic external influence was the fall in purchasing power of exports.

Table 2
Recent Balance of Payments Experience of Commonwealth Caribbean (US$millions)

Country and Item	1977	1978	1979	1980	1981
BARBADOS					
Current Acct Balance	-52	31	-35	-27	125
Capital Acct Balance	30	40	40	61	121
Basic Balance	-32	-10	-10	16	-47
International Reserves	37	60	67	81	75
JAMAICA					
Current Acct Balance	-42	-87	-143	-181	-427
Capital Acct Balance	69	10	-10	148	262
Basic Balance	27	-77	-153	-34	-155
International Reserves	-196	-447	-759	-806	-1253
GUYANA					
Current Acct Balance	-99	-29	-82	-101	-198
Capital Acct Balance	69	16	28	14	181
Basic Balance	-30	10	-49	-85	-1
International Reserves	23	58	17	13	7
TRINIDAD AND TOBAGO					
Current Acct Balance	215	36	45	296	99
Capital Acct Balance	310	274	368	340	293
Basic Balance	525	310	413	636	392
International Reserves	1335	1646	2016	2640	3199
ST. VINCENT					
Current Acct Balance	-15	-9	-15	-17	n.a.
DOMINICA					
Current Acct Balance	-5	-6	-14	-354	n.a.
ST. LUCIA					
Current Acct Balance	-11	-23	-28	-33	n.a.
Basic Balance	0	-1	-1	-3	n.a.
BAHAMAS					
Current Acct Balance	66	42	17	-14	-73
Capital Acct Balance	40	-25	4	10	141
Basic Balance	106	17	23	-4	68

Source: Jamaica: Social and Economic Survey, National Planning Agency; Guyana: World Bank Country Report; Barbados: Annual Statistical Digest, Central Bank of Barbados; Trinidad: Annual Report, Central Bank of Trinidad and Tobago; Bahamas: Statistical Digest, Central Bank of the Bahamas; St. Vincent, St. Lucia, Dominica: World Bank Country Reports.

The oil importers, confronted with sharp increases in import prices, restricted real imports by non-price rationing of foreign exchange. Because of the high income elasticity and low price elasticity of energy demand—the World Bank estimates 1.3 and 0.3 respectively for LDCs--the burden of import restrictions fell on non-oil producer goods and on consumer goods. In countries such as Jamaica, real imports of producer goods decreased more rapidly than real imports of consumer goods. The reduced availability of imported producer goods resulted in substantial underutilized production capacity, and in less than full potential growth of output.

Prior to the 1970s, inflation in Commonwealth Caribbean countries was mild and due almost entirely to rising import prices. A ready availability of imports practically guaranteed aggregate commodity balance and prevented excess demand inflation. From the mid-1970s onwards stringent foreign exchange rationing frustrated this safety-valve role of imports. Administrative price controls partially suppressed the rate of open inflation. Nontheless, it is evident from the data in Table 3 that inflation rates accelerated after 1977.

In view of these trends in the macroeconomic performance indicators, it is important to analyze the prospects for improved export performance. It is useful to begin by identifying the main structural features of Caribbean exports in order to direct attention to the main commodities and markets for detailed analysis.

Structure of Commonwealth Caribbean Exports

The commodity composition of Commonwealth exports is highly concentrated. Even for the larger economies, one or at most two categories account for over 70 percent of total merchandise exports. Furthermore, typically a few specific primary commodities account for the greater proportion of merchandise exports. In Jamaica's case, bauxite and alumina together constitute 78 percent of total merchandise exports in 1981. Bauxite represented 44 percent and sugar 31 percent of Guyana's merchandise exports in the same year. In Trinidad and Tobago, the two largest export commodities are petroleum products and sugar. Barbado's merchandise exports are somewhat less concentrated, sugar and molasses accounting for 20 percent, clothing 18 percent, and electrical components 26 percent. Primary commodity concentration has several well-known limitations, among which the more important are weak supply sensitivities to international price changes, greater likelihood of instability in export values and domestic incomes, and low growth prospects. The Caribbean countries have made little progress in reducing the degree of commodity concentration; indeed, shifts in the structure of merchandise exports have largely taken the form of the replacement of old staples by new ones.

The nature but not the degree of commodity concentration is changed if one includes travel services (tourism) and examines the structure of exports of both goods and services. Tourism is a major export commodity for Antigua, St. Lucia, Barbados, Jamaica, and the Bahamas. A crude indicator of its importance is the ratio of travel expenditures to exports of goods and services. In 1980, the percentages are 50 percent for Barbados, 11 percent for Jamaica, 51 percent for the Bahamas, 52 percent for St. Vincent and 46 percent for St. Lucia. In the tourist economies, tourism is evidently the new staple.

There is little country diversification of merchandise exports. The United States, the United Kingdom, and Caribbean Community countries are the main markets for the region's exports. The United States has replaced the United Kingdom as the major market for merchandise exports. Caribbean Community countries emerged as a sizable market as the regional import substitution scheme developed momentum early in the 1970s. The geographical composition of tourism exports has been more dynamic. Travel exports are now mainly to the U.S., Canada, the U.K., Germany, and France. The Caricom market is also significant for Barbados. The major changes in the geographical

Table 3
Annual Percentage Changes in Real GDP and Consumer Prices: Commonwealth Caribbean, 1976-81

	1976	1977	1978	1979	1980	1981
REAL GDP						
Barbados	4.3	3.7	4.8	7.9	4.9	-2.6
Guyana	1.0	-2.9	-2.8	-0.1	1.0	-0.5
Jamaica	-6.1	-1.7	0.0	-1.5	-5.4	2.0
Trinidad & Tobago	n.a.	n.a.	7.9	5.3	7.4	5.4
Dominica	n.a.	3.4	9.1	-9.5	-10.1	n.a.
St. Lucia	n.a.	5.8	13.5	4.4	-4.5	n.a.
St. Vincent	6.4	3.5	14.7	-0.6	0.1	n.a.
CONSUMER PRICES						
Barbados	5.0	8.2	9.5	13.2	18.3	14.5
Guyana	9.0	8.2	15.3	17.7	14.2	24.7
Jamaica	9.6	11.4	34.9	29.1	27.1	12.8
Trinidad & Tobago	10.5	11.8	10.2	14.7	17.5	14.3
Dominica	n.a.	27.1	7.7	20.0	30.4	n.a.
St. Lucia	n.a.	8.9	10.9	9.4	19.6	n.a.
St. Vincent	12.2	7.4	11.1	17.5	18.9	n.a.

Source: Jamaica: Social and Economic Survey, National Planning Agency; Guyana: World Bank Country Report; Barbados: Annual Statistical Digest, Central Bank of Barbados; Trinidad: Annual Report, Central Bank of Trinidad and Tobago; Bahamas: Statistical Digest, Central Bank of Bahamas; St. Vincent, St. Lucia, Dominica: World Bank Country Reports.

distribution of tourism exports since 1970 are the relative decline of the U.S. and Canadian shares, and the growth of those of the European countries and the Caribbean Community region. The significant point about market diversification and flexibility is the protection they offer against demand contraction or stagnation in any single country or region. In this respect, Caribbean merchandise exports are more vulnerable than travel exports. It is shown in subsequent sections that, while country diversification of tourism exports afforded quick recovery and expansion in the face of global economic recession, the country-rigidity of merchandise exports served as a drag on merchandise export performance.

The small share of Commonwealth Caribbean exports in global exports is the final structural feature to which attention is drawn. Except for bauxite, the major commoditities exported constitute relatively small proportions of import demand in the region's major external trading partners and even smaller proportions of world production and trade. Output expansion in these circumstances has little or no influence on export prices.

The Components of Recent Export Performance in Extra-Regional Markets

Some insight into this performance can be obtained by decomposing the change in the purchasing power of exports into its constituent parts. The purchasing power of exports is defined as the foreign currency value of exports divided by the foreign currency price of imports. The foreign currency value of exports itself is defined as the product of the volume of exports and the foreign currency price of exports. Accordingly, the percentage changes in export volumes and the export prices minus the percentage change in import prices. The analysis focuses on each of these constituent changes.

On examination of the relative weight of changes in import prices and changes in export values for aggregate exports, three points can be made. First in each country, import prices have risen annually, frequently by substantial amounts. Thus it is clear that import prices have been a major depressant on export performance. Second, the export value data for Barbados in 1976 and 1981, Guyana in each year except 1978, and Jamaica in 1978, reveal that even if import prices had not risen, export performance would have deteriorated in some years. Furthermore, the experience of Barbados in contrast to that of Guyana and Jamaican invites inquiry into the relative roles of export volume and export price changes. It can be argued that the differences in trends for export values reflect the stronger production performance of the Barbadian economy, the greater share of tourism exports in total exports, and the lesser degree of commodity and geographical concentration of exports.

The main underlying determinant of the foreign currency price of imports has been the rise in petroleum price and other prices of the sub-region's industrial trading partners. The world export price of crude petroleum increased by 10 percent between 1976 and 1977, 45 percent in 1978-79, and 73 percent in 1979-80. Given the high energy intensities of imported products, these price increases exerted a strong push on import prices. The main supplier of imports to the Caribbean are the U.S., Canada, the U.K., and Japan. According to OECD estimates, these countries' export prices continued to rise substantially between 1978 and 1980. For example, the U.S. export price inflation rate rose from 8 percent in 1978 to 16 percent in 1979, that of the U.K. rose from 7 to 15 percent, and Canada's from 8 percent in 1978 to 21 percent in 1979. In each case, export price inflation has slowed down since 1980, but still remains considerable (e.g. between 5 and 8 percent).

Table 4
Percentage Changes in Value, Volume and Foreign Currency Price of Main Commodity Exports

COMMODITY AND COUNTRY		1977	1978	1979	1980	1981
BAUXITE						
a) Guyana:	Value	15	0	0	47	19
	Volume	-3	-12	-14	20	19
	Price	18	12	14	27	0
b) Jamaica:	Value	9	80	12	-6	-13
	Volume	1	1	0	-6	13
	Price	8	79	12	0	0
ALUMINA						
a) Jamaica:	Value	60	70	30	47	9
	Volume	25	5	-3	15	6
	Price	35	65	30	32	3
3. SUGAR						
a) Barbados:	Value	6	-6	23	88	-53
	Volume	8	-4	3	45	-47
	Price	-2	-2	20	43	6
b) Guyana:	Value	-28	26	2	34	12
	Volume	-31	23	-3	-8	21
	Price	3	-7	5	42	-9
c) Jamaica:	Value		30	13	-7	-14
	Volume	-7	-8	-6	-30	-8
	Price	3	-7	5	42	-9
d) Trinidad:	Value	-29	-36	58	20	
	Volume	-10	-37	-1	-27	
	Price	-19	1	59	-7	
BAHAMAS						
a) Jamaica:	Value	54	47	28	-50	-50
	Volume	-1	-1	-13	-50	-44
	Price	55	48	41	0	-6

Sources: Annual Report, Bank of Guyana; Annual Report, Central Bank of Trinidad and Tobago, and Review of the Economy, Government Printer; Annual Statistical Digest; Central Bank of Barbados; Social and Economic Survey, National Planning Agency, Jamaica; World Bank Country Reports.

Turning now to the foreign currency value of exports, it is more fruitful to pursue the decomposition at the commodity-specific level. Percentage changes in export volumes and export prices are computed for the main exports. These are shown in Table 4. Buoyant prices have been the dominant positive influence on the values of the major merchandise exports. Export prices increased considerably for sugar, bauxite and alumina in the years between 1975 and 1980, while banana export prices rose steadily. In 1981, the prices for these commodities declined or stagnated. While ready statistics are not available on prices of travel services, the foreign currency price of hotel and other travel services appears to have kept pace with other basic price series such as the domestic consumer price index and the import price index.

Granted the positive contribution of export prices to export performance in most of the recent years, it must be inferred that the weaknesses discerned in the export performance of the main commodities are attributable to sluggish or decreasing export volumes. Export volumes declined for bauxite and sugar in Guyana, and either grew at a decreasing rate or declined in Jamaica. Barbados' sugar export volumes also fell continuously during this period.

Tourism volumes, measured by the number of stopover visitors and by the average length of stay, increased overall as Table 5 shows. In Barbados and the Bahamas both the number of stopover visitors and the average length of stay increased between 1975 to 1980.

Table 5
Selected Tourism Statistics

	BAHAMAS		BARBADOS		JAMAICA	
Year	Stopover Visitors (000)	Days Stayed	Stopover Visitors (000)	Days Stayed	Stopover Visitors (000)	Days Stayed
1975	903	6.9	221	8.6	394	8.8
1976	940	6.7	224	8.5	328	8.6
1977	891	6.5	269	9.0	264	8.7
1978	1083	6.4	317	9.1	382	8.5
1979	1129	7.5	371	9.9	426	8.1
1980	1181	7.6	370	9.8	395	10.2
1981	1029	7.7	352	9.6	407	10.1

Sources: Annual Statistical Digest; Central Bank of Barbados; Statistical Digest, Bank of Jamaica; Statistical Digest, Central Bank the Bahamas.

In Jamaica, the number of visitors has fluctuated with no discernible upward trend, while the average length of stay declined between 1975 and 1979. In the smaller island economies, e.g. St. Lucia and St. Vincent, the number of tourists and the average length of stay increased. The overall situation therefore has been one of volume depression and price increases for merchandise trade, and both volume and price increases for travel exports. However, as the decline in tourist arrivals in Barbados in 1981 and 1982 indicated, some uncertainty also surrounds tourism exports in at least one of the regional tourism centers.

Short-Term Prospects for Export Performances in Extra-Regional Markets

The immediate prospects for Commonwealth Caribbean export performance hinge upon many factors affecting import prices, export prices, export demand, and export production. Only the major ones will be discussed. It is probable that import prices will decline. The two main influences on the import price index are international energy prices and the export prices of the OECD countries. Energy prices have already started to decline. Crude petroleum prices declined by 2 percent during the first quarter of 1982, and by February 1983 plummeted an additional 23 percent, as the major producing countries began a round of competitive price cutting. Whether price competition continues or not, it seems that fundamental demand and supply forces are making for at least price restraint, if not for substantial price decline. The industrial economies with lower income elasticities and higher price elasticities of energy demand (1.0 and 0.4) have reduced energy intensity by 8 percent and oil intensity by 23 percent between 1978 and 1981. Substitution away from oil and greater economy in use of oil fuels have weakened aggregate demand for petroleum. On the supply side, several oil producers (Iran, Nigeria, Libya and the U.K.) have been inclined to expand output and cut prices.

Depressed world prices for crude petroleum should in all likelihood lead to a reduction or slower rate of growth of OECD export prices. In addition, there are indications that restrictive monetary and fiscal policies in the OECD countries are succeeding in lowering their inflation rates. Unit labor costs in manufacturing declined in the major economies in 1981 and 1982, and factor income distributions shifted against wage incomes, except in the U.S., where there was a small shift towards wages. The rate of growth of export prices for the entire OECD has slowed down appreciably since 1980. In 1980, export prices rose by 12 percent compared to 9 percent in 1981 and 7 percent in 1982. For the Commonwealth Caribbean's major import markets, the decelaration of export prices is even greater. The U.S. rate slowed from 16 percent in 1979 to 6 percent in 1982, Canada's from 21 percent to 4 percent in the same period, and the U.K. from 15 percent in 1980 to 8 percent in 1982.

With respect to their export prices, the immediate future does not augur well for the Commonwealth Caribbean, despite the fact that the main merchandise exports are either intra-company in the case of minerals, or sold in administered markets under stable commodity agreements for agricultural commodities. Caribbean export prices move in the same direction as world prices. There has been a distinct drop in world prices fo the pertinent primary commodities since 1980 (and 1979 in some instances). Reference has already been made to recent petroleum prices and to the dim short-term prospects for this commodity price. Aluminum prices (to which bauxite and alumina prices are indexed) decreased by 14 percent between 1980 and the first quarter of 1982, essentially returning to the slower trend of price increases characteristic of the 1970s. World sugar prices were halved during same interval. The U.K. sugar price series--a better indicator for Caribbean exports--also fell, though not as rapidly, e.g. 30 percent 1980-81 versus 39 percent for world prices. Significant export price declines were also experienced by the minor staples (some of which form a larger part of the smaller island economies' exports). For instance, world export prices of oranges fell by 16 percent between 1980 and the first quarter of 1982, while cocoa and coffee prices decreased by 35 percent and 20 percent respectively between 1979 and the first quarter of 1982. Bananas and natural gas are the only primary commodities of interest that exhibited upward world export price trends since the start of the 1980s. Banana prices (of considerable importance to Jamaica, and of major significance to Grenada, St. Vincent, Dominica and St. Lucia) increased by 9 percent and natural gas by 60 percent between 1980 and the first quarter of 1982. In both cases, world export prices have risen in every year since 1978. However, Jamaica's banana output has consistently declined, while Trinidad and Tobago has not become an exporter of natural gas.

It is probable that stagnant export demand will further depress primary commodity prices. The World Bank has forecast that LDC export volume growth rates will be considerably slower between 1975 and 1985, and between 1974-76 and 1990 for primary commodities. Sugar demand is expected to grow at 2.7 percent per annum between 1974-76 and 1990 compared with 2.8 percent between 1960 and 1976. For bananas the corresponding percentages are 2.1 percent and 3.3 percent. Real exports of fuel and energy are expected to grow at 3.4 percent between 1975 and 1985 in contrast to actual growth of 6.2 percent per annum between 1960 and 1975. Some commodites are expected to experience rising export demand. Non-fuel minerals, the World Bank estimates, will expand at an average annual rate of 5.8 percent 1975-1985 versus 4.8 percent in 1960-75, cocoa at 2.5 percent in 1975-76 to 1990 versus 2.2 percent in 1960-76, and coffee at 2.6 percent in 1974-76 to 1990 versus 1.7 percent in 1960-1976. These export projections reflect both supply and demand assumptions, not solely the latter. Nonetheless, they do provide some guidance to market prospects.

Prognoses about Caribbean export demand must reflect some judgement about income growth and production structures, commodity substitution, and domestic market production in the major industrial economies. Real income grew less rapidly, and in some cases declined in the OECD countries during the first few years of the current decade than during the 1970s. In the U.S., real income, having expanded at an annual average of 3 percent between 1969 and 1979, fell by 0.2 percent in 1980, then recovered by 1.7 percent in 1981, only to slump again by 0.5 percent in 1982. In the U.K., the corresponding percentage rates of change were 2.2 percent, -1.8 percent, -2 percent, adn 0.25 percent. Only in Canada did real GNP not decline between 1980 and 1982. The OECD has made some optimistic forecasts about future income growth in these countries on the basis of further anticipated falls in OECD inflation rates, the cessation of inventory decumulation, and buoyant export demand, especially from the OPEC countries. These forecasts are already being revised downwards, perhaps in response to the now visible downswing in petroleum export prices. Longer-term predictions have been made by the World Bank, which has forecast minimum annual average rates of growth of 2.6 percent in 1980-85, 3.0 percent in 1985-90 for industrial market economies. Even if these forecasts err on the side of optimism, it is reasonable to expect some income growth and therefore export demand expansion by the industrial countries.

Nonetheless, proportionate rates of growth in the demand for Commonwealth Caribbean primary commodity export volumes are unlikely for several reasons. First, income elasticities of demand for primary commodities are low. Second, commodity substitution in energy demand is likely to accelerate as the long gestation periods of nuclear and solar energy programs come to an end. These two reasons explain the slower annual rate of growth projected for primary commodities in world trade. Third, the competitive position of Commomwealth Caribbean countries has been eroded by the comparatively faster rate of increase in production costs and by fiscal measures adopted in relation to the mineral sector. As a consequence, other primary commodity producers have emerged as important price rivals to the Commonwealth Caribbean suppliers.

In theory, the export demand prospects for manufactured commodities should be better. The World Bank projects average annual growth rates of 12 percent between 1975 and 1985 for exports by LDCs as a group, a slight deceleration from the average annual of 15 percent achieved in 1970-75. Faster than average annual rates of expansion are forecast for machinery and transport equipment, iron and steel, and chemicals. However, the prospects for sustained growth of LDC exports of manufactured goods should be viewed cautiously. The developed countries, faced with an apparent rise in the share of LDC exports in their consumption of manufactures from about 1.7 percent in 1970 to 2.9 percent in 1978, have intensified their protection of domestic industry. Yeats (1974) has shown that tariff protection increases significantly, as the level of processing embodied in developing-country exports increases. Tariff protection, though likely to diminish significantly as Tokyo Round agreements are implemented, will still serve as a barrier to labor-intensive commodities. Non-tariff protection has also increased. Various specific protection schemes, e.g. multi-fibre arrangements, and trigger price mechanisms, have been introduced or extended. Under the Caribbean Basin Initiative, the U.S. government intends to reduce tariff barriers to manufactured exports from the Caribbean countries. It remains to be seen whether these intentions will be immune to U.S. producer lobbies.

Whatever the export demand situation, the prospects for enhanced merchandise export performance are weakened by obstacles on the supply side. One serious obstacle is the weak production performance of these economies. Overall growth rates have decelerated and production stagnation or decline has been evident for primary commodities. For example, between 1975 and 1980 sugar production decreased by 44 percent in Jamaica, fluctuated around the stationary trend in Guyana, fell 43 percent in Trinidad and Tobago, and except in 1980 stagnated in Barbados. Substantial output decreases were recorded for the lesser agricultural staples in Jamaica, St. Vincent and Trinidad and Tobago. Mineral output also contracted. In Jamaica, bauxite production was stationary between 1976 and 1981 while alumina production fell by 6 percent between 1975 and 1979, before recovering to its 19 peak output. Guyanese output of bauxite diminished by 20 percent, and alumina by 43 percent between 1975 and 1981. In Trinidad and Tobago, crude oil production, having increased from 78.6 million barrels in 1975 to 83.8 million barrels in 1978, decreased to 69 million barrels in 1981. Though not as critical a constraint on extra-regional merchandise export performance, for the simple reason that output is not geared to extra-regional markets, domestic manufacturing production has grown in an unsteady fashion in Barbados and in Trinidad and Tobago, two of the countries with sizeable manufacturing sectors. In Jamaica, the third country, manufacturing output declined in every year of the 1976-81 period. These trends in primary commodity and manufacturing output indicate that a better production performance is a requisite for enhanced export performance.

Serious domestic disincentives to merchandise export supply exist in all Commonwelath Caribbean economies. Official input and output policies for commodities and foreign developments have together resulted in under-capacity production and low profitability. Furthermore, the quota and tariff systems and the fiscal incentive mechanisms have biased manufacturing output against exports, particularly to extra-regional markets. In a study of Jamaican manufacturing industry, Ayub (1981) estimated effective protection coefficients of 1.68 on domestic sales, 1.19 on Caricom sales, and 0.90 on exports outside of Caribbean Community market. These connote a substantial bias against exports. A later study (Ranis, 1982) reveals that the degree of effective protection varies greatly among various categories of commodities (effective protective coefficients of 4.6 for durable goods, 1.2 for non durables, 0.7 for processed foods and 0.05 for producer goods).

A final obstacle to merchandise trade, which can only be mentioned briefly here, is the apparent inability of Commonwealth Caribbean producers to penetrate new commodity and geographical markets. There has been little change in the commodity composition of trade and in the spatial balance between traditional and new markets. This inflexibility, which is as much a problem of rigid production structures as it is of marketing skills and communication, has limited the region's ability to take advantage of differential rates of growth for various commodities and of differences in economic fortunes among nations.

Paradoxically, perhaps, the potentials and limitations of market flexibility in enhancing export performance are vividly illustrated by recent developments in tourism exports. Caribbean tourism is a product with high income and price elasticities of demand. Bond and Ladman (1972), and Ffrench (1972) estimate income elasticities of 1.1 to 1.5, and Ffrench aslo estimates a relative price elasticity of -2.5 to -3.8. Given greater than unitary income elasticity of demand for tourism services, tourism export performance will respond negatively to falling per capita incomes in the source countries. Moreover, a switch in the composition of source countries towards those with rising or less rapidly falling incomes can boost or moderate the depression of tourism exports. Barbados and the Bahamas, which reoriented their tourism product towards the higher growth economies of W. Germany, France, Scandinavia and Canada, and away from the more slowly growing U.S. and U.K. economies, were able to sustain a growth in tourist volumes until 1980. In contrast, Jamaica maintained its concentration on the U.S. market and experienced stagnant demand (admittedly also due to the Jamaican socio-political problems).

Future growth of tourism exports is contingent upon income growth in the OECD countries. There is a limit to the scope for output expansion through market diversification when, as happened since 1980, national economic growth rates converge. Domestic price trends in the Caribbean relative to per capita income of tourists and relative to price trends in competing tourism centers are also critical to future prospects. Not only is tourism demand sensitive to the import purchasing power of foreign income and to relative prices, but the degree of responsiveness to relative prices is likely to have increased as real foreign income decreased. From this standpoint, continuing high rates of inflation in the Commonwealth Caribbean portend problems for the tourist industry.

Granted this less than sanguine appraisal of prospects for extra-regional export performance, the final issue addressed briefly is whether the prospects are any better for intra-regional exports.

Intra-Caribbean Trade Prospects

The Caribbean Community was established in 1973 to provide an integrated market for regionally produced goods. Four countries predominate in Caricom trade: Barbados, Guyana, Jamaica, and Trinidad and Tobago. Manufactured goods constitute more than two-thirds of intra-regional trade. Nonetheless, intra-regional trade in manufactures are a small proportion of manufacturing output. Domestic enterprises display a marked preference for their own national markets. The share of intra-regional trade in total trade has declined from 7 percent in 1970 to 4 percent in 1980. The purchasing power of Caricom exports rose by 29 percent in Jamaica between 1976 and 1980. In Barbados it rose by 6 percent overall between 1976 and 1979, but had declined substantially between 1978 and 1979. Trinidad and Tobago's export purchasing power declined by 28 percent between 1976 and 1979, but recovered by 27 percent over the next two years. Guyana, the other major country, experienced a more or less steady decline (totaling 29 percent) in purchasing power of exports between 1976 and 1979. Thus, it is evident that the intra-regional trade performance of Commonwealth Caribbean countries is far from impressive.

Intra-Caribbean export performance during the 1970s has been affected principally by the following factors: (1) income stagnation or decline in some importing countries, e.g. Jamaica and Guyana; (2) increases in export prices; (3) decreases in export supply due to increased domestic demand and to sluggish domestic production in the exporting countries; and (4) increases in import prices for regionally produced intermediate goods. Assuming that the export performance characteristics which prevailed during 1978 to 1981 remain unchanged, the export performance of Caricom countries is likely to deteriorate perceptibly in the near future.

The issue of the effect of import prices on the purchasing power of intra-Caribbean trade can be dispensed with very quickly by extending our earlier conclusions to state that import prices substantially depreciated the purchasing power of intra-Caribbean exports.

The cost of intra-regional exports have been increasing rapidly, particularly since the oil price shock in 1973. Though there has been some lowering of costs through adoption of improved technology, the greatest impact has been in the electronic products group, which represents a small proportion of intra-regional exports. In each country, wage costs have risen pari passu but in a lagged relationship with the rate of general price inflation. Because labor intensity of production is uniformly high among the countries, differences in national inflation rates imply differences in comparative costs of production within the region.

Two conclusions follow from these observations on costs of production. First, differences in export performance among countries reflect differences in comparative costs depending on the price sensitivity of import demand in the several countries. Estimates of price elasticities of Trinidad, Barbados and Jamaican import demand for a range of manufactured goods by Adams (1971), and Joefield-Napier (1981, 1982) range between -0.064 and -2.363. Producer goods exhibit low price sensitivity, while consumer goods are price-sensitive. Because consumer goods are the largest proportion of intra-regional trade in manufactures, differences in national cost levels partly explain the differences in export performance. The second conclusion is that Caribbean producers are price-efficient foreign producers from penetrating the Caricom market to the degree implied by differences in price margins. However, official policy seems to be shifting towards opening up Caribbean markets to extra-regional suppliers with the hope of providing a spur to more price-efficient and more export-oriented production by domestic firms.

An important obstacle to the growth of intra-regional trade is the stagnation or retardation of output and per capita incomes throughout the Commonwealth Caribbean. An earlier section presented some details on the recent trends in output and by association income, and speculated about the immediate future course of these variables. On the demand side, the retarding effect of income stagnation depends on the income elasticities of demand. Estimates of these elasticities have been provided by Adams (1971) and Joefield-Napier (1981, 1982). These indicate low income elasticities for non-agricultural consumer and producer goods (1.2 to 2.3). It can therefore be inferred that income declines will adversely affect the potentially high growth commodity groups in intra-regional trade, and thereby depress overall export performance in the regional market.

Granted the influence of domestic production costs and domestic income growth on the behavior of intra-Caribbean trade during the 1970s and thus far in the 1980s, the appraisal of recent trends of income and cost factors leads to the judgement that there is little prospect of the Caribbean Community market acting as a buffer in the event of slow growth of extra-regional trade.

Conclusions

On the basis of the analysis of the main features and trends in the export performance of the Commonwealth Caribbean and the review and prognosis of the short-term future of income and prices in the sub-region and its trading partners, the following broad conclusions are ventured. First, the prospects for extra-regional export demand in volume terms are likely to improve during the later years of the current decade. Second, primary commodity export performance is likely to be adversely affected by future declines in commodity prices. Third, Commonwealth Caribbean import prices may continue their deceleration, thereby offsetting to some extent commodity export price depressing. Fourth, the Commonwealth Caribbean is not in a position because of current production difficulties and the rigid, static nature of its export structure, to take advantage of export demand growth in the immediate future. Fifth, intra-regional export performance is likely to be further hampered by income stagnation and the comparatively faster rates of inflation among the Commonwealth Caribbean countries.

Medium-term prospects may be improved by the effective implementation of policies designed to increase and diversify domestic production capacity, to raise real incomes, and to improve the price-competitiveness of Caribbean exports. Policies are also being proposed for the reduction of the economic bias against exports and for up-grading marketing skills. However, the anlysis of the specific character and dimensions of these policy proposals and initiatives and their likely effects cannot be pursued here.

REFERENCES

1. Adams, Nassau, "Import Structure and Economic Growth in Jamaica 1954-1967" Social and Economic Studies, Mar. 23, 1971.

2. Ayub Mahmood Ali, Made in Jamaica. The Development of the Manufacturing Sector, World Bank Staff Occasional Papers #31.

3. Bond, M.E. and Jerry R. Ladman, "Tourism a Strategy for Development" in Charles E. Gearing et al. Planning for Tourism Development (New York, Praeger, 1976).

4. Bourne, Compton (ed), Inflation in the Caribbean (Kingston, Jamaica: Institute of Social and Economic Research, UWI, 1977)

5. Ffrench, Rudolph, A., "The Effect of Devaluation on the Foreign Trade Balance of Jamaica", Social and Economic Studies, 21,4 Dec. 1972.

6. Joefield-Napier, Wallace, "Trinidad and Tobago's Economic Growth and the Balance of Trade: 1954-1968," Social and Economic Studies, 27,4, 1978.

7. Joefield-Napier, Wallace, The Demand for Imports: The case of Barbados, 1954-1970 (Kingston I.S.E.R. U.W.I. 1982).

8. OECD Economic Outlook 30, Dec. 1981.

9. Ranis, Gustav et al. "Production and Export Incentives in the Caricom Region," Report of a Group of Experts to the Caribbean Community Secretariat, May 1982.

10. World Bank, World Development Report, 1981.

11. Yeats, Alexander, J., Trade Barriers Facing Developing Countries (New York: St. Martin Press, 1970).

MEXICO'S PERSPECTIVES UNDER A THREE-YEAR AGREEMENT WITH THE IMF*

Juan Lara

Mexico's current economic crisis brings into sharp focus the constraints that the external environment imposes on the economy's growth and development. Burdened with a large external debt and facing a sharp cut back in external financing, the Mexican economy is suffering a drastic curtailment of its ability to import, and will probably continue to suffer from an imports bottleneck in the medium and long terms.

After three decades of pursuing an inward-looking, import-substitution strategy of economic development, Mexican authorities are likely to put more emphasis on export performance in the coming years. With oil exports found not to be the panacea they were once thought to be, non-oil exports will be expected to become a major source of growth and employment generation, and to bear the burden of relaxing, if not breaking, the foreign exchange bottleneck that has become the authorities' chief concern.

While exports will probably play a leading role in the recovery from the current recession, it appears unlikely that they will be a leading sector in the medium and long terms. Many obstacles of a bureaucratic, institutional, and economic nature must be overcome for Mexico to become an outward-looking, export-oriented economy. Indeed, a reorientation of the whole development strategy may be required to achieve that goal. It is nonetheless interesting and encouraging that the authorities and the private sector seem to have become aware of the urgency of moving in that direction. However, an analysis of such change in development strategy is beyond the scope of this paper.

This paper presents an outlook for the Mexican economy for the period 1983-85, with special emphasis on the evolution of the external sector. The first section presents an overview of the developments that led to the current crisis, and sets the background for understanding the economic policies assumed to be implemented by the authorities. The second section analyzes the short-term outlook, focusing on the role of exports in leading the economy out of the recessionary cycle that started in early 1982. In a brief closing section, the factors that could change the outlook for 1983-85 are listed.

The Making of the Crisis

The underlying causes of the current crisis can be traced back to 1978. After achieving remarkable success in breaking the inflationary process inherited from the Echeverria admininstration, the Lopez Portillo administration, then in its second year, changed course to pursue rapid growth and employment generation via expansionary fiscal and monetary policies. The recently-discovered oil wealth of the country became the basis for an ambitious development program that was later to become formalized in the Global Development Plan of 1980. Over a period of four years (1978-81), real government expenditures grew at an average annual rate of 14.9 percent, with investment expenditures growing at an average of 20.4 percent per year in real terms. Money supply growth over the period was around 33 percent per year.

The private sector, given a psychological boost by the early success in turning around the accelerating trend of inflation and by the discovery of vast oil reserves, joined in the expansion. Private fixed capital formation grew at an average annual rate of 13.6 percent during the period, and private consumption expanded at an average rate of 8.2 percent per year. As a result, real GDP grew over 8.0 percent per year, and the

*This paper is based on the DIEMEX-Wharton February Forecast for the Mexican economy. Thus, it reflects the contributions of Abel Beltran del Rio, Vaughn Montes, and Francisco Gutierrez. The author alone assumes responsibility for the interpretations and opinions expressed in the paper.

ambitious employment goals of the Global Development Plan were overfulfilled.

The oil boom, as this period has come to be known, was not based on oil alone. The availability of abundant and relatively cheap external financing also played an important role in supporting the expansion. From 1978 to 1981 the external debt of the public sector grew from US$26.2 billion to US$53 billion. The private sector also borrowed heavily to finance ambitious investment programs. As a result, Mexico's total external debt rose to US$74.9 billion at the end of 1981 (see Table 1).

The rapid pace of the expansion generated a situation of excess demand that was reflected almost immediately in a reactivation of inflationary pressures. As measured by the implicit GDP deflator, inflation rose to 20.2 percent in 1979 and to 28.7 percent in 1980, from the low of 16.8 percent attained in 1978 as a result of the stabilization efforts in the first year of the Lopez Portillo administration. However, inflation was moderated by the rapid growth of imports. As Table 2 shows, domestic aggregate demand grew much faster during these four years than domestic aggregate supply, with the gap being filled by the dramatic growth of imports. This growth was encouraged by the rapid expansion of the economy, the availability of external financing, and the policy of keeping the exchange rate virtually fixed at close to 23 pesos per dollar.

Table 1
External Debt at the End of the Year
(Billion dollars)

Year	Total Debt	Public Debt		Private Debt
		Long Term	Short Term	
1970	7.1	3.3	1.0	2.8
1975	20.0	11.6	2.8	5.6
1976	26.1	15.9	3.7	6.5
1977	29.7	20.2	2.7	6.8
1978	33.4	25.0	1.2	7.2
1979	40.2	28.3	1.4	10.5
1980	50.7	32.3	1.5	16.9
1981				
June	n.a.	33.4	4.6	n.a.
December	74.9	42.2	10.8	21.9
1982				
August	79.3	48.4	8.9	22.0

n.a.: Not available

Sources: Statistical Appendix, Historical, Informe de Gobierno, 1980 and 1982, Ministry of Planning and the Budget; Banco de Mexico.

As the current account deficit widened and inflation continued on the rise, the peso became increasingly overvalued. A simple purchasing-power-parity calculation, presented in Table 3, illustrates this phenomenon. Non-oil exports were discouraged by the overvaluation of the peso and the strong internal demand, while imports continued to grow at a fast rate. Nevertheless, a corrective devaluation seemed out of the question given the availability of external financing.

The ambitious goals of the Global Development Plan were predicated on high oil prices. When these dipped in July of 1981, confidence in the government's policies began to erode at home, and among bankers abroad. Other aspects of the external environment also took a turn for the worse. The recession in the United States limited the growth of non-oil exports, and the dramatic rise of interest rates increased the burden of debt service. At the same time, a bitter disagreement over Mexico's fiscal and financial stimuli to non-oil exports developed with the United States.

Mild corrective policies were introduced in the second half of 1981, including a move to fiscal austerity, a moderate slide of the peso against the dollar, and the reintroduction of import-licensing requirements. Nevertheless, the year ended with an US$12.5-billion deficit in the current account, and a record increase in the net external borrowing of the public sector. It was clear then that the oil boom was over, and that 1982 would be a year of adjustment.

Table 2
Aggregate Demand and Supply
Real Growth Rates

	1978	1979	1980	1981	1978-81	1982
Aggregate Demand						
Internal Demand (1)	9.2	10.9	11.2	9.7	10.3	-5.0
Private	7.7	10.8	8.5	9.0	9.0	-3.8
Consumption	8.1	8.8	7.5	8.1	8.2	0.6
Investment	5.1	22.7	13.7	13.7	13.6	-25.3
Public	19.8	13.3	13.2	13.3	14.9	-6.6
Consumption	9.9	9.6	9.5	9.1	9.5	-0.4
Investment	31.6	17.1	16.7	17.0	20.4	-11.7
External: Exports	11.6	12.1	6.1	5.7	8.8	-10.4
Aggregate Supply						
Internal Supply (GDP)	8.2	9.2	8.3	8.1	8.5	-0.7
External Supply: Imports	21.9	29.9	31.9	18.5	25.4	-35.5

(1) Includes changes in inventories
SOURCE: Ministry of Planning and the Budget

Table 3
Purchasing-Power-Parity Exchange Rate
(pesos/dollar)

Month	Prices Mexico[1]	Prices U.S.[2]	P-P-P Ex. Rate[3]	Ordinary Ex. Rate (controlled)	Ratio P-P-P to ordinary Ex. Rates
January 1977	100.00	100.00	22.18	22.18	100.00
December 77	115.46	105.45	24.28	22.74	106.77
December 78	133.71	115.57	25.66	22.72	112.94
December 79	160.33	132.59	26.82	22.87	117.27
December 80	202.66	149.28	30.11	23.26	129.45
December 81	257.79	157.17	36.38	26.23	138.70
February 82	281.88	158.73	39.39	44.64	88.24
June 82	339.67	159.07	47.36	48.04	98.59
August 82	398.99	159.62	55.44	49.81	111.30
December 82	496.83	162.83	67.68	96.48	70.15

1 Wholesale Price Index for Mexico City. January 1977 = 100.00
2 Wholesale Price Index, "All Commodities." January 1977 = 100.00
3 Assumes that the prevailing exchange rate in January 1977 was the P-P-P exchange rate.

SOURCE: Banco de Mexico and DIEMEX-Wharton calculations

Space limitations preclude a careful discussion of the many dramatic events in 1982. To put it in a nutshell, the year can be best characterized as one of frustrated adjustment. Successive attempts to implement a stabilization program ran afoul of rapidly deteriorating expectations at home and abroad. Following the devaluation of the peso on February 18, the economy slid rapidly into a state of disarray. Capital flight and a sharp cutback in external financing led to another devaluation in August and the imposition of exchange controls. At the end of the year, the economy was already in the grip of recession and hyperinflation, and the acute scarcity of foreign exchange had led to a near-paralysis of imports. Negotiations on a loan from the International Monetary Fund (IMF), begun in August by the Lopez Portillo administration, culminated in agreement on an IMF-sponsored stabilization program with the de la Madrid admininstration in December. With assistance from the IMF, negotiations began on rescheduling the public external debt and on a US$5 billion commercial-bank loan for 1983. The IMF program—covering the period 1983-85—sets the policy background for the short-term outlook.

The Short-Term Outlook

The de la Madrid administration has moved swiftly to implement the stabilization measures agreed to with the IMF. These call for a reduction of the fiscal deficit as a fraction of nominal GDP to 8.5 percent in 1983, from the nearly 17 percent of 1982. They also require the accumulation of at least US$2 billion in foreign exchange reserves, and a limit on net external borrowing by the public sector of US$5.0 billion this year.

The program also constrains monetary policy by placing a limit on central-bank financing of the public sector deficit and encouraging increases of interest rates. Wage policy, although not explicitly included in the agreement, is to be conservative. Minimum wages were increased 25 percent in January, and are to be revised again in July. So far, wage settlements in various industries have stayed close to the 25-percent signal sent by the authorities in January, suggesting that organized labor is willing, at least for the time being, to toe the line set by the authorities.

The outlook presented here is taken from the Alternative 1 forecast produced by the DIEMEX-Wharton Mexican Service in February 1983. The major assumption in this scenario is that the onus of adjustment in the short term will be compounded by a drop of 5.50 dollars in the average price per barrel of Mexico's oil exports.* The authorities are assumed to absorb the impact of the drop in oil prices to maintain reasonable compliance with the terms of the IMF agreement, especially during the current year.

The major assumptions and results in this forecast scenario are presented in Table 4. The specific numerical assumptions are:

- The average price per barrel of Mexican oil is assumed to drop by US$5.50 from its February level. Oil exports are assumed to average 1.6 million barrels per day (mbd) and to rise by 100,000 barrels per day each year thereafter.

- A level of government spending that results in a real drop of 25.3 percent in investment expenditures and of 3.0 percent in current expenditures is assumed for 1983. Total government spending drops 14.5 percent in real terms.

- Owing in part to the impact of the drop in oil prices on the free foreign exchange market, the controlled (official) exchange rate is assumed to slide faster than the current slippage rate. For 1983 as a whole, the controlled rate is assumed to rise 81 percent, ending the year at 174.55 pesos per dollar.

- The authorities are assumed to apply strict import controls to keep the current account deficit to a level consistent with the availability of external financing and the goal of accumulating foreign exchange reserves. As a result, imports drop 2.8 percent in real terms in 1983.

- Money supply growth is assumed to be 66 percent in 1983, a figure that appears to be consistent with the guidelines in the IMF agreement.

The assumptions in this scenario lead to a drop of 5.5 percent in real GDP in 1983, to be followed by low positive growth (1.9 percent) in 1984. The accelerating trend of inflation is broken, however, and the current account deficit is substantially reduced,

---

*The outlook presented in this article was prepared in February, at the height of uncertainty about oil export prices. The actual reduction in Mexico's oil export prices, announced on March 14, was less than that assumed for the purpose of this forecast. The average price per barrel was cut $2.75, instead of the $5.50 assumed here. Consequently, the projection for the current account deficit in this forecast is likely to be an overestimate, and the controlled (official) foreign exchange rate is not likely to reach the 174.55 pesos/dollar envisioned in this forecast scenario. Other assumptions underlying the outlook are based on the IMF-sponsored stabilization program, and remain valid.

although at the cost of seriously hindering imports. While the average inflation rate in the Consumer Price Index (CPI) and the GDP deflator peaks at nearly 100 percent, the December-to-December rate in the CPI drops to 76 percent from the high of 98.8 percent reached last year. The current account deficit is reduced to US$2.9 billion.

Except for exports, all components of real aggregate demand drop in 1983. Real government spending drops 14.5 percent, private consumption declines by 5.2 percent, and private investment contracts by 20 percent. The severity of the recession is underscored by the fact that private consumption has never dropped in Mexico's recent economic history.

The results for the balance of payments are summarized in Tables 5 through 8. Total exports of goods, services, and factors in current dollars increase 4.0 percent in 1983, which represents a real growth of 16.4 percent. The value of oil exports declines 14.3 percent due to the assumed drop in prices, but the export volume increases 7.4 percent to the assumed 1.6 mbd from last year's 1.49 mbd. Non-oil merchandise exports, which are estimated to have dropped 20 percent in real terms last year, increase by 12.5 percent in 1983. In current dollars, these exports reach US$5.5 billion, which represents a 15.8 percent increase over last year's value. Exports of services also post a substantial growth rate (19.7 percent in real terms), after a drop of nearly equal magnitude last year.

The value of merchandise imports increases only 8.5 percent in 1983, following an estimated 38 percent drop last year. In real terms, however, merchandise imports increase only 1.7 percent. Imports of capital goods drop 25.3 percent in real terms, following an estimated 51 percent drop last year. This is due to the sharp contraction of private and public investment that began last year and is expected to continue throughout the current year. The only imports showing substantial growth in real terms (11.8 percent) are raw materials, which reflects the selective control of imports in favor of those needed to keep the industrial plant in operation. Consumer-goods imports, which are estimated to have dropped 51.4 percent last year, post a moderate real growth rate of 2.5 percent in 1983.

The slow growth of imports follows from the need to exercise strict and selective control of imports in light of the acute scarcity of foreign exchange. The limitations on external financing and the target for accumulation of foreign exchange reserves defined in the IMF agreement leave the authorities no choice but to curtail imports in order to accommodate the strong pressure of debt service on the current account. In 1983, interest payments on the public external debt are estimated at US$7.55 billion, which amounts to more than half the earnings from oil exports projected for the year. In the two following years of the adjustment period, interest payments on the public external debt continue to be a sizable fraction of total exports, reaching US$7.1 billion and US$7.9 billion dollars in 1984 and 1985, respectively. Indeed, the external financing constraint and the burden of interest payments will force the economy to operate with a merchandise-trade surplus in the foreseeable future. A surplus in merchandise trade emerged last year for the first time in Mexico's recent economic history, reaching nearly US$6 billion. For 1983, the merchandise-trade surplus is projected at 3.14 billion dollars.

The fact that exports are the only component of real aggregate demand showing positive, and respectable, growth rates suggests that this sector may lead the recovery out of the 1983 recession. There are several reasons to believe that this will be the case. In the first place, exports are stimulated by the large devaluation of the peso last year and the depressed state of internal demand. In the second place, the recovery of the U.S. economy, which appears to be under way, should have a strong effect on the performance of non-oil exports, and especially of services.

Two factors are critical in order for non-oil exports to respond as expected. One is that the U.S. recovery actually materializes. The other is that supply constraints, arising from the inability to import production inputs, be substantially relaxed. The successful negotiation of the US$5 billion loan requested from Mexico's creditor banks should ease the import constraint and enable established and potential exporting industries to increase production. The recovery of the U.S. economy, on the other hand, is critical to generate demand for that production.

Historical evidence indicates that Mexican non-oil exports respond strongly to the level of economic activity in the United States. Estimates of the elasticity of non-oil merchandise exports and service exports, obtained from simple regressions of U.S. GNP on these variables, are substantially larger than one. This responsiveness of non-oil exports to U.S. activity levels is also illustrated by the behavior of Mexican exports during business cycles in the United States. Merchandise exports dropped 12.7 percent in real terms in 1975, a recession year in the United States, and rose 12.3 percent the following year as the U.S. economy recovered. In the same fashion, exports of services rose by 13.2 percent in 1976 following a 19.3 percent drop the year before.

The assumptions underlying the performance of exports in 1983 point to two major risks associated with this forecast. One is that the U.S. recovery could be weaker than assumed. The other is that the scarcity of foreign exchange could be such as to seriously hamper imports of raw materials and intermediate goods required to produce for export.

The year 1984 would witness a weak recovery, with real GDP growing 1.9 percent. Inflation would continue to abate, dropping to 40 percent on a December-to-December basis as measured by the CPI. The average inflation rate as measured by the CPI is 47 percent, and as measured by the GDP deflator it drops to 43.3 percent. The current account deficit drops further to US$2.2 billion, as the authorities continue to enforce import controls to stay within the external financing constraint. The merchandise-trade balance shows a surplus of US$2 billion, resulting from an 18 percent increase in the value of merchandise exports and a 28 percent increase in the value of imports. In real terms, imports of consumer goods rise by 84 percent, but their level is still below that attained in 1980. Imports of capital goods recover moderately, rising 22 percent over their level of 1983, but still below the level of 1979.

The onset of sustained growth begins in 1985, with real GDP rising 4.9 percent. The current account deficit rises to US$4.8 billion as the growth of aggregate demand gains momentum, but this figure appears in line with reasonable assumptions about the availability of external financing.

It must be pointed out that the limits imposed on the fiscal deficit as a fraction of nominal GDP are not met in 1984 and 1985, according to our results. The agreement with the IMF specifies that this ratio must drop to 5.5 percent and 3.5 percent in 1984 and 1985, respectively. Instead, the ratio for the two years turns out to be 7.2 and 7.3 percent, respectively. This results from the assumption that fiscal policy will turn moderately expansionary after 1983 to speed up the recovery—an assumption that appears plausible in light of the social and political pressures that the 1983 recession will very likely generate. In real terms, government expenditures grow 2.7 percent in 1984 and 6.6 percent in 1985. Strict adherence to the IMF guidelines would result in a stronger dosage of fiscal restraint than assumed in this forecast, and would, therefore, lead to a weaker recovery than that described here.

Inflation is moderated in the years 1984-85 by the weakness of the recovery and a relatively slow slide of the official peso against the dollar. The controlled exchange rate rises only 25 percent in 1984 and 14.8 percent in 1985, since the authorities are assumed to slow down the slippage rate to gradually eliminate the undervaluation of the official peso. Simple purchasing-power-parity calculations, as well as other less simple calculations, indicate that the official peso was undervalued at the official rate prevailing at the end of 1982 and would still be undervalued at the rate foreseen for the end of this year.

Another moderating influence on inflation is monetary policy. In 1984, money supply growth is assumed to drop to 47 percent, from the 66 percent growth rate assumed for this year, and in 1985, it decelerates further to 33 percent. Wage policy, on the other hand, does not exert a moderating effect on inflation, since the average nominal wage is assumed to increase 55 percent in 1984 and 45 percent in 1985.

The social cost of the adjustment shows up most clearly in the evolution of employment. Following an estimated 0.3 percent drop in 1982, total employment is expected to drop an additional 1.3 percent this year. In the years 1984-85, employment grows only 0.6 and 0.9 percent, respectively. By the end of 1985, total employment is projected to be still below the level attained in 1981.

The outlook for employment is the most worrisome aspect of this forecast because of the potential for social and political unrest that it raises. Indeed, a major risk associated with this forecast is the fact that the adjustment program is assumed to be carried out throughout the entire period 1983-85. This assumption could fail to materialize if political pressures become unmanageable, forcing the authorities to push for a faster recovery.

Other Forecast Risks

Some factors that can make the outlook for the short term more pessimistic than described here have already been mentioned. These include the possibility of a weaker U.S. recovery than assumed in this forecast scenario, the failure to relax the supply constraint imposed by the inability to import production inputs, and the possibility that social unrest may lead to a departure from the IMF-sponsored stabilization program. Other factors that would result in a more pessimistic outlook are a sharper drop in oil prices than that assumed, and an increase of international interest rates. Both of these are regarded as clear possibilities by many observers.

There are some factors that could result in a more optimistic outlook. These include the following:

- The drop in oil prices could be lower than assumed in this forecast.
- The volume of oil exports could be higher than assumed here.
- International interest rates could drop further.
- A drop in oil prices could result in a stronger recovery of the U.S. economy this year and higher sustained growth thereafter.
- International banks might be persuaded to extend more credit to Mexico in the event of a drastic drop in oil prices.

Should any of these events occur, the recession could be less deep and shorter, and the recovery could be stronger than predicted in this forecast.

REMARKS BY MANUEL GOLLAS

About a year ago, in this same room, I said that Mexico was the darling of the international banking community. Today things have changed. Mexico is now portrayed as an irresponsible country. The one which lightly succumbed to the temptations of easy credit and excessive indebtedness. Let us discuss this subject in the context of Mr. Juan Lara's paper and my comments on it. My observations on his presentation could be only as good as my knowledge of the details of the model on which he bases his predictions. But these are not available to me. I only have the results. With such a complex, sophisticated model composed of numerous equations, I cannot at this point evaluate the results. There is only one thing left to do and that is to elaborate a little bit about what we are doing in Mexico in relation to the problems facing the country.

Apparently the solution to the difficulties we have in Mexico now, that is, high levels of unemployment, recession in the economy, high rates of inflation, and so on and so forth, depends upon the following variables: (1) the price of oil, as it has already been said; (2) the behavior of the U.S. economy; (3) the behavior of international interest rates; and, of course, (4) our capacity to increase exports.

We are dealing with the only variable open for us to manipulate decisively and with a modicum of certainty, which is our own economy. In this context, it is appropriate to ask what is it that we are doing about increasing exports. One of the most important policies that has been recently implemented in Mexico addresses the issue of allocating scarce resources and foreign exchange to key export industries.

There have been plans before aimed at resolving this question. Along these lines, policies designed to control wages have been implemented. Naturally, we do not want the benefits of possible increases in export capacities, opened up by the devaluation, to be offset by increases in domestic prices. Otherwise, we'll be in exactly the same position in which we began. We are also cutting down subsidies on food, oil, gasoline, transport, and all other kinds of goods. I think there is an awareness among the financial authorities of the Treasury that in all likelihood to undervalue the peso will benefit us. That is, the view exists that the undervaluation of the peso should be pursued as a concious policy decision to attain the goal of promoting exports. Tourism is an important activity that will benefit from our new approach to economic policy. Our attention to it had been distracted because of our concentration on oil. But now we are trying to revive it again as one of the important sources of foreign exchange. Approximately four million people visit Mexico every year and spend about $400 per capita. As a result, almost one million jobs are created by that activity. So, obviously, it is very important for us to maintain and develop it.

Border Industries

In 1981, for instance, 20 percent of the non-oil exports can be attributed to our border industries. These are subcontracts that foreign companies have with the national companies in Mexico. We are also trying to diversify not only the products of those border industries, but also the destination of the products. In other words, we are looking for companies other than from the U.S. that want to do certain stages of their manufacturing in Mexico. Besides, we are encouraging foreign investment and we are also trying to use our excess industrial capacity.

It should be noted that not all of the loans that we received during the last six years were spent irresponsibly. Many of them have been invested in productive sectors of the economy. That investment is in place. Now we have to use the fruits of it. We are trying to expand the barter economy, in the sense of being able to draw contracts for international goods based on these transactions. We are also realizing that if we are going to increase our exports, then we had better specialize in a few select goods. We cannot try to export everything. One important program is to bring agriculture back to its feet, and hopefully to the point where it could be one of the main sources of foreign exchange in Mexico.

A number of years ago, our main source of foreign exchange was that sector. That is no longer the case. Nonetheless, I think we have the capacity and the potential markets to reestablish our position. It has been estimated that an increase in exports of between 20 and 25 percent annually need be attained in order to help solve the unemployment problem. That is not a very unrealistic possibility, given the fact that from 1970 to 1974 exports increased on the average about 23 percent annually. It has also been estimated that exports in manufactures can now increase by one billion dollars with respect to 1982. There are about 250 key industries and 60 key products in which we are going to have special kinds of programs that will increase our capacity to export. Now the main question that we should ask ourselves in Mexico (and certainly there are people who are doing this) is the following: Will the expansionary effects of a higher demand for exports due presumably to the depreciation compensate for the depressing influence of lower domestic demand? How are we going to handle the respective behavior of these two variables?

Previous to this current devaluation, we last had one in 1976. It also involved a decline in economic activity which, in fact, was quite severe. All components of aggregate demand declined. Additionally, price increases took place which were very steep--of about 20. By today's standards this was a very mild occurrence. Then there were capital outflows, even massive ones. But the economy somehow picked up again in 1977, mainly because we had oil. Despite the differences, the experience of 1976 is not totally irrelevant today. As I said before, we have an economy with a very high unemployment rate and a very high inflation rate. And that, incidentally, was not said to me by a taxi-driver, which as a group seem to constitute a very important source of information at this meeting--twice they have already been mentioned as such.

Finally, the relevant query is this. How do we then get out of this predicament? In 1976 we found oil, as I said before. But we keep on living in a sort of fictional economy—overvaluation of the peso, heavy subsidies for all kinds of activities, ravel for all of us, the distorted allocation given to our resources, and so forth and so on. I am optimistic, believing that the new set of prices in the economy will give us a chance to adjust and to put our affairs on a more realistic basis. Besides, all those other measures that I have previously noted also point in the right direction.

Lastly, if Secretary of State Schultz is correct, in the sense that the final objective of the present Central American turmoil and unrest is Mexico, then I am sure that we are going to receive a lot of help from the U.S. In that case, our difficulties will be considerably diminished and the situation correspondingly alleviated.

TRADE PROSPECTS FOR THE OIL EXPORTERS: THE CASE OF VENEZUELA

Mostafa F. Hassan

Introduction

Given the appropriate international environment, international trade can play an important role in the economic development of nations. It contributes to economic development in a number of ways:

- It expands output and provides additions to income, which enlarge domestic demand and as a result create further economic activities.
- The expansion of the market enables the economy, especially the small ones, to benefit from a more productive division of labor and from economies of scale.
- Trade also provides important ingredients essential to economic development, such as technical assistance, foreign capital, raw materials, etc.

The extent to which a country can achieve the benefits realized from international trade depends on the relative importance of its foreign sector, as well as on its trade policy and economic strategy. These last two factors, in turn, must be tailored to the specific growth and development needs of the country. For nations which rely heavily on the foreign sector, the benefits from trade are affected in part by the volume of their export proceeds and also by the effective use of these resources. Export proceeds depend on the type of markets in which the country's exports are exchanged, and on the country's trade promotional policies. A few developing countries have been fortunate to be endowed with minerals and other resources which have provided them with a relatively large sum of foreign exchange. However, they vary in their economic strategy which affects their ability to use their foreign exchange effectively to promote economic development and raise the standard of living of their people.

Venezuela is one of the fortunate economies which is endowed with not only petroleum, but with other resources, though the latter are yet to be efficiently exploited. While the foreign sector has played an important role in Venezuela's economic development, in several cases economic policy has not been a factor inducing accelerated economic development. Economic policy has not capitalized on the possibly propulsive role of the oil industry in Venezuela, and in many cases it has slowed down the momentum of development that the foreign sector has created.

International Trade Contribution to Venezuela's Development

In the past three to four decades both the international and domestic oil conditions were favorable for the rapid development of the oil industry in Venezuela. As a result the oil industry was able to substantially facilitate the process of economic development in Venezuela. It was able to do so in several ways.[1] First, it provided a substantial amount of foreign exchange which enabled Venezuela to import a variety of goods and services and at the same time maintain, until recently, a surplus in its balance of payments. Because of its dependence on oil (and not on other unstable exports) Venezuela's terms of trade have been, until recently, stable, and as a result it was able to avoid balance of payments crises which have frequently interrupted economic development in other countries. Second, the development of the oil industry has created a net inflow of foreign capital which has, until the current recession, contributed to the high rate of capital accumulation in Venezuela which created several productive activities and facilitated further the process of economic development. Third, the large amount of revenues generated by the foreign sector led to an increasing sense of security in the managerial class that helped to encourage a spirit of venturesome enterprise.[2] Fourth, the oil sector provided the government with a substantial amount of revenues which enable it to increase its level of spending. At the beginning, this was primarily used for the social expansion of overhead facilities, which consequently stimulated other economic activities. Later (as will be explained) as government revenue increased substantially, the authorities began to spend inefficiently on huge and unproductive projects that created the current high level of external public debt.

Capital Flight and Public Debt

In the past three decades Venezuela experienced two periods of capital flight crisis. The first occurred in 1958-63[3] and the second seems to have started in 1980, though there has been an outflow of capital since 1978. The causes for both capital flights are similar: lack of clear government economic policy, absence of business confidence, inability of the government to balance the budget, and the recent huge public debt. The first crisis was cured by, among other things, a devaluation of the bolivar. Confidence was restored, and economic activites were returned to their normal level before the crisis occurred. In fact, the first capital flight crisis occured in the middle of one of the most prosperous periods of Venezuela, i.e., from the early 1950s to the early 1970s. This is a period that was characterized by a relatively high rate of economic growth and also a high degree of price stability. In this period oil prices were very low (about $2.50 a barrel) compared to their current level, and as a result government revenues were a small fraction of their current level. Despite the relatively rapid growth in the economy's infrastructure, external public debt was very small and could be ignored (e.g. in 1961 external public debt was $387 million). Ironically, it was when petroleum prices increased to $35 a barrel that the public external debt became a major problem reaching about $20 billion by early 1983. When petroleum prices increased from about $3 to $14 in 1973, obviously the government expected to receive a substantial increase in petroleum income. As a result a decision was made to create an investment fund, Venezuelan Investment Fund, through which most of the income was to be channeled. Such an investment fund was designed after the Kuwaiti investment fund, which was created several years earlier and which served as an example of good investment management by a developing country. The government then decided to utilize these funds for the purpose of bringing about the structural transformations of the society. However, this was to be done in a relatively short period of time, possibly in the five-year term of office of the new government. As a result, large sums of money were spent on lavish but inefficient industrial plants, great public works, and grandiose projects. The large increase in government revenues was no match for the rapid expansion in government spending. Banks, domestic and the more important international ones, were eager to participate in the prosperity of Venezuela. They were, in a way, competing to finance Venezuela's debt, thus facilitating the rapid acceleration of public expenditures. Every government agency acquired its own debt with national and international banks. The private sector also was able to get government loans or loan guarantees for its projects. By the end of the five-year term, the government was not only unable to save part of the additional billions of petroleum income, but it had to borrow an unidentified amount, probably about $15 billion.

The new government taking office in 1979 was shocked by the huge Venezuelan external debt. However, instead of adopting a clear policy that dealt with the problems, such as imposing an austerity program, the government has continued the policy of the rapid increase in government spending. Fortunately for Venezuela, petroleum prices increased once again, to about $34 a barrel. Obviously, government income increased faster than in the period of the previous administration. However, government spending continued to advance at a higher pace, ending up with a national debt of probably $30 billion in 1983.[4]

The question now arises: Why did lending to Venezuela expand so rapidly in such a short period of time? The following are several factors that have facilitated the rapid expansion of Venezuela's external debt:

1) In general, lending to prosperous developing countries like Venezuela was considered to be a profitable business for banks especially in a period of an expanding world economy. The profit margins for banks were considered to be higher on government loans than on first class corporate loans. In addition, the risk involved was considered to be lower in the former than in the latter case.[5]

2) The high prices of oil, reinforced by views that prevailed in the second half of the 1970s regarding the expectation of major raw materials shortages,[6] encouraged further optimism about the ability of Venezuela and similar countries to support a higher level of debt service than would otherwise be the case.

3) The competition among major banks to capture a share in the promising market of Venezuela and other prosperous economies facilitated the flow of loans into these countries.

4) This international "easy money policy" of expanding credit by major international banks to the prosperous developing countries stimulated the Venezuelan government to devise new grandiose projects and to accelerate the rate of increase in its expenditures. As previously noted, this was one of the major causes of the economic crisis and capital flight from Venezuela.

As a result of the banks' desire to expand credit to prosperous countries, and the latter's desire to increase their expenditures, the external public debt of Venezuela and other countries increased rapidly, as shown in Table 1.

Table 1
External Public Debt
Selected Countries
(millions of $)

	1961	1970	1975	1978	1979	1980
Venezuela	387	924	1,393	7,384	10,239	11,144
Mexico	1,191	3,792	13,829	31,139	36,686	38,994
Brazil	2,200	4,698	17,600	40,116	47,510	51,458
Argentina	1,871	2,455	5,224	9,023	10,995	12,249
Latin America	8,149	20,786	59,087	122,497	146,052	159,633

Source: Inter-American Development Bank, External Public Debt of the Latin American Countries (Washington, D.C. 1982).

While data for recent years on external debt are scarce and not accurate, one may guess that Venezuela's external debt in 1983 stands at between $20 billion-$30 billion. Table 1 shows the high rate of increase in the external public debt in Venezuela for the period of 1975 to 1980. This rate is much higher than the average for Latin America and also for each of the other countries listed in Table 1, which are considered to be among the most highly indebted nations in Latin America. The rapid increase in the external public debt of Venezuela is also demonstrated by its relation to GNP. As a percent of GNP, external public debt increased from 6.3 percent in 1975 to about 30 percent in 1980 (see Table 2 below).

Table 2
External Public Debt as a percent of GNP

	1960	1970	1975	1978	1979	1980
Venezuela	7.6	7.7	6.3	23.6	29.9	30.4
Mexico	9.7	12.1	24.4	40.7	40.2	37.2
Brazil	13.3	10.7	17.9	29.5	29.3	27.1
Argentina	10.5	11.3	15.4	21.9	23.1	23.3
Latin America	11.0	13.6	17.5	31.9	33.2	31.7

Source: Inter-American Development Bank, External Public Debt of the Latin American Countries (Washington, D.C. , 1982).

However, as a percent of the value of exports, Venezuela's external public debt service had been increasing at a moderate rate until 1980, as shown in Table 3. In fact, this ratio compares favorably with the corresponding ratio in other developing countries in Latin America and other parts of the world. After 1980, however, the ratio of external public debt service to the value of exports has deteriorated very rapidly for Venezuela.

Table 3
Ratio of External Public Debt Service
to Value of Exports of Goods & Services

1961-70	1971-75	1975	1978	1979	1980	
Venezuela	2.7	5.2	5.8	7.7	10.3	14.8
Mexico	21.5	23.0	25.5	56.7	65.6	33.2
Brazil	22.2	15.1	17.5	31.9	38.5	36.1
Latin America Ave.	13.4	13.6	14.8	27.7	28.6	23.8

Source: Inter-American Development Bank, External Public Debt of the Latin American Countries (Washington, D.C. 1982).

End of International "Easy Money Policy"

The optimism that prevailed in the second half of the 1970s began to change into a mood of pessimism as these favorable conditions began to deteriorate in the 1980s. Several factors can explain this turning point:

1) The extended recession, and its depth in the U.S. and Europe, has resulted in a more conservative approach in the lending policy of banks to developing countries in general.

2) The sudden eruption of the financial problem of Mexico, which was due to the build up of external debt not associated with commensurate levels of trade, has caused

great concern in the financial circles and reinforced the conservative approach in their lending policy.

3) The rapid increase in international interest rates in 1980-82, accompanied by the recent decline in the price of petroleum, has adversely affected Venezuela's burden of its external public debt. While the decline in the interest rate that began last August (1982) did not produce immediate relief, the weakening international oil market has reduced Venezuela's oil exports to 1.5 million barrels a day, 300,000 barrels less than initially estimated at a price of $4 per barrel below that projected in the 1982 government budget. As a result, Venezuela's exports fell by about $6 billion in 1982.

4) The collapse (in November 1982) of the largest commercial bank, Banco de los Trabajadores, created an uncomfortable feeling about Venezuelan economic conditions in the international financial community.

5) Venezuela's entanglement in the Falkland war, as well as Standard and Poor's lowering of the country's bond rating, has added to the difficulty of securing further loans.

6) Capital flight reached an alarming level in 1982. By the end of that year the dollar sales of commercial banks averaged $80 million per day. As a result, Venezuela's international reserves suffered a serious decline of $5 billion, lowering international reserves to the $15 billion level by year-end. This created a widespread fear that the country was heading for devaluation and exchange controls, and in turn stimulated further capital flights.

Earlier in the year, and in order to bolster confidence in Venezuela's financial conditions, the government revalued the central bank's gold reserves from $42 to $300 an ounce. This move boosted Venezuela's international reserves by about $3 billion. In addition, the dollar holdings of all government enterprises were consolidated at the central bank, including about $6 billion belonging to Petroleos de Venezuela. Unfortunately, instead of improving confidence, that measure had the opposite effect. Many viewed the transfer of Petroleos de Venezuela's reserves to the central bank as harmful to the long-run viability of Venezuela's petroleum industry.

Exchange Controls and Public Policy

All these factors have finally forced the government to institute an exchange control system by which three exchange rates are determined. The first is the old rate of 4.3 bolivars to the dollar for the import of necessities, and the second is that of 6 bolivars to the dollar for items needed for economic development. The third rate is the free market rate which is applied to the remaining transactions.

It is obvious that devaluation is not an adequate solution to the general economic problem in Venezuela. In fact, devaluation could worsen economic conditions in the short run. Usually after a devaluation aggregate demand falls, especially when the economy was not badly overheated before the devaluation, as was the Venezuelan case. This leads to a further drop in profits and a subsequent increase in unemployment, which will provoke calls for expansionary actions by the governments. This, of course, would be impolite when the major solution to the economic ills of Venezuela is contraction of government activities, as will be explained later in this paper.

Another immediate effect of devaluation is the increase in prices. With devaluation, importers attempt to pass on to their customers all or most of the increased cost of foreign goods. The higher the level of imports, the greater is the effect of devaluation on increasing domestic prices. In Venezuela a relatively large portion of domestic consumption goods is imported and this obviously will be reflected in higher prices.[7] In addition, producers of domestically manufactured goods also usually raise their prices since competition from imported goods is reduced. Such inflationary pressure could provoke further increases in wages and in other local costs. These, in turn, may offset the decline in the foreign prices of the relatively limited Venezuelan quantity of exports, which would otherwise have resulted from the devaluation. Obviously, the major export of Venezuela, petroleum, will not be affected by devaluation since its price is determined in dollars according to international market conditions. On the other hand, imports in the short run will be reduced. In the long run, imports could rise to their former or higher level once the Venezuelan consumer becomes used to the new level of higher prices. This would be the case in the absence of an effective and successful import substitution policy[8] geared to international markets and not only to the relatively small Venezuelan market. Additionally, exchange controls, with their sharp alteration of relative prices and hence of factor incomes, may result in major economic distortions in the allocation of resources.

From the above brief and general analysis of the effects of devaluation[9], one may conclude that the exchange control system may contribute very little to the solution of the Venezuelan problem.

Government Expenditures

It is obvious that exchange controls are only temporary measures, and for most part they do not cure the underlying economic problems. Ultimately, one has to delay with the basic cause of the problem, which has created a business "confidence crisis." An expanded and detailed research is badly needed to outline and analyze the various types of policy and measures that are necessary to improve economic conditions in Venezuela. In this section, however, some of the urgent measures needed are briefly outlined.

A major cause of the crisis in confidence is the fiscal problems created by the losses of government-controlled industrial and public service enterprises. The following table gives a general idea of the magnitude of the debts of government enterprises.

Table 4
Debt of Venezuela's Public Enterprises
March 31, 1982

Enterprise	Amount (in $ Million)
SIDOR (Steel Co.)	2,060
C.V.F. (Venezuela Development Corp.)	2,010
National Water Institute	1,190
Housing Authority	955
National T & T	726
Hydorelectricity Development	685
National Urban Development	613
National Savings Fund & Loan Bank	418
National Port Institute	392
Centro Simon Bolivar	355
ALCACA (Aluminum Co.)	309
Caracas Metro	309
Western Venezuela Electricity	190
Iron Company	97

The losses and debt of government-controlled industrial and public service enterprises have been fostered by the problems of industrialization. In Venezuela, the pattern of industrialization has been different from that of successful small developing countries such as Taiwan, where the emphasis has been on export-oriented production, due to the small size of the market and the existence of relatively low wages. By contrast, in Venezuela industrial export orientation has been of secondary importance. Many of the industrial projects have little or no comparative advantage. They depend on imported capital-intensive equipment, high levels of wages,[10] and protection from foreign competition. Because of the high level of wages and the capital-intensive techniques of production, the process of industrialization does not solve the problem of unemployment.[11] The state enterprises have accentuated these features of industrialization in Venezuela. Usually well-intentioned politicians use state enterprises to push through particular projects which require an immense amount of capital and which turn out to be inefficient for lack of proper planning and management. The only beneficiaries of these projects are public officials who maneuver these salespeople. In addition, public services and public utilities are often used by the government as a means of subsidizing the cost of living of the urban population.

In recent years, despite the rapid increase in petroleum revenues, government expenditures on unproductive public projects have by far exceeded these revenues, resulting in the huge public debt which has contributed to the current crisis in Venezuela. The most important single measure that may contribute to the solution of the problem is the drastic decline in public expenditures. While the public enterprises issue cannot easily be resolved, a quick solution must be found. For this purpose two groups of public enterprises should be identified. Those that provide public services and those which are supposed to be industrial or commercial in nature. The first provide important services at reasonable and sometimes very low cost to consumers. These will have to continue to offer their services, though they must improve their efficiency. The second group must be eliminated or sold off totally or at least in part. Given their size, selling off these enterprises to nationals is not easy. The case may be different if foreign enterprises are invited to participate in these projects. Foreign enterprises will not only provide capital, but also management and technical skills which are badly needed in Venezuela. This suggestion is contrary to the current attitude toward foreign investment in developing countries. The rise of economic nationalism in the late 1950s (as stimulated by the writings of such economists as Hla Myint, Paul Baran, Paul Sweezy, and others[12]) and the attack on the multinational corporation[13] as a means of not only exploiting and exhausting their resources but also corrupting their governments, have encouraged developing countries to change their attitude toward foreign investment. Because it was felt that foreign investment created more foreign "dependency" than foreign loans, developing countries began to substitute loans for foreign investment to finance their development projects. However, these projects must be productive in order to yield a profit from which the debt can be serviced. In the case of Venezuela, the unproductive projects together with the rapid increase in the interest rates have made it very difficult to service the country's debts. In the absence of productivity resources that generate profits, the servicing of the debt can be achieved only through refinancing which increase further the burden of the debt and also the level of "dependency" on foreign resources. Such "dependency" may be reduced if foreign corporations (which need to change their attitude and reduce the conflict between their objectives and those of developing countries[14]) are able to participate in these projects, sharing both the risk and the reward from the operation of them. In this case, not only will these corporations bring the other ingredients necessary for the productive functioning of these projects, as well as for the general economic development of the country, but they will also contribute to the lowering of the burden of the public debt. In short, the payment of profit to foreign corporations will be a far less problematic burden to the Venezuelan government than its current international obligation of servicing the public debt.

Other Needed Policies

There are several other measures that may also contribute to the solution of Venezuela's problem. These are stated briefly as follows:

1) A well-defined and clear economic policy is badly needed to reduce the uncertainty from which investors are currently suffering.

2) A drastic reduction in government red tape procedures in almost all aspects of business is required to facilitate and stimulate economic activities.

3) Greater efforts are needed to create new incentives and stimulate a greater volume of savings by Venezuelans.

4) Greater care and attention should be given to private basic industries. One of the most important industries in Venezuela is construction. Production in that industry declined by about 10 percent in 1979, 15 percent in 1980, and 3 percent in 1981. Production capacity in the industry is running below 70 percent and unemployment is about 40 percent. This activity needs adequate financing and increased domestic savings, elimination of complex red tape procedures and clear policies regarding the contracting and payment of public works.

5) Helping industries to increase productivity and efficiency by improving import-substitution programs, as well as by meeting foreign competition domestically and possibly also in the international market, will make an important contribution to the healthy functioning of industry.

Conclusion

While oil exports have played an important role in the economic development of Venezuela since the 1940s, the country has not been able to take full advantage of international trade as an engine of growth and a means of transforming the economy into a more mature and developed one. Given the growth potential resulting from the relatively high incomes of petroleum exports, the availability of other resources, and an appropriate economic policy, Venezuela could have achieved a higher degree of economic development than it is currently experiencing. While most of the ingredients for the rapid transformation of the economy are available, two important factors are missing: 1) skills and entrepreneurship and, 2) efficient public administration and clear public economic policies. While labor and management skills, as well as other required ingredients for the transformation of the economy could be imported, Venezuela has not encouraged the attraction of these resources for several reasons.[15] Among these factors, an important one is the fear that the distribution of the gains from development will be mostly in favor of the foreign resources. However, in this respect, one must take a long-run approach of the future acceleration of development that may result from the current use of imported resources. Another factor is fear of an increased predominance of foreign interests in Venezuela in an age of rising national aspirations. This is considered by many to be both politically and economically undesirable. The past experience of Venezuela provides an example of the foreign influence when oil has contributed to the maintenance of corrupt governments.[16] While the conditions now are different from those which prevailed four to six decades ago, economic nationalism seems to be one of the factors that slows down the rapid transformation of the Venezuelan economy. In addition, the private sector has not shown willingness to make sacrifices to attain the necessary transformation of the Venezuelan economy. Such willingness has been reduced by Venezuela's large capacity to import, which provides the domestic economy with a large variety of imported consumer goods. In addition, the small size of the domestic market, foreign competition, and the preference for foreign products discourage further the inducement to industrialize and transform the economy. Development is also discouraged by the lack of a well-defined social and economic policy that stimulates and provides incentives for the transformation and industrializaton of the Venezuelan economy.

While a more detailed and adequate analysis is needed of the factors and policies that are required to accelerate development in Venezuela, a brief outline of these factors has been explained above. While in most other countries the most pressing need is for the government to do "more," in Venezuela the extreme urgency is for the government to do "less." The latter term is used here in two important aspects. First, "less" of grandiose projects that the government is unable to manage, either now or in the near future. Also, less of a whole line of other expenditures that have created a mammoth public debt responsible for the current crisis and which, if not resolved, soon may result in an economic disaster in an economy that has almost all the ingredients for successful development. And second, "less" of government regulations of industrial development and other activities which have discouraged incentives and reduced economic activities.

As mentioned earlier, the fiscal problems of Venezuela have created a business "confidence crisis" which is the major cause of the current economic problems. The fiscal difficulties have been created by the great losses and waste of government-controlled industrial and public service enterprises.

In conclusion, the trade prospect for Venezuela will continue to be good in terms of the exports of petroleum and the imports of products, basically consumer goods. The question is whether the relatively high volume of Venezuela's trade will contribute to more enduring benefits for Venezuela in terms of a more rapid expansion and transformation of the Venezuelan economy, which in turn would induce further expansion and diversification of Venezuela's foreign trade. It is important to note that Venezuela has not been able to secure greater and more lasting benefits from the accelerated development of the petroleum industry and from such favorable conditions as the availability of basic natural resources, the accumulation of large amounts of foreign exchange, and the absence of balance of payments problems for many years. Economic nationalism, foreign competition, inefficient government projects, lack of a defined economic policy, and absence of managerial and manpower policy are the basic factors that prevented Venezuela from maximizing benefits accruing from its foreign sector. Whether Venezuela will be able to derive more enduring benefits from its foreign sector depends on the ability of the government to adopt the appropriate policies, and also on the initiative of the private sector. Under current conditions, the possibility of improvement is remote. However, if the government changes its economic policy, reducing substantially its expenditures and the regulations that discourage economic activities, and goes on to and develop an appropriate monetary and fiscal policy, and if the private sector takes the appropriate initiative and makes the necessary sacrifices, the task of rapid economic development in Venezuela becomes much less difficult than that in many developing countries, and the prospects for trade expansion and diversification for Venezuela become very promising indeed.

FOOTNOTES

[1]For more details on the contribution of the oil industry to Venezuela's economic development, see Mostafa F. Hassan, Economic Growth and Employment Problems in Venezuela: An Analysis of an Oil Based Economy (New York: Praeger Publishers, 1975) Chapter 2.

[2]Cordiplan, Social Change in Venezuela (Caracas, 1965).

[3]M. F. Hassan, "Capital Flight: Venezuela 1958-1960," Inter-American Economic Affairs, Autunm 1963.

[4]One must bear in mind that it is not easy to find accurate, consistant data on the external debt of Venezuela and of most other developing countries.

[5]For more details, see Pedro-Pablo Kuczynski, "Latin American Debt," Foreign Affairs (Winter 1982/83).

[6]Among the publications predicting shortages in major raw materials are Jay Forrester's World Dynamics (Cambridge, Mass.: Wright-Allen Press, 1971), The Club of Rome's Limits to Growth (New York: Universe Books, 1972) and the British "A Blueprint for Survival" (The Ecologist, 1972).

[7]For more details, see M. F. Hassan, "Inflation and Growth Once Again: The Latin American Case," Rivista Internazionale di Scienze Economic e Commercial (March 1971).

[8]In the 1950s many Latin American and other developing countries implemented import substitution projects in order to promote industrialization and overcome some of their balance of payments problems. At the beginning they were successful, but by the end of the 1960s they had exhausted the potential of this strategy due to the small sizes of the domestic market and other reasons. For more details, see, for example, Albert Hirschman, "The Political Economy of Import Substitution Industrialization in Latin America, "Quarterly Journal of Economics (February 1968), and Werner Baer "Import Substitution and Industrialization in Latin America," Latin American Research (Spring 1972).

[9]For more adequate analysis of the effects of devaluation, see Richard N. Cooper, "Currency Devaluation in Developing Countries," Essays in International Finance (June 1971).

[10]M. F. Hassan, "High Growth, Unemployment, and Planning in Venezuela," Economic Development and Cultural Change. (July 1967). See also John Beyer, "High Growth, Unemployment, and Planning in Venezuela: Some Observations," Economic Development and Cultural Change, (January 1970), and M. F. Hassan, "High Growth, Unemployment, and Planning in Venezuela: A Reply," Economic Development and Cultural Change, (January 1970).

[11]For more details, see M. F. Hassan, "Unemployment in Latin America: Causes and Remedies," The American Journal of Economics and Sociology, (April 1973).

[12]See, for example, Hla Myint, "An Interpretation of Economic Backwardness," Oxford Economic Papers (June 1954); Paul Baran, "The Political Economy of Growth," Monthly Review, (1968); Paul Sweezy, The Theory of Capitalist Development: Principles of Marxian Political Economy (New York: The Monthly Review Press, 1964) and Raul Prebisch, "Commercial Policy in Underdeveloped Countries," American Economic Review (May 1959); and Hans Singer, "The Distribution of Gains between Investing and Borrowing Countries," American Economic Review (May 1950); and Hans Singer, "The Distribution of Gains from Trade and Investment-Revisited, "The Journal of Development Studies (July 1975).

[13]For more details, see M. F. Hassan, "The Role of the Multinational Corporation in Land Development in Latin America," Rivista Internazionale Di Scienze Economic E Commerciali (May 1980).

[14]For more details, see Richard Bennet and Ronald E. Muller, Global Reach: The Power of the Multinational Corporations (New York: Simon and Schuster, 1974).

[15]For more details, see M. F. Hassan (1975) op. cit. pp. 39-40.

[16]For more details, see Edwin Lieuwen, Venezuela (New York: Oxford University Press, 1961) p. 50.

TRADE PROSPECTS FOR LATIN AMERICA: THE CASE OF COLOMBIA

Juan Jose Echavarria

Introduction

It is not very encouraging to know that last year Colombian growth was among the highest in Latin America; only Ecuador did better. This "successful" figure is one of the lowest of the post war period, and most people believe that in 1983 economic growth will be nil or even negative. Of course, the behavior of the foreign sector is not the only reason for those meager results, and many economists today argue that there are some other more important explanations. After all, the negative impact of the foreign sector could be compensated through fiscal and monetary policies, or through subsidies to agriculture and industry. Fortunately, this important issue is not our main concern here.

Rather, we want to examine those factors related to the foreign sector which contributed to place Colombia in a better position than most of the other Latin American countries. First, policies adopted by the Colombian government toward foreign loans and imports were rather conservative. Ex-post, risk-averse countries do much better than risk takers, when the world system becomes unstable and falls into depression. Also, export promotion policies were relatively successful. Second, Colombian terms of trade improved after 1975, when the price of coffee increased dramatically. However, other Latin American countries were not so fortunate. Also, exports of cocaine and marijuana were a new and significant source of foreign exchange for the country. On the other hand, oil was never important in terms of total imports. All these factors allowed Colombia to accumulate reserves at rates unknown in the past. Third, the Andean Pact played a role, not so much because "trade creation" policies were effective, but rather because the Venezuelan market was very dynamic. Of course, the Pact had the advantage of declining commercial results from developments of bilateral discussions in other areas.

Nevertheless, the situation is not particularly favorable at present. Colombian unemployment is high and increasing.[1] Moreover, the country will badly need foreign exchange in the near future. In 1981, imports were higher than exports for the first time in more than five years. This trend continued in 1982, when the difference between imports and exports of goods represented 3.6 percent of GNP. Reserves dropped more than 15 percent in 1982, and something similar will in all likelihood happen this year. Colombian dependency on a single export commodity is the highest in Latin America after Venezuela.[2] Besides, the terms of trade will not improve in the near future.

In the first section of the paper we will review the Colombian experience during the seventies. In the second we will see how export perspectives are not very encouraging. Something should be done to regain our shares in the international market and to promote the dynamism of regional markets despite the difficulties attending this task. We now conclude with some remarks on imports substitution.

I. Colombia in the 70s

We start with a description of those policies related to borrowing and export promotion in Colombia. Next, we see how our high dependency on coffee turned out to be convenient, at least for the period 1975-80. Finally, we consider some points related to the influence of the Andean Pact.

A. Government Policy

Borrowing. Until 1974 the situation was not very different in Colombia from that in other Latin American nations: the country borrowed more resources abroad than those strictly needed to compensate for the deficit in the current account. The Eurodollar market was rapidly expanding, real interest rates were low or negative, and two or more years were allowed for repayment. It was convenient to borrow, even if the commodity boom of 1972-73 allowed exports to be higher than required imports. In retrospect, the accumulation of "unneeded" reserves during this period was a good policy. It allowed the country to sustain high import levels during the recession of 1974-75. Accommodation to oil price increases and to the international recession was obtained at near zero cost.

From 1976-80, however, the Colombian experience was very different. All the countries continued borrowing, but while Colombia showed increasing surpluses in its payments, other countries were less fortunate, their current accounts remaining negative.[3]

First, it is not a secret that the Colombian government was very conservative in its attitude towards loans: Euromoney (June, 1978) classified the country as "Latin America's prickliest borrower." The different governments argued, for example, that foreign exchange did not belong to the government but to the private importers. Nobody ever understood the argument and the truth is that aversion towards government intervention in the economy was showed once more. A different strategy could of course have been followed. For example—and this was suggested by many Colombian economists—in a way similar to the one followed by Brazil, the government could have forced public owned firms to increase their investment, or subsidize private investment in those sectors with a high propensity to export. Once reserves were exhausted, the government could have borrowed in the Eurodollar market. It is still very early to evaluate the merits of various policies; the results depend on how deep and how long the world recession will be.

Second, similar to Brazil and contrary to Chile or Argentina, the government tried to accommodate foreign loans to internal and external requirements. The "invisible hand" was not allowed to operate freely in the international financial markets. Import barriers were not dismantled, and private sector borrowing was rather discouraged, at times even prohibited.

Exports and Imports. Many people still consider Colombian policies to be among the most successful in the management of the external sector in Latin America. According to this view, Decree Law 444 of March, 1967, was a good example of policy-making intended to avoid the impact of trade shocks. The decree codified and rationalized existing regulations and practices in the field of trade and payments and, even more important, it reinstated the crawling peg that had been abandoned since 1958.

Colombia was one of the first countries to promote exports in Latin America.[4] In 1967 the country rationalized a draw-back system known as Plan Vallejo, which had been created in 1959, and an income tax reduction tied to exports (CAT).

Our economic growth between 1967 and 1974 was the highest ever recorded prior to 1974 and, according to Diaz Alejandro (1976, p. 208), the Colombian experience indicated that drastic import liberalization was neither a necessary, nor a sufficient condition for export growth. Also, that large output gains could be obtained by avoiding stop-go cycles, through the coordination of fiscal, monetary, and external policies.

Export quantum--excluding coffee--almost tripled in less than seven years, and manufactured exports increased five times between 1967 and 1974. As in many LDCs, euphoria was at its highest level ever, and some people even thought that the "structural" foreign exchange deficit experienced by the country throughout most of its history was no longer a problem. Export "miracles" were spreading in the under-developed world, and those successful experiences showed that exports could and should be the new engine of growth. In 1974, the newly elected President Lopez called Colombia "the new Japan of South America."[5]

In this last year the quantum of non-coffee exports decreased 5 percent, and manufactured exports more than 40 percent, notwithstanding an increasing real exchange rate. Studies undertaken during 1977 and afterwards showed that things were more complicated than were originally thought to be the case. Even for a "small" country like Colombia, with a share of less than 0.15 percent in world exports, the market was not "infinite." World demand was one of the crucial determinants of Colombian exports. It had an important role to play, perhaps because the international market is very segmented, particularly in manufacturing. Moreover, the stability of the exchange rate, praised before as one of the most favorable characteristics of Colombian policy, was no longer an important variable in the explanation of exports. Finally, contrary to what could have been expected, the export quantum increased faster between 1960 and 1967 than between 1967 and 1977,[6] although the opposite occurred in most LDCs (Echavarria, 1980a). After all of this it can be asked, how important was the package implemented in 1967? My answer is that it had some positive influence, but it was not as important as was originally thought.

Coffee, Other "Commodities" and Oil

Bad weather in Brazil saved Colombia from the traumatic experience faced today by many Latin American countries. Due to exogenous reasons, coffee price almost tripled, in real terms, from 1975 to 1977.[7] Production stayed almost constant from 1974 to 1977, but increased from 7.4 millions of bags in 1976-77 to 12 million in 1979. Only a small portion of production is consumed internally, and coffee exports—quantum wise—doubled between 1976-77 and 1980. The share of non-coffee exports in registered exports was reduced from 56 percent in 1974-34 percent in 1978.

Marijuana and cocaine exports were also significant as a source of foreign exchange, though it is very difficult to estimate their precise importance. Junguito and Caballero (1978, p 131), estimate that they increased from US$1 million in 1970 to US$500 million in 1977. However, other studies (Ruiz, 1979; Ruiz and Lopez, 1981) indicate much larger figures. These last studies estimate that Colombia exported 10,000 tons of marijuana in 1978 and 15,000 tons in 1979. If we accept their price of US$70 per pound FOB, this could represent US$1,400 million in 1978 and $2,150 million in 1979. In cocaine, the "value added" in Colombia represented between US$154 and US$420 million in 1978. The figures of these last two studies would indicate that non-official exports of cocaine and marijuana were higher than coffee exports, even in those years when the value of coffee exports was at the highest level ever recorded.[8]

Oil was never too important in terms of total imports. On the contrary, until 1974, oil-crude petroleum and fuel oil-exports were the main source of foreign exchange after coffee. Things changed after 1975, when the country had to import oil for the first time in many years, but, as Table 1 shows, the share of oil in total imports was very limited. Even in 1981, the figure of 6 percent contrasts with that of 20 percent for the Latin American non-oil producing countries as a whole. For Brazil, oil represented almost 50 percent total imports in 1981.

The Andean Pact

In 1967 more than 65 percent of manufactured exports from the "south" went to other countries in the "south" (Echavarria, 1980b), and Colombia was not an exception. Today, with a share higher than 30 percent, Venezuela constitutes the most important market for Colombian non-coffee exports. This is an important development, if we consider that this share was less than 5 percent in 1970. On the other hand, Diaz Alejandro (1976, p. 73) found that the Colombian minor exports to LAFTA and to the

Table 1
Participation (percent) of Crude Oil Imports in Total Imports

	Colombia	Latin American Producers	
		Arithm. Average	Weighted Average
1960-64	0.00	6.14	3.99
1965-69	0.00	7.27	4.76
1970-74	0.00	9.25	9.10
1980	3.19	17.60	18.33
1981	5.97	n.a.	19.96

Sources: IMF, Financial Statistics; DANE, "Anuario de Comercio Exterior."

Methodology: Arithmetic Averages for each period.
Latin American Non-Oil Producers: Argentina, Brazil, Costa Rica, El Salvador, Guatemala, Honduras, Nicaragua, Panama, Paraguay and Uruguay.

Andean Group were more capital intensive than those shipped elsewhere, indicating that those markets could be obvious candidates for the promotion of manufactured exports.

Colombia signed the "Cartagena Agreement" more than 10 years ago, and it is now time to ask ourselves about the effectiveness of the policies adopted. Of course, the Agreement had many important elements: a common treatment of foreign capital, an industrial programming system, a common external tariff and the freeing up of intra-regional trade. Our main concern, however, are those aspects of the Agreement which could contribute to the promotion of trade.

It seems, in retrospect, that the Andean Pact played an important initial role, but its impact has decreased with the passage of time. Moreover, the very impressive case of Venezuela is explained mainly by the dynamism of its market, by the exchange rate between Colombia and Venezuela, and by other factors such as proximity and lower levels of competition. Exports would have increased anyhow, even without the "Cartagena Agreement." The analysis is similar for the relative capital intensity for our exports: it could have been expected, even without the existence of preferential trading arrangements, since the Colombian factor endowment is closer to that of the rest of the Latin America than to those of North America and Europe.

All of the empirical studies on Colombian exports undertaken before 1976 concluded that the Andean Pact played a very important role in the expansion of trade. The variable which tried to incorporate its effects was always significant in the econometric models. However, later studies (Echavarria, 1980a), did not obtain the same result, suggesting the diminishing impact mentioned above.

The conclusions of L.J. Garay (1981) are rather similar. As an explanation of exports to those markets, it was found that import reductions were not important. Actually tariffs increased for those products with the best export performance. Garay also concludes that Colombia did not "learn" by first exporting to the Andean Pact countries.[9] Finally, the case of Venezuela is rather an exception. The Peruvian share of Colombia non-coffee exports is down to 2.6 percent today from 8 percent in 1970, and for Ecuador the figures have been almost constant around 6 percent over more than 10 years. In turn, Bolivian participation is almost nil.

What, then, is the importance of the Andean Pact? We believe the main advantage would be to have a "cushion" against the recession in the developed capitalist countries. Once the recession starts affecting our nations, trade could be diverted to neighbor countries. However, paradoxically, it seems that the stronger the world recession hits our economies, the higher become the barriers between Andean Pact countries.

Export Perspectives

In comparison with other Latin American countries, Colombia finds itself in a privileged situation. Borrowing was high in terms of the past record, but cannot be compared with the borrowing histories of Brazil, Argentina or Mexico. It is not advisable to renegotiate loans today, when banks are panicking over the debt situation of Poland or the Latin American countries just mentioned and, even less, when real interest rates are higher than 25 percent in terms of export prices.[10] Profits, amortizations and interests payed abroad by Colombia in 1978 represented only 14 percent of exports. It could be close to 20 percent today. This ratio was 43 percent for Latin America, and more than 45 percent for the non-oil Latin American countries. Nevertheless, reserves have been falling considerably since 1981 and its amount could be negligible in the next few years, unless new loans can be obtained. To reduce imports will not be the best solution.

Latin America as a whole is in a worse situation. Exports decreased almost 20 percent in real terms during 1982—10 percent in nominal terms—,and higher loans were required in order to sustain imports. But the required loans did not materialize, so that the only solution at hand was to cut imports drastically. In order to sustain the level of real imports of 1981, and be able to service the debt, the continent needed a surplus in the "capital account" of more than US$60,000 million. However, this surplus was only US$19,000 million at the end of 1982. Capital flows towards Latin America decreased from an index of 224 in 1981 (1973=100) to 145 in 1982 (CEPAL, 1983).

How is Latin America going to avail herself of the foreign exchange needed? Loans will not be readily forthcoming during the next several years and export perspectives, which basically depend on world demand, look rather poor. Although something could be done to regain markets, the emphasis should be placed on internal demand and, in the case of some medium income countries like Colombia, Chile or Peru, on import substitution. In the following paragraphs we will review various factors related to exports, and conclude with some comments on import substitution.

World Demand

According to some projections (see F.G. Adams in this book), the industrialized countries will grow at an annual rate of just 2.9 percent in 1983-87. However, this rate could be lower, if we consider how projections made in the past have been systematically more optimistic than ensuing results.[11] It seems that the huge expansion of the post war period has ended and that fiscal and/or monetary policies are not as powerful as originally thought.[12]

If growth rates are low, protection will be high, and even more so for the products exported by the LDCs, which have a weak position at the international negotiating tables. Paradoxically, the industrialized countries should understand that only with low protection and a deficit in their current account--at least with respect to our countries--will Latin America be able to repay loans.

Terms of Trade

In 1982, the terms of trade for the non-oil Latin American countries were the lowest since 1930 (Table 2). Taking 1952 as a base year (100), the index for 1982 was 58.40, and the drop betwen 1972 and 1982 of 30 percent--especially acute between 1980 and 1982, when it fell by 15 percent. It is also clear that the behavior of the terms of trade has been more favorable for the other non-oil LDC's than for the Latin American nations.

Countries like Chile or Peru were most adversely affected due to the fact that the relative price of copper and iron ore fell more earlier than any other commodity. Nevertheless, the terms of trade for agriculture also moved perversely: the index for 1982 is lower than that of the worst period of 1940-49. The only countries which did not do so badly were those dependent on oil or, as is the case of the big southeast Asian exporters, on manufactured products like apparel.

As previously mentioned, it is impossible to guarantee an improvement in the terms of trade, even if the projected growth rate of 2.9 percent, which we consider optimistic, happens to materialize.

Table 2
Terms of Trade
Latin America (Non-Oil)
And Non-Oil Developing Countries
(1952=100)

	Latin America	LDCs	Different Groups of Products: Apparel	Agricult.	Non-Oil Minerals	Oil
	(1)	(2)	(3)	(4)	(5)	(6)
1930-39	73.17	n.a.	122.09	90.08	102.32	97.91
1940-49	85.77	n.a.	124.94	89.95	98.05	101.48
1950-59	101.87	95.11	105.24	107.12	116.13	100.63
1960-69	82.11	87.75	109.34	89.48	116.11	116.52
1970-74	84.55	90.15	98.40	126.24	134.93	179.69
1975-78	78.43	84.84	119.65	112.50	87.72	343.73
1980	68.88	78.24	144.78	116.68	83.70	511.26
1981	60.96	n.a.	187.26	96.43	66.93	561.77
1982	58.40	n.a.	n.a.	87.20	55.55	591.42

Sources:

IMF Financial Statistics, United Nations, Cuadernos Estadisticos de la CEPAL, (1976) "America Latina: Relacion de Precios de Intercambio" (P.25); Historical Statistics of the United States, Bicentenial Edition; CEPAL, "Estudio Economico de America Latina, 1981 " (Cuadro 27); CEPAL, "Balance Preliminar de la Economia Latinoamericana durante 1982" (Cuadro 10).

Methodology:

Arithmetic averages for each period.
The weights used for Columns 3-6 correspond to the relative importance of the different products for the period 1970-72. This explains the differences between the first and the second part of the table. Figures for columns 1 and 2 are more reliable.

Column 1.1930-709. based on CEPAL (1976).
1970-82. CEPAL (1981 and 1982).--non oil--.

Column 2. From IMFFS. Export and Import unit values for "Non Oil Developing Countries."
Column 3. 1930-70. U.S. Historical Statistics. Serie E-156
1971-82. From DANE, Anuario de Comercio Exterior. Arithmetic Average between implicit prices in Chapters 61 and 64 (clothing and footwear).
Column 4.Weighted Average of prices for beef, coffee, cotton, sugar, wheat and wool. Between 1952 and 1982 it also includes bananas, cocoa and fishmeal. Weights were taken from total Latin American exports for 1970-72. Prices for 1930-52 were taken from US Historical Statistics; for 1952-82 from IMFFS.
Column 5.Weighted Average of prices for copper and iron ore (weights for Latin American exports 1970-72).
Column 6.From IMFFS and U.s. Historical Statistics.

C. **Latin American Share in the International Markets**

Latin American participation in world exports decreased from 11 percent in 1950 to 8 percent in 1960 and 5 percent in 1975-77 (Tironi, 1982, and Movarec, 1982), and this was not only due to the behavior of oil exports. Participation increased in manufacturing (from 1 percent in 1960 to 1.4 percent in 1982), but it was reduced for almost every other good. Between 1960 and 1977 the Latin American share dropped in 13 out of the 18 products considered by UNCTAD as important for the LDCs. Markets were lost to other LCDs in coffee, rubber, copper and bauxite, and to the industrialized world in sugar, beef, oil seeds and phosphate rock. Moreover, the events just described occurred for almost every country. The only exceptions were Brazil and Costa Rica in coffee, and Nicaragua in cotton.

Low growth in Latin American exports has been due, then, not only to the behavior of world demand, but also to the fact that the continent lost participation in almost every international market. However, it is difficult to conclude from these facts that our countries can regain the shares obtained in the past, at least in relation to other LDCs. Maybe, the results just described are the "natural" outcome of the industrialization process followed by Latin America in the last twenty years or more. As described, the continent gained participation in manufacturing. On the other hand, when some Latin American countries have a "monopoly power" in some goods--e.g., Brazil or Colombia in coffee--it is almost inevitable that, in order to keep prices high by means of export restrictions, participation will decrease. Other countries know that they can act as "free riders." Finally, some of the results just mentioned are the result of the policies adopted by those multinationals which control an important share of the market. If they decide not to invest or export from Latin America, there is not much that can be done.

Nevertheless, shares can be increased in some commodity markets. We cannot accept the view that the continent and every country lost ground due merely to "natural" are exogenous factors. More aggressive and selective policies have to be undertaken, and the exchange rate should be kept at parity levels or even devalued in real terms. On the other hand, we lost participation with the industrialized countries, partially because large subsidiaries were given by those countries to exports. Definitely, this is an important issue which should be the subject of negotiation. Clearly, we need to export in order to repay our debt.

Conclusions

In this paper we have seen how the favorable behavior of exports--coffee, drugs and minor exports--and a conservative policy towards borrowing have placed Colombia in a better situation than most other Latin American countries. The proximity to Venezuela and a low dependency on oil were also favorable factors. However, export prospects are not good. World demand will not increase much during the next several years and it is likely that protection will only exacerbate the situation. It is clear that something needs to be done to regain participation in the international markets.

The main concern of the different governments should be, then, how to continue with a selective process of import substitution and how to increase internal demand. Exports played an important role for some countries during the 60s and 70s, but the world will not be the same in the future. At least in Colombia, the main source of growth during the 60s and 70s was the evolution of internal demand (Ocampo, 1982, p. 26), and exports played only a minor role. Poor export prospects do not necessarily mean low rates of growth. Moreover, even if the process of import substitution is exhausted in countries like Brazil, Mexico or Argentina--which remains debatable--it is not in Colombia, Chile, Venezuela or Peru. The size of our markets is comparable to the Brazilian one in 1950, or to the Mexican or Argentine markets around 1958. At the same time, those countries followed an import substitution process which was very fruitful.

Although we saw how barriers increase even for "south-south" trade in times of crisis and recession, our countries have to understand that the Andean Pact and ALADI constitute one of the few possibilities to make the process of import substitution more viable. The lesson to be learned from these experiences is that a successful developmentally oriented trade strategy must heavily rely on mechanics or regional cooperation.

REFERENCES

CEPAL, "Balance Preliminar de la Economia Latinoamericana en 1982".

----. Statistical Yearbook for Latin America.

Diaz, Alejandro C. (1976) Foreign Trade Regimes and Economic Development Colombia, NBER, Columbia University Press.

Echavarria J.J. (1980a), "La Evolucion de las Exportaciones Colombianas y sus Determinantes. Un Analisis Empirico," Revista del Banco de la Republica, Agosto.

Ffrench, Davis R. and E. Tironi (1982), Latin America and the New Interantional Economic Order, Macmillan.

Garay L.J. (1981), El Pacto Andino. Creacion de un Mercado para Colombia, Fedesarrollo.

Junguito R. and C. Caballero (1978), "La Otra Economia," Coyuntura Economica, Dic.

Lewis, W.A. (1982), Economic Record, 1919-1939.

Movarec M. (1982). "Exportaciones de Manufacturas Latinoamericanas a los Centros y su Significado", en Revista de la CEPAL, Agosto.

Ocampo, Jose A. (1982), "Politica Economica bajo Condiciones Cambiantes del Sector Externo", en Ensayos sobre Politica Economica. Colombia, Sept. 1982, Rev. No. 2. Banco de la Republica.

Ruiz H. (1979), "La Produccion y el Comercio de la Marihuana en Colombia", ANIF, Carta Financiera, Enero-Marzo.

---- . and J.F. Lopez (1981), "Economias Clandestinas, Economia Subterranea y las Perspectivas del Sector Externo", ANIF, Carta Financiera, Enero-Marzo.

Tironi E. (1982), "National Policies towards Commodity Exports", in French-Davis and E. Tironi.

ACKNOWLEDGEMENTS

I want to thank Carlos Caballero, Leonard Villar, and Sonia Weill for their valuable comments.

FOOTNOTES

[1]The absolute level of industrial employment today is similar to the level in 1972. The level of unemployment in Medellin is the second highest in Latin American after La Paz.

[2]The country produces today more than 12 million bags. With world surpluses, Colombia will not be able to export more than 9 million (Ocampo, 1982, p.8).

[3]Of course, this does not mean that the policy followed by Colombia was without cost. The government was not able to sterilize foreign exchange, and this was for the country. Inflation rates were much higher than in the previous years or even decades. They had been increasing since 1969—less than 8 percent in 1969—and moved to over 20 percent after 1976, an unprecedented level.

[4]And it did so without dismantling import tariffs and restrictions. Protection was even increased during the period. The average tariff for consumer goods, raw materials and capital goods increased from 53, 26 and 21 percent in 1964, to 99, 50 and 38 percent in 1970, respectively (Coyuntura Economica, Dec. 1982, p. 95).

[5]Imports increased but, on the whole, exports were higher.

[6]After a very marked increase between 1967 and 1974 they remained relatively stagnant.

[7]Even in 1980, after a drastic drop in the previous years, it was higher than in the first part of the 70s. The nominal price for 1977 (US$2.29 per pound) was over five times higher than the average price for the 60s (around US$0.40).

[8]The main difference between the studies cited seems to be the export price. For Junguito and Caballero, the export price of marijuana in the Colombian port was US$12.50 per pound in 1977; according to the other two studies, it was US$70.

[9]According to this view, Colombia would export first to the Andean Pact Group, and then, once the country has learned how to produce and compete, exports would go to

[10](CEPAL, 1983) This indicates, in one figure, what Kuczynsky calls the "scissors effect." Sharp drops in commodity prices and rapid increases in interest rates (quoted by E. Sanchez in his paper in this book).

[11]In the OECD "Economic Outlook" of 1980 it was predicted that for 1982 the growth of rate would be 2 percent for the 24 OECD countries. This prediction was reduced to 1 1.25 percent in the "Outlook" of 1981, and to 0.5 percent at the beginning of 1982. All of them were wrong. The growth rate was negative (-0.5%).

[12]It is not the recent problem of inflation versus unemployment. Fiscal policy was not effective even in the 30s, a period chosen by many economists as the best example of the power of demand policies. W.A. Lewis (1949) shows how the world expansion came very late, after 1938, despite the enormous year-to-year fiscal deficits in the United States and in the other developed countries. The Second World War was "effective" but with an amount of expenditures and government intervention not even dreamt of by Keynes.

TRADE PROSPECTS FOR BRAZIL AFTER THE DEVALUATION

Roberto Fendt, Jr.

The recent devaluation of the cruzeiro last February has raised a lively round of discussion about the merits of the devaluation to improve trade prospects for the economy in 1983. Opponents of the devaluation pointed out that (1) export markets for Brazilian products are still much too contracted to assure success in increasing exports; (2) the import demand elasticity is too low to assure a sizeable reduction in imports via devaluation; and (3) in any case, in a highly indexed economy like the Brazilian economy the devaluation will not produce permanent changes in relative prices. Those who favor the devaluation claim that export markets, like any other markets, depend on supply and demand conditions and that a reduction in export prices will always produce an increase in quantities sold abroad, provided the change in relative prices is seen as a permanent change. In addition, although acknowledging that the world economy is still not under a clear drive to full recovery--and thus not imparting yet a significant push in exports from the developing countries--the proponents of the devaluations point out that Brazil hardly takes one percent of world trade. A slight increase in, say, one-tenth of 1 percent share in total world trade would be enough to increase Brazilian exports by 10 percent, the target growth rate for 1983. Of course, if, as expected, world trade were to recover growth with the expected world economic recovery, that increase in export revenues would be forthcoming even at unchanged market shares. The devaluation, according to this view, would expedite export growth and allow a faster change in relative prices toward tradables.

This note has the purpose of exploring some of the arguments raised in favor and against the devaluation and its impact on trade prospects for Brazil in 1983. These prospects depend on two sets of variables. The first set encompasses variables associated with the domestic stabilization program negotiated with the IMF. Although not formally a part of this program, the devaluation must be seen against the background of this stabilization effort. The second set of variables encompasses data associated to international market conditions, which are taken for granted by the domestic economy. Of particular interest, of course, are the effects of the expected recovery in the OECD countries' economies on international interest rates, Brazilian terms of trade and Brazilian export volumes. These effects will determine much of the results, while the first set of variables will impact mostly on import volumes.

The Domestic Stabilization Program and the Devaluation

As will be recalled, as a part of the scheme negotiated with the IMF, the Brazilian crawling peg policy was expected to produce a 12.7 percent devaluation over and above whatever the domestic inflation happened to be in 1983. This acceleration was supposed to take place in quarterly installments, in such a way that roughly one would observe a compounded 3 percent additional quarterly devaluation above inflation. Since the beginning of the year, however, it had become clear that the scheme would not work. First, because it accelerated devaluation compounded on the overall expected devaluation in the computation of real rates of interest for domestic loans. In an open economy like the Brazilian one this meant the <u>real</u> domestic rates of interest climbed to 30-40 percent above expected domestic inflation, with obvious implications on investment and growth. Second, the change in relative prices between tradables and non-tradables became too painful and long: one would have to wait for a full semester to expect to observe a mere 6 percentage point increase in the rate of return of export activities, certainly not enough to compensate just the appreciation of the dollar vis-a-vis the currencies of Brazil's major partners. Finally, by assuring a known gain for exporters in delaying exports—and putting pressure on importers in the opposite direction—the scheme also contributed to reduce trade surpluses in the first half of the year.

Resorting to a sudden change in parity instead of applying a gradualistic scheme previously in force requires, however, some complementary policy actions to validate the move. It is well known that, when successful, a devaluation can offset some of the side effects on output growth which accompany any balance of payments adjustment program. What is at stake, of course, is the ability of the devaluation in producing a permanent change in relative prices. To do so, two sets of conditions are required. First of all, aggregate demand must be reduced relative to aggregate supply, for otherwise the change in relative prices to restore equilibrium in the balance of payments would be beyond any reasonable range. Second, the change in relative prices which would be implemented simultaneously with the reduction of the excess of aggregate demand in the economy should not be perceived as a transitory phenomenon by the economic agents.

The widespread indexation of the Brazilian economy raises several questions in connection to the basic need to make the devaluation permanent. A devaluation has an immediate impact on the prices of all traded goods, both importables and exportables. But over and above this obvious fact, close substitutes, both in consumption and in production, of traded goods will also have their domestic prices raised by the devaluation. In a previous study of the present author,[1] it was estimated that the impact of domestic prices of any change in the prices of trade goods was very high. Every 10 percent increase in prices of trade goods transmited an increase of 7 percent to the prices of non-tradable goods. Indexation, though not the only way to transmmit these price increases—as the experience of countries without formal indexation mechanisms shows-nonetheless helps to make the transmission faster.

Being reality as it is, one precondition for full success of the devaluation clearly is the change in the indexation mechanisms. It is important to prevent that prices of factors of production be immediately raised by the effect of the devaluation; by the same token, there are no reasons to transmit to non durables, compulsorily and immediately, changes in prices of tradables goods. Finally, one cannot allow the rise in prices of tradables to be transmitted to the rates of return of financial assets. The standard monetary approach to the balance of payments clearly shows that the major impact of a devaluation arises primarily from the depreciation of the real cash balances and from the efforts to replenish them. Monetary and fiscal restraint, in this connection, is a precondition for the success of the devaluation itself.

One final point deserves to be mentioned. Since the Brazilian Central Bank is today virtually responsible for Brazilian foreign external debt, a devaluation has a fiscal implication which differs from the simple depreciation of the community's real cash balances. Since borrowers service their external debt with cruzeiros at the Central Bank, an immediate capital gain accrues on international reserves held the Central Bank, while a flow gain accrues over time as the service of the debt of the private sector is performed over time. Given the magnitude involved, this is no small amount.

The External Conditions

Of course, success in managing the balance of payments imbalance depends very much on domestic actions, since the balance of payments itself—i.e., changes in the international reserves account—merely reflect changes in the supply of domestic money and credit relative to demand. But the management of foreign external debt is another story, since it has very little to do with actual actions of policy makers. Changes in international interest rates and the actual stock of the debt, resulting from decisions taken in the past relative to the absorption of foreign savings, determine much of the present events, while being outside the command of domestic policy makers.

In a recent statement before the Subcommittee on International Economic Policy of the Senate Foreign Relations Committee, Rimmer de Vries has pointed out cogently that a blueprint for a manageable solution of the debt problem requires both a major adjustment effort in the debtor countries and a sustainable recovery and growth of the world economy.[2] Any of the two, taken in itself, will have minor impacts on key variables, such as current account balance as a percentage of exports of total debt as a percentage of exports. Over 1982 the world recession has contributed significantly to enlarge difficulties with balance of payments management in Brazil. As a direct effect of the recession, export volume declined 6.9 percent in 1982 relative to 1981, already a year of not so bright performance; to compound matters, export prices declined 5.2 percent. On the import side, despite a huge effort which resulted in a reduction in import volumes of 11.3 percent, import prices rose 0.5 percent. As a result, terms of trade declined for Brazil in 1982 some 5.7 percent, compared with a decline of 4.6 percent for 21 major LDC borrowers in the international market.

It is anticipated that in 1983 import volumes will continue to drop from current depressed levels. This will be achieved with a full knowledge of the implications of further decline in import volumes on output growth and employment. But all this effort will be meaningless if export volumes cannot resume growth, if the terms of trade do not improve and if the international interest rates do not, at least, stay at current levels. In the de Vries study mentioned above, three scenarios are constructed for the 21 major LDC borrowers in the international market. One scenario assumes a major LDC adjustment coupled with a moderate OECD recovery over the period 1983-86; the second scenario assumes the same OECD recovery but only a partial adjustment in the LDC economies; the last scenario assumes a major LDC adjustment with a minimal OECD recovery. Not surprisingly, the scenario with the worst results is the third: total debt, as a percentage of exports, increases, while it declined both in the most favorable case—scenario 1—as in the case of the OECD recovery and a minimal adjustment in the LDC economies.

Concluding Comments

The conclusions that emerge from the analysis are the following: first, Brazil is undertaking a major adjustment in the economy in order to produce external balance, even at the cost of losing other domestic objectives, such as a reduction in the domestic rate of inflation. This major adjustment effort intends both to reduce the excess of aggregate demand in the economy and to change permanently domestic relative prices, in order to create conditions for an improved competitiveness of Brazilian exports abroad and a higher rate of return of import substitution opportunitities at home.

Second, this major effort requires a strong recovery of the world economy, through which Brazilian export volumes increase, Brazilian terms of trade improve and international interest rates at least remain at the current levels. The adjustment program itself will be responsible for a further decline in import volumes.

Third, the role of the international banking system and the international multilateral lending institutions in the process of adjustment is crucial. It is a meaningless adjustment in a single country if the system is not responsive to the needs of the whole and not up to the responsibilities raised by the needs of coordination and expansion of the multilateral sources. Provided the borrowing countries perform their adjustment programs, it is up to the system as a whole to continue to create the conditions for an orderly way out of the current difficulties. The system has performed these duties and has been up to its responsibilities over all of the previous decade, contrary to the opinion of many who did not believe it would be able to. By consistently working in the same direction, borrowers and lenders can continue to perform in the eighties the successful tasks of adjustment and financing initiated in the seventies.

REFERENCES

[1]Roberto Fendt Jr., "Brazilian Trade Liberalization: A Reassessment," paper presented at the Conference on the Free Trade Movement in Latin America, Haus Risen, Hamburg, Germany, June 21-24 1981.

[2]Rimmer de Vries, "Global Debt:" Assessment and Prescription," statement before the Subcommittee on International Economic Policy of the Senate Foreign Relations Committee, Washington, D.C., January 19, 1983, published in World Financial Markets, February, 1983.

LATIN AMERICAN INTEGRATION IN THE EIGHTIES

Eduardo R. Conesa

Integration in the Sixties: an Option

In the 1960s, when the formal integration schemes were created in the Latin American region, the world economy was growing at rates on the order of 5-6 percent annually. In the face of the dynamic impact that growth of the industrial centers was having on our region, Latin America could also grow at very high rates. This happened mainly because the expansion of the industrial countries called for imports of raw materials, as well as other types of goods. As a result of this demand, our region exported and obtained foreign exchange that enabled us to make investments to stimulate our own production, which in turn demanded imports from the industrialized countries. In other words, there was synchronization between the development of the industrialized countries and that of Latin America.[1]

During the 1960s and early seventies, Latin America's economic development including the period 1963-73 proceeded at the rate of 6 percent annually. This was an exceedingly high rate, in fact one of the highest in the world. In these circumstances, the development strategy of our countries could logically have been based on the outward looking development approach which emphasizes the promotion of exports. This applies particularly to manufactured goods, inasmuch as the region's traditional exports were, and still are, hampered by a multitude of restrictions prevailing in world markets for primary products after World War II. In fact, during the sixties and early seventies many of our countries pursued a successful combination of export promotion and import substitution strategies that resulted in the above mentioned high growth rate.

Integration in the Eighties: a Need

At the present time, however, and since 1973, the world economy has undergone the shock brought about by the upsurge of oil prices. Not only oil, but also the majority of raw materials increased in price, and thereafter the prices of all of them fell, with the exception of oil. The impact of the rise in oil prices has been strong in the industrial countries. As a result of their balance-of-payments deficits, these countries have reacted by letting their economies grow more slowly, on the average, at a rate of around 1-2 percent annually. Because of this slow growth, the demand for oil imports in the period 1974-82 also increased much more slowly than would have been the case if the economies of the industrial countries had maintained their rapid expansion.[2] This was an strategy designed to prevent OPEC from exercising unrestricted monopoly power. It was a way of alleviating the internal demand for oil in the developed countries themselves.

Despite these conditions, Latin America continued to grow during the period 1973-81 at rates of about 5 percent annually. There has been a substantial positive differential in the Latin American growth rate over the one registered by the industrial countries up to 1981. The slow growth of the latter provoked increasing difficulties for the marketing of Latin American exportable commodities. Furthermore, Latin America's rapid growth caused the region to demand sizeable volumes of imports. In the face of the resulting widening gap between exports and imports, foreign loans were resorted to with increasing frequency. The Latin American foreign debt, which in 1973 was on the order of $30 billion, reached by the end of 1982 the $300 billion mark. This situation is, as mentioned above, the result, to a degree, of the rapid development of the region, compared with the slow growth of the economies of the industrial countries. Should these nations have had a high rate of growth in this period, it would have not been necessary for Latin America to incur such heavy indebtedness and our region would have been able to finance its growth to a greater degree from the proceeds of increased exports, thus keeping the foreign debt at a lower level.

In any case, this process of growth based on foreign indebtedness has come to an end. The majority of the countries in our region face problems in this respect. The foreign debt is rising to such high levels that it makes it difficult to continue to move along the path provided by this model. In the face of this situation, the Latin American countries should change the direction of their imports by importing more from Latin America itself. Our purchasing power should be channelled to a greater extent towards our own region. This will be achieved through the reciprocal opening of our markets,[3] which will bring about a better division of labor and increased competition within the region, thus leading to a better allocation of resources and to improved operation of the price system, which in turn is vital to a sustained economic development.

None of the countries in the region has a domestic market large enough to attempt autonomous development. Development in the Korean style—through encouragement of industrial exports to the industrial world—has strong limitations of its own at the present time because of the international semi-recession referred to previously. Consequently, if we want to continue to grow, the best way is the reciprocal opening of our markets. Hence, the validity of the integrationist idea in the eighties.

The Margin of Tariff Preference

Latin American integration finds itself today at a very favorable juncture. On the one side, there is great integrationist fervor in the region on account of the South Atlantic conflict and, on the other, we have several legal instruments available which, although in an embryonic state, provide the constitutional basis to move forward in a practical way. In particular, mention should be made of the Latin American Integration Association Treaty, signed in 1980 between eleven countries of the region: Argentina, Bolivia, Brazil, Chile, Colombia, Ecuador, Mexico, Peru, Paraguay, Uruguay and Venezuela. Specifically, Article V of the Treaty provides that: "The member countries shall grant to each other a regional tariff preference which shall be established on the basis of that prevailing for third countries and shall conform to the appropriate implementation regulations."

The tariff preference consists simply of a tariff reduction that each country of LAIA would grant to imports from other countries of the Association. Thus, if the preference level were fixed at 20 percent, and Venezuela, for example, had a custom duty of 50 percent on the importation of a given product, in the case that the product is imported from Argentina or Brazil, the duty would fall from 50 percent to 40 percent.[4]

A problem of the preference margin is how to make it work when the import duty is zero as well as when it is extremely high. In such cases it is apparent that the preference is not operative. If the tariff is zero, a preference margin cannot be given. In this case, what should be done is to raise the tariff for products from outside the region to a level similar to that of the margin of preference. This margin can start from a low level, for instance of 10 percent, and then gradually can be increased to levels of 50 percent or 100 percent. In the latter case we would have attained a formal free trade zone.

The Margin of Preference and its Generality

The regional tariff preference mechanism would encompass all the products of the tariff universe, with very few exceptions. This feature of the margin of preference is important because one of the factors leading to stagnation in the Latin American Free Trade Association was the casuistic method of negotiating concessions on a product-by-product basis. This new device means that creators of LAIA have realized the need to improve the former mercantile system. It is preferable to have a 10 percent tariff reduction across the board than multiple concessions for 30 percent of the products. It should, once again, be stressed that there are reasons—institutional, political and, particularly, economic in nature—that make it advisable to place all the products on an equal footing in regard to this type of tariff reduction. International experience indicates this. For instance, as long as GATT negotiations were conducted on a product-by-product basis, very slow progress was made from 1950 through 1963. Only at the Kennedy Round, when it was decided to negotiate uniform and generalized tariff reductions for all products, was it possible to make rapid progress in negotiations. And so, the Kennedy Round achieved great success, leading to a reduction in tariffs of about 35 percent between industrialized countries. This was one of the key factors in promoting trade and growth in the sixties.

The Margin of Preference, Reciprocity and the LDCs

A second advantage of the margin of preference is reciprocity, inasmuch as everything would have a "quid pro quo." A given country, Venezuela for example, would grant a margin of preference—of, say, 20 percent—to Brazil, but the latter would grant Venezuela a similar preference. However, with regard to reciprocity, the guidelines for the margin of preference allow for greater tariff reductions across the board to be given by the more developed countries of the region to the less developed ones. Conversely, the latter would give the former tariff reductions across the board but of a smaller percentage.

A further major advantage of the regional margin of preference is that it permits access of other Latin American countries to the system of LAIA. This Association excludes the five Central American countries, Panama, the Dominican Republic and others in the Caribbean. In Article 24, the Treaty of LAIA provides for a possibility of granting the margin of preference to Latin American countries which are not signatories of the Treaty.[5]

The Grounds for Protectionism in Latin America

Before ending this presentation, a short exposition should be made on a subject of theoretical importance for Latin American economic integration: the justification that our countries have to protect industry with tariffs.

There is no question about the advantages of a competitive price system as a lever to promote development. If this is so, then why not adopt the world price system? That is, the prices actually ruling in the international economy which supposedly have not been distorted by protectionism and other interferences. In other words, why not impose a protection equal to zero on all economic activities? This line of argument is attractive from the theoretical standpoint and deserves an in-depth analysis to see whether or not it is applicable in the case of Latin America.

At INTAL we have undertaken many studies on the relevancy of the theory of comparative advantage versus protection for the case of Latin America.[6]

The subject is vital for Latin American integration inasmuch as if protection to our industries were eliminated, Latin American integration would be impossible. In this case, we would integrate our economies within the world economy. But this approach has some problems. The main economic activities be stimulated would be the exports of certain primary products such as coffee, sugar, beef, wheat, corn, cotton, oil and bananas. As a result, our countries would have to channel a large part of their investment resources towards the production and exportation of these commodities in which we have a great competitive capacity at the international level.

Accordingly, a basic point for the design of a Latin American economic strategy consists of investigating whether or not a vital assumption of the theory of comparative advantage is valid. This assumption is that the price elasticity of demand for the region's exportable primary products is infinite. If the price elasticity of demand is infinite—in other words, if the demand curve that our countries face in exporting these commodities is wholly horizontal and we could then triple, quadruple or increase tenfold our exports of coffee, bananas, wheat, beef, sugar and the like to world markets without causing prices to fall as a result—then it would be obvious that the theory of comparative advantage would hold. In that case, the best avenue open to our development would consist of adopting the world price system, eliminating all kinds of protection, and concentrating our investments on these traditional export sectors, with a view toward using the proceeds of these increased exports to import more goods in the production of which we have no comparative advantage.

But if our countries faced less than infinitely elastic demand curves for these products, that is, if on account of quintupling, for example, the exports of coffee its price was to fall by 70 percent, then we ought to give serious thought to the question of whether or not we would gain any advantage by increasing these exports fivefold. Of course, this would also be the case with sugar, cotton, wheat corn, copper, bananas and so forth.

It is obvious that Latin America affects its own terms of trade either by exporting more or by exporting less of her traditional export commodities. Latin America, however, does not have a monopoly power with which to exploit other countries. Nothing would be farther from reality than such an assumption. Most of the region's exportable commodities have not, even remotely, had an elasticity pattern similar to that which enabled OPEC to exercise monopoly power. It is merely a question of how to best allocate the region's own resources in the light of existing relationships between volumes exported and prices received. In order to optimize the use of our own resources, we should equalize marginal incomes and marginal costs of exportable commodities. For this purpose, we should establish a common external tariff and a system of taxes in our foreign sector.

Thus, the new import substitution that integration would entail should be formulated on the basis of an enlarged Latin American market. It would be of sufficient size to permit competition and, accordingly, to give rise to an adequate allocation of resources. This would enable a sound growth of production to be achieved without distortions and, particularly, to do so with a more uniform effective protection. By proceeding in this fashion, we would turn the price system into an invigorating factor for resource allocation and growth.

In short, in order to overcome the antagonism between the need for protection on the one side, and the narrowness of domestic markets on the other, we Latin Americans should reciprocally open our markets to each other. At the same time, we would maintain a not-too-high degree of protection—say, between 20-30 percent against imports from outside the region. The appropriate level would be mainly, but not exclusively, on terms-of-trade considerations regarding our exportable commodities. In this way we could sustain high rates of economic growth with only a slow increase on our indebtedness.

In the context of an integrated Latin American market with a tariff wall of about 20-30 percent, direct exports from industrial countries to Latin America will have a slower growth rate than in the past. This is consistent with the constraint imposed by the size of our foreign debt.

Thus imports financed by debt will have to slow down their increase substantially. However, the tariff wall of 20-30 percent protecting an integrated Latin American market will present excellent opportunities for direct foreign investments. In this way, I believe that in the eighties the economic relations of Latin America with the North will have to rely much more on foreign investment and less on indebtedness than in the past. This will entail substantial improvement for Latin America because direct foreign investments are agents for transfers of technology, which is itself a key factor for Latin American growth.

FOOTNOTES

[1] Conesa, Eduardo R., "La Integracion de America Latina en el Decenio del 80," *Integracion Latinoamericana*, N° 36. June 1979, pp. 3-10.

[2] Conesa, Eduardo R., "La Integracion de America Latina en el Decenio del 80", *Integracion Latinoamericana*, N° 36, June 1979, pp. 3-10.

[3] Lewis, Arthur, "The Slowing Down of the Engine of Growth," *The American Economic Review*, September 1980, Spanish version in *Integracion Latinoamericana*, No. 56, April 1981, p. 13-21.

[4] See De Maria, Luis, "Perspectivas de la Preferencia Arancelaria Regional en la Asociacion Latinoamericana de Integracion," *Integracion Latinoamericana*, No. 70, July 1982, pp. 12-20.

[5] Conesa, Eduardo R., "La Integracion de America Latina en el Decenio del 80," *Integracion Latinoamericana*, No. 36, June 1979, pp 3-10.

[6] Conesa, Eduardo R., "La Aplicabilidad de la Tarifa Optima en Argentina," *Integracion Latinoamericana*, No. 62, October 1981, pp. 6-22.

Kravis, Irving B., "Aranceles Aduaneros Optimos, Integracion y otras Estrategias Comerciales para America Latina," *Integracion Latinoamericana*, No. 64, December 1981, pp.2-13.

Lonof, Marc, "Panorama Economico del Mercado Mundial de Cobre y Computo de la Elasticidad de Demanda que Enfrentan Chile y Peru," *Integracion Latinoamericana*, No. 64, December 1981, pp. 14-26.

Adams, Gerard F., "Las Relaciones entre el Mercado del Cafe y la Economia Brasilena: Sus Consecuencias para la Politica Comercial," *Integracion Latinoamericana*, No. 66, March 1982, pp. 4-12.

Pizano Salazar, Diego, "Cafe y Politica Economica: Aspectos de la Experiencias de Colombia y Brasil," *Integracion Latinoamericana*, No. 66 March 1982, pp. 13-36.

Lord Montague, J., "Commodity Export Demand of Latin America," paper presented at the Seminar on optimum trade policies, INTAL, Buenos Aires, 22-24 June 1981.

Behrman, Jere, R., "Mercados Segmentados para las Exportaciones Latinoamericanas de Productos Primarios: Implicaciones de la Estimaciones Disponisbles para Identificar las Fuentes Dominantes de la Perturbaciones de los Mercados y Politicas para Explotar el Poder Monopolico, *Integracion Latinoamericana*, No. 73, October 1982, pp. 25-41.

SOME THOUGHTS ABOUT LATIN AMERICAN INTEGRATION IN THE EIGHTIES

Hugo M. Hervitz

The clear message of Dr. Conesa's paper is that given the current conjuncture of the world economy, the only way in which Latin American countries can reasonably expect to go back to a sustained growth path is through the reciprocal opening of their markets. Furthermore, Dr. Conesa goes on to suggest a particular form in which such a liberalization should take place, based on the concept of a "margin of tariff preference."

In this note I intend to present a number of questions that arise from reading the paper which, in my view, need to be considered in order to enable a thorough assessment of the merits of the integrationist idea in general and the "margin of tariff preference" mechanism in particular.

Why has integration had a very limited success in the past?

It is essential to identify those factors that in the past have prevented the success of economic integration schemes, and the extent to which they are likely to constitute serious obstacles in the future. Dr. Conesa suggests that one such major factor has been the pattern of "complementary" growth between Latin America and the industrialized countries experienced in the 60s and early 70s, which resulted in a reduction in the incentives of Latin American countries were readily available to absorb their exports. I believe that this line of analysis poses a serious question about the future probabilities of survival of any integrationist program: if and when the industrialized countries go back to a more rapid growth pattern with an increased ability to absorb exports, would not many Latin American countries prefer to trade again with them to the detriment of trade within the region?

To what extent will an integrated Latin American market be able to absorb the products that the region currently exports elsewhere?

If exports currently being sold to industrialized countries are going to be diverted to countries in the region, it is essential to establish whether or not there will be a significant market for them, even in the most optimistic scenario of very low or non-existent tariffs. It must be taken into account that various countries in the region enjoy similar comparative advantages and are to a great extent in a competitive position with each other.

If exports are diverted away from industrialized countries, how is hard currency going to be earned?

Even if integration proceeds swiftly without major obstacles, Latin American countries are still going to need a significant amount of hard currency for two major purposes:

- repayment of the huge foreign debt, which, even under the most generous debt rescheduling scheme, will pose a heavy burden for many years; and

- imports of products and services not available in the region, most notably the ones related to high-technology.

What type of relationship is envisioned between an integrated Latin American market and industrialized countries with respect to trade and foreign investment?

An integrated economic entity may be highly protectionist, placing stiff restrictions on foreign investments, or it may seek to promote its large-scale market to attract foreign goods, capital, and technology. The particular types of policies to be followed are crucial for determining the likelihood of success of integration.

To what extent does the "margin of tariff preference" provide for the harmonization of protection policies among the member countries?

The "margin of tariff preference" consists of a generalized accross-the-board tariff reduction among member countries, which seems particularly attractive on the grounds of its simplicity, generality, and political feasibility. However, one major drawback is that by introducing only relative changes such that a tariff reduction leaves untouched the overall tariff structure of each country. The tariff structures of various Latin American coutries are likely to be highly conflicting and incompatible, thus preventing the integrated entity from possessing a coherent overall protection policy.

The issues raised in this note do not attempt to suggest that integration in Latin America is not feasible or not desirable. Rather, the objective has been to increase the awareness of the broad range of factors that have to be analyzed before a final assessment of the promise and danger inherent in integrationist experiments is made.

INTERNATIONAL FINANCIAL DISORDER

Roger Bird

Overview

Despite some optimism recently in the financial press regarding the international debt situation based on recent IMF actions, the facts remain that new credit extensions are slowing down, big banks are still vulnerable, and LDCs are not receiving the credit they need to cover their deficits while meeting their IMF obligations.

New credit extensions from BIS reporting commercial banks to all non-oil less developed countries totaled approximately $45 billion in 1981. In 1982, however, net new credit extensions to this same group amounted to at most $25 billion, and indications are that this amount will be even lower in 1983. In a recently completed study we have examined the implications of a significant slowdown of credit available to LDCs, and what this would mean in terms of resulting LDC import restrictions and drastically reduced growth for all countries involved. We have thereby analyzed the risks inherent in the current debt structure, and have produced complete world forecasts on a country-by-country basis based on three sets of assumptions about the international financial outlook. The analysis also contains warning signs to look for when trying to assess the stability of the international financial situation.

The conclusion of the study is that the debt crisis is still unresolved, and new initiatives may be needed, in addition to the evident need for continuing surveillance of the situation in the next two to three years.

Initially, analysis of three levels of financial disorder was prepared to examine the effects of strains in the world financial system on the world economy. The idea was to focus on the interrelationships between financial flows, world economy activity, the growth of world trade in a world economy that has become more integrated. The nature of the integration means that the effects of economic developments or the aims of policies in one country can lead to results that are difficult to anticipate due to the responses in other economies.

The three cases examine the effects of tight credit on the world economy:

- The first case, which we label a credit crunch, represents the current situation in which world credit conditions had been tight from late 1979 through mid-1982. In mid-1982 the Federal Reserve moved to ease credit conditions in the United States and short-term interest rates fell. The international lenders of last resort, the IMF, the BIS, and to some extent the World Bank, successfully arranged short-term bridge financing for the major debtor countries in the LDC block, with the cooperation of commercial banks.
- The second case we label a mild financial crisis. This case assumes that credit conditions were to remain tight through 1983. The financial risk to international lending results in a lower rate of net new lending by commercial banks to the LDCs; capital flight to the relative security of U.S. financial markets raises the value of the dollar; tight credit and a high dollar further squeeze the world economy and lead to a reduction of world commodity prices (including oil prices), world trade and world growth.
- The third case, that of a severe crisis, occurs in the event that international commercial banks further reduce net credit extensions to the non-oil LDCs, and U.S. authorities, worried over high money growth and the growing budget deficits in 1983, turn monetary fiscal policies tighter. This has its most important impact in 1984 and

results in another year of firm interest rates, a high dollar, and reduced growth in the United States. The deflationary effects on the world economy are so severe that protectionist policies are introduced to protect jobs. This limits trade between the developed countries and the LDCs and among the developed countries themselves, further contributing to an outlook of sustained slow growth.

Whether the international economy spirals downward into these progressively deepening stages of crisis will depend importantly on the willingness and ability of private and official international lenders to help out financially troubled debtor countries and their lenders. Presented below is an overview of those portions of the study focusing on the U.S. economy and the international economy as a whole with a special table covering Latin American effects.

In the appendix section we have included a taxonomy of the financial disorders scenarios as well as an explicit listing of the different sets of initializing assumptions about credit extensions, interest rates, exchange rates and oil and non-oil commodity prices.

Summary of the Results for the United States

Although the economic outlooks of heavily-indebted developing countries have been most dramatically affected by the present international financial crunch, tighter conditions of international liquidity have had important consequences for the U.S. and other industrial economies as well. Close financial ties, due to greatly expanded developing-country debt owed largely to industrial-country banks, provide only part of the picture; increased international competition has greatly heightened the importance of developing-country markets to industrial economies. The U.S. economy, for example, now directs 40 percent of its exports to developing-countries.

The Crisis Scenarios. In the baseline case, the U.S. economy recovers mildly in 1983 before registering a 5 percent growth rate in 1984. Although unemployment and the federal deficit are currently breaking post-World War II records, the U.S. economy is able to power itself away from deeper recession. After 1983 the recovery is secure. Growth should average better than 3 percent per year.

In the mild crisis case, a decline in net new lending initially reduces exports from developed countries to LDCs and also undermines confidence in the viability of many developing countries. There is a general flight to quality assets, including the U.S. dollar, which appreciates, and government bonds in developed countries, which also increase in value. The demand for liquid assets increases faster than the supply of money and credit, however, forcing up commercial interest rates. The increased uncertainty and consequent increased demand for liquidity mean that investors and consumers are more cautious, the latter saving more and spending less. This further aggravates the deteriorating economic situation of the United States, making 1983 a year of very low growth.

In the case of the severe crisis, greatly reduced new net lending and inappropriate fiscal and monetary responses reduce aggregate demand and lower growth in the United States. The U.S. fiscal authorities are assumed to view with horror the ballooning projections of deficits based on reduced growth and reduced inflation. They respond by instituting a deficit-reduction package in 1983, which has its greatest impact on the 1984 fiscal year. The U.S. monetary authorities are forced in 1983 to increase liquidity substantially. This occurs as a result of the Federal Reserve's activities as lender of last resort. In 1983, the large deficits and the high rate of growth of the money supply relative to growth in nominal GNP are assumed to lead the authorities to believe that a tighter monetary policy is necessary to avoid increasing inflation. The tightening of the money supply is assumed to occur in 1984, and interest rates remain high for yet another year. This has severe consequences for the health of the U.S. economy.

Summary of the Assumptions. In summary, the judgmental assumptions for the two scenarios include the following.

- Monetary Policy:

  Mild Crisis: accommodative monetary policy throughout accompanied by increased liquidity due to lending of last resort by the Fed. Greatly increased liquidity preference due to uncertainty overcomes this effect, however, and short-term interest rates are 230 basis points higher than in the baseline case for 1983.

  Severe Crisis: accommodative monetary policy in 1983 and more lending of last resort. A sharp reduction in money growth occurs in 1984, however. This causes short-term interest rates to remain 200 basis points above the baseline in 1984.

- Investment:

  Mild Crisis: increased uncertainty helps bring about an autonomous decline in business investment of 1.8 percent over and above the effects of income and interest rates for 1983 only, as well as an autonomous decline of 5 percent in residential investment in 1983 only.

  Severe Crisis: increased uncertainty helps bring about an autonomous decline of 3.6 percent in business investment for 1983 and 5.4 percent from 1984 through 1987 as well as an autonomous decline of 10 percent in 1983 and 1984.

- Consumption:

  Mild Crisis: increased savings due to heightened uncertainty helps bring about an autonomous decline of one-half of 1 percent in consumption from 1983 through 1987.

  Severe Crisis: increased savings helps bring about an autonomous decline of 1 percent in consumption from 1983 through 1987.

- Exports and Imports:

  Mild Crisis: tighter international liquidity, reducing the scope for trade finance, and heightened protectionism help to produce an autonomous decline of about 5.8 percent into exports and imports from 1984 through 1987.

  Severe Crisis: tighter international liquidity and heightened protectionism help produce an autonomous decline of about 6.5 percent in exports and imports from 1984 through 1987.

- Fiscal Policy:

  Mild Crisis: passive response to lower inflation, higher interest rates and unemployment.

  Severe Crisis: a deficit-reduction package amounting to a 7 percent increase in taxes by 1987 and a 3.5 percent reduction in government purchases of goods and services by 1987.

Results. The mild crisis assumptions set forth above have a much less grevious impact on the economy, of course, than do those of the severe crisis case. GNP growth in the mild crisis scenario averages 3.2 percent per year in real terms from 1982-87, which is just less than in the base forecast. In the severe crisis case, GNP growth averages only 2.0 percent. Inflation is lower in both crisis scenarios because of lower import prices and reduced economic activity. Price increases average 5.7 percent in the base case, 5.4 percent in the mild crisis case, and 5.2 percent in the severe crisis case.

In both crisis cases, consumption is reduced and investment falls. Unemployment tends to remain high through 1987, especially in the severe crisis scenario. The potential for political and social unrest is, of course, greater. This makes an eventually active fiscal response more likelier.

Lower inflation increases the scope for monetary intervention. This is especially true in the severe crisis case, in which capacity utilization also falls. Since very large deficits are likely to inhibit any attempts at a fiscal response to an international crisis, increasing pressure will fall on the monetary authorities to respond with a looser policy. Congress is already discussing regulating the activities of the Federal Reserve System. Were the Fed not to step in and lower interest rates in a crisis situation, Congress could eventually force such intervention. An increase in inflation would, after all, be more politically palatable than prolonged depression. Increased inflation would help increase the revenues of the federal government as well as cheapen the debt burden of developing countries. Were interest rates to fall substantially due to a looser U.S. monetary policy, the interest payments of the U.S. federal and developing-country governments would decrease as well.

A reallocation of fiscal expenditure would be likely in a financial crisis, although none was assumed in these crisis scenarios. The Congress and perhaps even the Administration would want to intervene in some way to lower the unemployment rate. Given very large deficits, this reaction would imply a shift of expenditures away from defense spending and, most likely, toward public works projects. The latter type of spending has been shown to have a higher employment multiplier than defense spending. The effects of such stimulation would not be great, however. No significant impact would be expected on the economy as a whole, and only slight effect on unemployment.

Summary of the Results for the International Economy

Using the baseline case as a basis for comparison, Table 1 shows that the world economic recovery is delayed for at least another year—until 1984 under the mild crisis and until 1985 under severe crisis. Even in the base case, the week recovery largely due to the high level of real interest rates and low investment expectations.

Growth. The developed countries are led to recovery in all three cases by the United States, judging by comparative growth rates. Japan is severely hurt in both crisis cases due to her dependence upon developing-country markets, high dollar costs of imports (in spite of reduced oil prices), and the effects of higher interest rates on investment and consumption. Europe also suffers relatively more than the United States. This is especially true in the case of Germany. Her export dependence on the developing countries of the Middle East and on the centrally planned economies bloc shows up in the crises in the form of reduced net exports in 1983 and 1984 and reduced investment for future export production.

Compared with the credit crunch, the two crisis cases assume that the developing countries initially reduce their imports by a combination of quantatitive controls and weak internal demand. This drop in imports from the developed countries lowers economic activity in those countries. The lower growth in the developed countries, in turn, lower the demand for exports from the developing-country bloc, thus limiting any improvement in the developing countries' current accounts. Oil exporters are especially affected in the severe crisis, even after the oil importers have started to recover because the shock to oil export revenue prolongs the growth recession. Non-fuel commodity price recovery after 1983 permits the balance of payments constraint to be somewhat relaxed for the oil importers. By contrast, the rise in oil prices after 1983 does not compensate oil exporters for the reduced longer-term expectations of oil revenues, which are the basis for both capital inflows and development expenditures.

Inflation

Table 2 shows inflation rates for the developed countries in the three cases. Under all scenarios, the U.S. recovery means that 1983 is a low point for inflation, with rates continuing to fall in Europe for the whole forecast period.

The underlying improvement in inflation is related in all cases to the removal of oil price shocks—and the disappearance of lagged effects from the last shock—as well as the fundamental slowing of unit labor costs as wage bargains are affected by unemployment. Monetary policy is kept moderately restrictive after recovery in all cases. The reasons for the differences in patterns in the two crises across countries are mainly related to the different exchange rate patterns and their effects upon import prices for the U.S. versus the other developed countries. The stronger dollar in 1983-84 compared with the base contains U.S. inflation and retards improvement outside the US. Thereafter, as the dollar weakens and unemployment pushes down wages even more, the rate of inflation improves outside the United States compared with the credit crunch case.

Balance of Payments. The balance-of-payments effects of the three scenarios are set out in Table 3. Even in the case of the credit crunch, the shift of current account deficits between developed and developing countries is evident for 1983 versus 1982; lower LDC growth reduces LDC imports from the OECD as OECD recovery aids the LDCs exports. In 1984 and thereafter, the balance of payments of the developing countries slowly improves as recovery of export volumes and prices proceeds and domestic absorption is held in check. The oil exporters show a significant deterioration as oil prices and export volumes flatten while imports associated with development expenditures continue to grow. As recovery takes hold, their accounts also improve.

The results for the mild crisis demonstrate the inability of the oil-importing LDCs to reduce their current account deficits to the levels consistent with lower net lending by commercial banks. Their steps to reduce imports feed back on the developed countries' ability to export, and hence, to grow. It should be expected that LDC import restrictions would have global effects upon world growth as would developed countries' import restrictions. The strong dollar-high interest-low commodity price nexus means that the current account balance improvement for the non-oil LDCs is less than the reduction in commercial bank lending from 1982 to 1983 (a fall of $8.6 billion versus a cutback of $10 billion). Thereafter, the sluggish recovery track takes hold and balances of payments improve for this group.

The oil-exporting LDCs as a group are assumed to need more credit during 1983 due to the decline of oil prices and their development needs. They are, as a group, considered to be a better risk than the other LDCs (who have the heavy weight of Latin America less Venezuela). Hence, credit will likely be available this year. Thereafter, the oil exporters follow a track of increasing current account deficits associated with their continuing development needs and lower oil prices.

In the severe crisis, the inability of the LDCs to reduce their balance-of-payments deficit again shows up—the deficit is reduced by $21.6 billion, capital inflows by $25 billion. In this case, the recessionary feedback effects are greater, overwhelming the effects of lower oil and commodity prices and higher interest rates. Moreove, the disequilibrium becomes greater through 1987—not less, as in the mild crisis. Overall, the borrowing requirement for all LDCs grows almost continuously to 1986 to much higher levels than for the other two cases.

For the Latin American countries as a group, debt service ratios worsen in both crisis cases—discouraging future bank lending still further in a cumulative decline of confidence. Evidently, the policy of "adjustment via recession" imposed on these countries makes them economically weaker, more vulnerable to political turmoil, and less attractive overall to private market investment whether from domestic or international sources.

Conclusion

Wharton's study of the effects of a possible international financial crisis suggests the following:

- International financial flows do play an important role in buffering the effects of changes in the rate of real economic activity. Petrodollar recycling after the first oil price shock helped the world economy to recover from a deep recession. A reduction or cessation of lending in 1982-83 will have longlasting effects on both developed and less developed countries.

- The increased integration of the world economy makes it impossible for any one country to shield itself from these effects.

- The effects of disintegration through rising protectionism might place the countries of the developing world in a hole from which they cannot extract themselves.

In conclusion, it should be stated that neither crisis scenario has a high probability of occurring. The chances of an international financial crisis are great enough, however, that simulation analysis can be a valuable means of acquainting ourselves with the probable consequences. The key decision makers--the IMF, the Treasury, the Federal Reserve System, the Administration, Congress and the private banks—all appear to have an acute awareness of the hazards of the current financial crunch. Though many of the policy actions taken thus far have been ad-hoc, it is Wharton's view that some of the responses needed to defuse the crisis are being taken. This does not mean that international financial crisis is no longer a threat to be taken seriously—only that the probability of its occurring is not increasing. That probability can be significantly lessened if more information on credit flows were available, and if concerted action to encourage a solid economic recovery under U.S. leadership were assured.

International Financial Crisis Scenarios
Summary of Results for the U.S. Economy

	1982	1983	1984	1985	1986	1987
GROSS NATIONAL PRODUCT						
(Billions, 1972 dollars)						
Credit Crunch	1477.7	1512.8	1588.3	1653.8	1685.7	1739.7
growth rate	-1.7	2.4	5.0	4.1	1.9	3.2
Mild Crisis		1482.1	1555.6	1606.5	1650.2	1725.8
growth rate		0.3	5.0	3.3	2.7	4.6
Severe Crisis		1461.6	1490.1	1536.8	1562.1	1635.3
growth rate		-1.1	2.0	3.1	1.7	4.7
FINAL DEMAND DEFLATOR FOR GNP						
(1972=100)						
Credit Crunch	207.4	218.2	230.0	244.5	259.5	273.8
growth rate	6.1	5.2	5.4	6.3	6.1	5.5
Mild Crisis		216.5	227.2	240.3	254.8	269.9
growth rate		4.4	4.9	5.8	6.0	5.9
Severe Crisis		215.5	226.6	238.4	252.2	266.9
growth rate		3.9	5.1	5.2	5.8	5.8
UNEMPLOYMENT RATE						
(percent)						
Credit Crunch	9.7	10.5	9.3	8.6	8.6	8.2
Mild Crisis		11.4	10.5	10.3	10.2	9.2
Severe Crisis		11.9	12.8	13.2	13.8	13.0
FEDERAL SURPLUS OR DEFICIT						
(Billions, Current Dollars)						
Credit Crunch	-143.4	-178.9	-166.0	-141.1	-138.6	-125.5
Mild Crisis		-209.1	-201.5	-199.5	-195.5	-164.6
Severe Crisis		-221.0	-207.6	-209.0	-196.8	-152.3

Table 1

Growth of Real GDP
(annual growth rates-%)

	1982	1983	1984	1985	1986	1987
Developed Countries						
Financial Crunch	-0.3	1.6	4.0	3.0	2.3	2.9
Mild Crisis	-0.3	-0.7	2.7	2.2	2.3	3.4
Severe Crisis	-0.3	-1.7	0.5	2.0	1.9	3.1
U.S.						
Financial Crunch	-1.6	2.5	5.0	3.6	1.7	3.5
Mild Crisis	-1.6	0.4	4.9	3.3	2.8	4.6
Severe Crisis	-1.6	-0.8	1.8	3.5	1.6	4.7
Japan						
Financial Crunch	2.6	2.4	4.7	3.2	2.9	2.5
Mild Crisis	2.6	-2.4	1.6	2.3	2.9	3.3
Severe Crisis	2.6	-4.2	1.8	1.6	2.4	2.3
Germany						
Financial Crunch	-0.8	-0.1	2.7	1.5	1.7	1.7
Mild Crisis	-0.7	-2.5	2.1	0.8	0.5	1.0
Severe Crisis	-0.8	-3.2	1.0	1.7	1.3	1.1
Oil-Exporting Developing Countries						
Financial Crunch	-1.6	1.1	4.6	4.7	5.4	4.8
Mild Crisis	-1.7	-1.8	0.6	3.2	3.8	4.6
Severe Crisis	-1.7	-4.4	-1.3	1.8	2.9	3.7
Oil-Importing Developing Countries						
Financial Crunch	0.9	2.4	4.4	4.2	4.7	5.0
Mild Crisis	1.1	-1.2	2.0	3.7	4.8	5.5
Severe Crisis	1.1	-4.1	-1.8	1.6	4.6	4.6

Table 2

Inflation: Consumption Price Deflator
(percent per year)

	1982	1983	1984	1985	1986	1987
Developed Countries						
Financial Crunch	10.9	9.3	8.5	8.8	8.5	8.2
Mild Crisis	10.8	9.9	9.2	8.1	7.3	7.2
Severe Crisis	10.8	10.0	9.9	7.8	7.0	7.4
U.S.						
Financial Crunch	6.0	5.0	5.1	7.0	6.6	5.4
Mild Crisis	6.0	4.2	4.7	5.6	5.8	5.5
Severe Crisis	6.0	3.5	4.9	5.1	5.6	5.5
Japan						
Financial Crunch	3.2	2.4	3.4	3.3	2.8	2.8
Mild Crisis	3.2	3.4	3.7	2.1	1.1	1.2
Severe Crisis	3.2	4.0	5.4	2.5	1.5	1.6
Germany						
Financial Crunch	4.9	3.9	3.0	3.0	3.3	3.6
Mild Crisis	4.9	4.8	3.8	3.2	3.6	3.7
Severe Crisis	4.9	5.4	4.5	2.9	2.8	2.9

Table 3

Current Account Balances
(billions of current US dollars)

	1982	1983	1984	1985	1986	1987
Developed Countries						
Financial Crunch	-36	-49	-41	-33	-15	-21
Mild Crisis	-36	-55	-68	-71	-72	-88
Severe Crisis	-36	-46	-61	-75	-74	-101
U.S.						
Financial Crunch	-5	-28	-22	-12	6	1
Mild Crisis	-5	-30	-36	-27	-11	-16
Severe Crisis	-5	-27	-29	-25	-1	-2
Japan						
Financial Crunch	4	11	15	17	15	9
Mild Crisis	4	13	13	13	6	-1
Severe Crisis	4	16	11	5	-6	-21
Germany						
Financial Crunch	-2	4	3	2	3	5
Mild Crisis	-2	4	-1	-5	-7	-8
Severe Crisis	-2	5	-1	-7	-9	-12
Oil-Exporting Developing Countries						
Financial Crunch	-13	-22	-15	-6	-5	7
Mild Crisis	-13	-20	-17	-20	-25	-16
Severe Crisis	-13	-25	-18	-27	-36	-27
Oil-Importing Developing Countries						
Financial Crunch	-58	-50	-51	-49	-48	-46
Mild Crisis	-59	-50	-43	-40	-39	-35
Severe Crisis	-59	-37	-46	-45	-50	-46

APPENDIX

Taxonomy of Financial Disorders

TAXONOMY OF FINANCIAL DISORDERS

	Crunch	Crisis	Crash
Insititutional Role (CBs, IMF, BIS)	Flexible: tight or loose as credit conditions warrant; accommodative to prevent crisis; "orderly credit markets" is a top priority.	Miscalculations: institutional delay in reaching decisions to accommodate; under-then-over-reaction.	Institutional failure to accommodate: situation deteriorates and feeds on itself.
Lenders Role (Banks)	Reduced positive net lending: willingness to roll over debts if adjustments by debtor are made, occasional bankruptcies of weak, poorly-managed firms; negotiation and rescheduling under generally accepted rules and procedures of IMF guidance and/or Paris club; banks do not fail.	Negative net lending: bankruptcies affect weak and not-so-weak alike; cumulative effects on other banks, lenders or firms who otherwise were prudent; delayed roll-overs; eventual renegotiation and rescheduling of debts; large banks do not fail, but are hurt; certain banks' CDs cannot be sold without great difficulty.	Capital positions are wiped out: new lending, no roll-overs: foreclosures, defaults, bankruptcies snowballing to low level of credit usage; banks fail, firms fail, institutions fail or are nonexistent, what were once thought to be assets are now valueless.
Borrowers (Firms or Countries) Role	Slowdown of growth: use of borrowing is reduced; three types of borrowers (prime, risky, and rationed) are in manageable proportions; selective bankruptcies of weakest firms.	Growth is stopped by major borrowers, negative for many others: more borrowers become risky or rationed; liquidity positions are changed by inventory liquidation (or export drives); weak <u>and</u> strong firms are bankrupted (or default) as demand falls.	Capital positions are wiped out: negative growth all around with many bankruptcies, defaults, etc.; situation stabilizes at low level of activity based on cash and barter.

TABLE A.1

Net New Credit Extensions by BIS Reporting Banks to Developing Countries
(Billions of dollars)

	1981	1982	1983	1984
Crunch	45	25	25	20
Crisis 1			15	10
Crisis 2			0	10

Note: These figures exclude the Middle East countries, who are primarily net lenders to commercial banks.

TABLE A.2
Interest Rate and Credit Market Assumptions
(Annual average percent)

	1981	1982	1983	1984	1985	1986	1987
UNITED STATES							
Short-term Interest Rates[1]							
Crunch	14.8	12.1	8.7	8.2	8.7	8.2	8.4
Crisis 1			10.9	8.8	9.3	8.7	8.8
Crisis 2			10.9	10.3	9.3	8.7	8.8
LIBOR[2]							
Crunch	16.5	13.6	9.6	8.9	9.0	8.5	8.6
Crisis 1			12.0	9.5	9.6	9.0	8.9
Crisis 2			12.0	11.5	9.6	9.0	8.9
DEVELOPED COUNTRIES							
Short-term Interest Rates[3]							
Crunch	13.5	12.0	9.5	8.8	8.8	8.3	8.3
Crisis 1			12.1	9.4	9.4	8.9	8.8
Crisis 2			12.1	11.2	9.4	8.9	8.8
DEVELOPING COUNTRIES							
Basis points[4]							
Crunch			-0-	-0-	-0-	-0-	-0-
Crisis 1			200	100	50	-0-	-0-
Crisis 2			200	100	50	-0-	-0-

1 Prime commercial paper, four to six months.

2 London Interbank Offer Rate on US dollar deposits for six months.

3 Weighted average of short-term interest rates in World Model.

4 Premia above Crunch case premia on LIBOR for individual developing countries. See Chapters 7, 8 and 9 on Latin America, Mexico, and the Philippines.

TABLE A.3

Exchange Rate Assumptions
(1975:100.0)

	1982	1983	1984	1985	1986	1987
US Dollar Effective Exchange Rate*						
Crunch	118.2	125.0	116.8	109.7	106.7	108.0
Change (%)	11.8	4.9	-5.9	-6.0	-2.8	1.2
Crisis 1		131.6	129.6	114.8	104.4	102.1
Change (%)		11.3	-1.6	-11.4	-9.0	-2.2
Crisis 2		136.6	142.1	125.8	112.4	109.8
Change (%)		15.6	4.1	-11.5	-10.7	-2.3

*IMF Multilateral Exchange Rate Model (MERM) weights

TABLE A.4

Price Assumptions:
Non-fuel Commodities and Fuels
(1975:100.0)

	1981	1982	1983	1984	1985	1986	1987
PRICE INDICES							
Crunch							
Non-fuel							
commodities	141.7	135.1	138.5	145.8	155.2	163.4	171.8
% change	-7.8	-4.6	2.5	5.3	6.5	5.2	5.2
Fuels	271.4	255.6	258.5	284.0	314.3	345.6	378.1
% change	11.0	-5.8	1.1	9.8	10.7	10.0	9.4
Crisis 1							
Non-fuel							
commodities			134.4	141.6	150.8	158.7	166.9
% change			-.5	5.4	6.5	5.2	5.2
Fuels			240.6	261.9	289.5	318.0	347.9
% change			-5.7	8.8	10.5	9.8	9.4
Crisis 2							
Non-fuel							
commodities			131.6	138.7	147.7	155.4	163.4
% change			-2.6	5.4	6.5	5.2	5.2
Fuels			225.0	232.9	268.5	295.1	322.9
% change			-11.9	8.0	10.5	9.9	9.4
Addendum: crude petroleum prices [1] ($ per barrel)							
Crunch	34.9	32.4	32.9	37.0	41.7	46.6	51.9
% change	10.2	-7.4	1.9	12.4	11.9	11.8	11.2
Crisis 1			30.0	33.8	38.0	42.5	47.3
% change			-7.2	12.5	12.7	11.8	11.2
Crisis 2			27.5	30.9	34.9	39.0	43.3
% change			-15.1	12.5	12.7	11.8	11.2

[1] Weighted average of official OPEC prices with discounts, spot market trades, and price estimates for non-OPEC suppliers.

Note: Dollar indexes of world export prices of fuels and non-fuel primary commodities, based on UN data.

WORLD ECONOMIC OUTLOOK AND THE PROSPECTS FOR U.S. EXPORTS TO LATIN AMERICA

Colin I. Bradford, Jr.

The prospects for U.S. exports to Latin America are determined by the import capacity of the region. Import capacity is, of course, dependent upon export growth and debt financing. Hence, we are immediately vaulted into the realm of the world economic outlook. Donald Keesing said at a conference just two years ago on this subject: "The major question in making projections today is how gloomy one should make them."[1] In the intervening period, the situation has become still more critical as the world problem has emerged as a central issue.

However, most analysts agree that the world debt problem, though most acute in Latin America, is more a world economic problem than it is a debt problem *per se*. The problems facing developing countries are largely determined by world recession, adverse shifts in the terms of trade, high interest rates, and slower growth in bank lending. The solution, then, would seem to be a global strategy for economic expansion.[2] This strategy would not only involve U.S. expansion but a coordinated expansion among the major OECD countries, as called for by the group of twenty-four economists brought together by the new Institute for International Economics in the fall of 1982.[3] It would involve continued lending by the private banks and it would involve, as Enrique Sanchez has rightly emphasized, a more flexible and growth-oriented outlook for the IMF.[4]

The basic idea is to get the international trade multipliers going again in a positive upward direction and to use the structural linkages that have developed between industrial developing countries to reinforce the process of world economic growth.

The strategy is built on past patterns. These patterns basically consisted of the creation, in effect, of a world pool of savings generated by the increase in oil prices by OPEC which was then recycled through private capital markets, with the intermediation of private banks, largely to the non-oil LDCs as medium- to long-term debt. The non-oil LDCs ran cumulative current account deficits amounting to $416 billion between 1974-81, nearly equivalent to the cumulative OPEC surplus for the period of $454 billion. This debt was highly concentrated in the more creditworthy LDCs, most notably the newly industrializing countries (NICs), which were emerging simultaneously in this period as major exporters of manufactured goods on a global scale. Investment growth outpaced GNP growth in almost all the and potential NICs. Saving rates also increased, but not sufficiently, such that the current account deficit financed the savings gap as capital goods imports increased. Advanced industrial countries increased their exports to LDCs significantly, and their trade surplus in manufactures just offset their trade deficit in fuels. The dynamic growth of LDC exports of manufactures increased LDC capacity to import from advanced countries and their capacity to service their foreign debt. As a result, growth rates in LDCs were higher than OECD growth in this period, and OECD growth rates were greater than they would have been in the absence of these patterns of world trade and financial adjustment.[5]

The capacity to import in LDCs is now an important stimulus to OECD growth. Developing country imports were 26 percent of OECD exports in 1981 and 4.2 percent of OECD- combined GDP. LDC imports in 1981 equaled 38 percent of U.S. exports, of which Latin American imports constituted 17 percent of U.S. exports. In terms of GDP, developing country imports were 3.1 percent of U.S. GDP in 1981, of which Latin American imports were 1.3 percent of U.S. GDP.[6] Despite the increase in structural interdependence between developing countries and advanced economies and the mutually reinforcing trends of the 1974-81 period, there are reasons why these patterns might not prevail in the future. The rest of this paper will explore why this strategy of global economic expansion might not work.

First, recovery in the United States alone is inadequate to spur global economic expansion. The relative weight of the U.S. in the world economy in not sufficient to make the decisive difference in the level of world economic activity, as it did in the 1950s and early 1960s. Precisely the lessons of the growing interdependence among OECD economies that were realized in the mid-1970s, and formalized in the LINK model, were that the new structure of interdependence required simultaneous and coordinated expansion to achieve the desired results.[7] Similar kinds of structural relations have now formed between the OECD, the NICs and the oil exporters, such that renewed expansion by the NICs and the oil exporters becomes a significant factor in world economic growth through feedback effects. But despite these new structural relations, it appears that the policies which would utilize them to reactivate world economic growth are not there.

A consensus does not exist among economists or among policy makers that expansionist policies are the appropriate or the desirable ones at this juncture. There is a continuing concern for inflation. Based on the role of expectations in driving economic behavior, some analysts believe that giving up too soon on stabilization policies in the industrial countries may undermine the gains already made.[8] The IMF has been exceedingly cautious in this regard.[9] Agreement within Europe and in Japan on the need for expansionist policies is not yet evident. Furthermore, there is no agreed upon process or mechanism for bringing about coordinated policies, though the OECD secretariat has tried admirably to serve such a function. Indeed, one European observer argues that "the network of institutions, norms, regimes, designed to provide the essential political framework for an integrated world economy, is indeed gradually disintegrating."[10] These factors constrain the coordinated expansion of industrial countries through deliberate policy design and execution.

IMF conditionality is still a burden on the growth outlook of LDCs. As necessary as adjustment is, there is a difference between adjustment through growth and adjustment through contraction alone. One of the key variables is time. In March 1970, the Executive Board of the IMF reached agreement on a new set of guidelines on conditionality. These new guidelines, for the use of both IMF general resources and stand-by arrangements, extended the period for stand-by arrangements from one to three years. This extension rested intellectually on the recognition that shorter periods forced more one-sided stabilization programs focusing on short-run demand management, and placing necessarily less emphasis on the need for adequate supply responses which require longer gestation periods. Second, there was concern for the effectiveness in implementing stabilization programs which historically had been disrupted by political reactions and discontinuities. The new guidelines made explicit the need to pay attention to domestic social and political objectives, as well as the economic priorities of the country itself.

These innvovations in the Fund's approach to conditionality provide a potential basis for negotiations with major borrowers which are consistent with a global strategy for economic recovery. The adoption of a more balanced stabilization cum development approach by the Fund in negotiating conditionality agreements with major borrowers would constitute a significant policy shift in the world economy, encouraging debtor-country adjustment through growth.

Nevertheless, IMF conditionality continues to be a problem, as indicated by the February 9, 1983, Communique of the Ministers of the Group of 24 on International Monetary Affairs, which states that the Group

> ...noted that the source of the imbalances in recent years has been mainly structural, requiring adjustment financing over a longer period....They expressed a regret that a large number of medium-term programs have had to be interrupted and cautioned against the current tendency for the Fund to shift from three-year programs to one-year programs. They urged that, in the implementation of adjustment programs, conditionality should be appropriately designed to take account of the cause of imbalances and emphasized that

adjustment programs should be framed in the context of growth-oriented policies. In this context, they urged that the guidelines on conditionality should be kept under review in light of the evolving world economic situation. Ministers also pointed out that adjustment has become difficult because of exogenous factors and the prescriptions of adjustment, and the review of performance should pay adequate attention to circumstances and factors which are beyond the control of countries....11

With the IMF moving back to center stage in international monetary affairs, the policy outlook and influence of the Fund on the economic policies of developing countries will be a major factor affecting the world economic outlook. The recently agreed upon Eighth Quota increase will expand IMF resources from 60 billion to 90 billion SDRs. In addition, the General Agreements to Borrow will be expanded from 6.4 billion to 17 billion SDRs and access to it extended to any country experiencing balance of payments difficulties, rather than limited to industrial countries alone as in the past. Finally, discussions have been concluded between the Fund and Saudi Arabia for a contribution parallel to the General Agreements to Borrow. J. de Larosiere, Managing Director of the IMF, indicated that together these constitute "a doubling of the effective usable resources" of the Fund.

These several actions are significant steps in expanding the supply of lendable funds to the IMF. The key issue now is whether these funds will be borrowed by debtor countries. In the past decade, borrowings by developing countries have been less than the amount of lendable resources. There are two manifestations of the impact of this reluctance to borrow on the resource balance of the Fund. One is the net flow of resources in a given year between the IMF and developing countries. Repayments of previous loans are continuous and cumulative, while the magnitude of drawings under stand-by arrangements in a given year may be relatively small. In several years during the late 1970s, the net flow of funds between developing countries and the IMF was actually negative because new drawings failed to equal repayments.

The other manifestation of low demand for the IMF funds has been that commitments are not drawn upon by countries which feel the conditions are too harsh, and hence do not engage the conditionality arrangements until absolutely necessary. For this reason, undrawn balances under stand-by arrangements are sometimes very large. In 1981-82 (the financial year ending on April 30, 1982) undrawn balances constituted 68 percent of commitments, the lowest since 1978. Stringent stabilization programs can generate serious constraints on the flow of the IMF resources to the developing countries. Hence, the ability of the IMF to design stabilization programs which are politically feasible appears to be critical to both its qualitative and it quantitative role in the next phase of world economic adjustment.

It is essential that the Fund reach a balance in its approach to developing countries between adjustment and financing which permits sufficient economic growth to make stabilization politically feasible in debtor countries. This challenge is even more critical in the 1980s than it has been before, because of the need for the full resources of the Fund to be drawn upon in this new period in which the flow of funds is the costraint on economic growth.

This is due to the fact that perhaps the most important factor militating against the expansion of LDCs and hampering their contribution to global growth is the slowdown in bank lending to the developing countries. Whereas the IMF has played a crucial role in 1982 and 1983 in keeping the private banks involved in external financing of LDCs, in the medium term it seems reasonable to expect that the smaller local and regional U.S. banks, particularly, are going to want to withdraw from global lending as soon as this becomes feasible. The capacity of the large U.S. banks to syndicate loan packages will decline in the medium run (1984-85) and with it the aggregate flow of finance to LDCs will decline also. Already the LDCs have moved from a period which can be seen as one of debt-led growth to a period of finance-constrained debt with concomitant dampening of LDC economic growth.

The tendencies of private banks to withdraw from international lending is but one part of a reorientation of world investment and growth patterns toward favoring the OECD countries. It seems more likely that savings generated in the OECD countries will be invested in those countries in a climate of international caution. The result may be that, whereas LDC growth exceeded OECD growth in the 1974-81 period, OECD growth will outpace LDC growth from 1982 and beyond. This may come as some relief to those who have viewed the rise of the NICs as challengers to U.S. industrial competitiveness.

Finally, the emergence of OPEC as a new class of debtor nations, which we thought of as creditor nations in the 1970s, is another factor limiting the outlook for world economic growth. The combined total debt in 1981 of Algeria, Saudi Arabia, Indonesia and Nigeria (according to OECD figures) was $44.7 billion, compared to Mexico's debt of $54.4 billion. Debt service payments in 1982 for these four OPEC countries was $14.0 billion compared to $15.2 billion for Mexico.[12] The debt burden to OPEC will limit its demand for imports, which was previously restrained by absorption rather than finance.

The growth prospects for OPEC have been changed by three fundamental shifts in the oil market. First, whereas OPEC constituted 68 percent of world oil supplies in the early 1970s, their share has now shrunk to 47 percent. Second, there is evidence of a shift in U.S. investment to less energy-intensive technology, which will make a difference in future oil demand. Third, the U.S. has shifted to less oil-dependent energy sources in the last decade. These are structural shifts which mean that OPEC oil revenues will not be as responsive to recovery as was the case in the past.

In conclusion, these several factors appear to constitute major elements in determining a slow-growth outlook for the world economy. Growth will be based, if not confined, to select industrial countries. Their policies are likely to be nationally determined, rather than internationally coordinated. LDC growth will be constrained by slower OECD growth, more limited bank lending, and IMF policies emphasizing adjustment more than economic growth. OPEC growth and import demand will experience a financial constraint for the first time in a decade.

More fundamentally, the net result of these various factors and forces is to place the world economy on the threshold of an era of inward-looking economic growth. After two decades of substantial economic growth of developing economies based on outward-looking growth strategies, there have now emerged some thirty developing countries which have become integrated into the world economy. These are the newly industrialized countries and the next tier NICs, which have become or are becoming major exporters of manufactures on a global scale, and the oil-exporting countries. These major LDC exporters are also the major debtor countries. Only Turkey and Morocco, of this group of thirty countries, have become debtor countries without becoming significant exporters of manufactures of oil.

As the financial cosntraint has its impact, it will inevitably mean that import capacity of the oil and non-oil developing countries will be sharply reduced, and with it the growth of U.S. and OECD exports to them, principally capital goods. This will limit the pace of invesment-led growth in LDCs that has characterized the 1974-81 period and eventually reduce the export capacity of these countries as well. Economic growth will depend proportionately more on internal savings and investment. Other lesser developed countries, in turn, will not adopt outward-looking growth strategies and will continue to rely on slower growing commodity exports and more limited flows of concessional finance.

Such an evolution of policies and patterns would constitute a major shift in signals of the world economy in the postwar period. This was based on the central idea that national economic growth could be fostered and, indeed, achieved through integration into an open world trade and financial system.

FOOTNOTES

[1]Keesing, Donald B., "Exports and Policy in Latin-American Countries: Prospects for the World Economy and for Latin-American Exports, 1980-90" in Export Diversification and the New Protectionism: The Experience of Latin America, Werner Baer and Malcom Gillis (eds), National Bureau of Economic Research and the Bureau of Economic and Business Research, University of Illinois, Champaign, Illinois, 1981, g. 25.

[2]Bradford, Colin I., Jr., "International Debt and the World Economy: Global Integration on Trial", Paper prepared for a meeting on International Debt and the World Economy organized by the Concilium on International and Area Studies of Yale University on February 17, 1983, in New York City.

[3]Institute for International Economics, Promoting World Recovery, A Statement on Global Economic Strategy, by Twenty Six Economists from Fourteen Countries, Washington, D.C., 1982.

[4]Sanchez, Enrique P., "Latin American Outlook Under IMF Conditionality," in this volume.

[5]Bradford, Colin I., Jr., "The NICs and World Economic Adjustment," in Louis Turner et al, The Newly Industrialized Countries: Trade and Adjustment, George Allen & Unwin, 1982, Chapter 11.

[6]Morgan Guaranty Trust Company, World Financial Markets, October 1982, Table 8, p. 8.

[7]OECD (1980) "Fiscal Simulations with the OECD International Linkage Model," OECD Economic Outlook, Occasional Studies, July 1980.

[8]Ehrbar, A. F., "Is Inflation Coming Back?" Fortune, March 21, 1983, pp. 60-63.

[9]See Colin I. Bradford, Jr. (footnote 2 above) op. cit. 16-20, and John Williamson, "The Lending Policies of the International Monetary Fund," Institute for International Economics, Washington, D.C., August 1982, pp. 43ff.

[10]Bressand, "The Whittling Away of the International Economic Framework" in Transatlantic Perspective, Washington, D.C.: The German Marshall Fund, No. 7 December 1982, excerpted from the introduction to RAMSES 1982: The State of the World Economy, Annual Report from the French Institute for International Relations, Cambridge: Ballinger Publishing Company, 1982.

[11]International Monetary Fund, IMF Survey, February 21, 1983, pp. 53-54.

[12]OECD (1982), External Debt of Developing Countries: 1982 Survey, Paris, p. 42.

ASSESSING COUNTRY RISK: LESSONS FROM THE RECENT EXPERIENCE WITH LATIN AMERICA

J. Antonio Villamil

Country risk, from an international lender's perspective, can be defined as the possibility of a country being unable or unwilling to allow its residents to service external financial obligations on a timely basis. In recent Latin American history, instances of the unwillingness of sovereign countries to allow repayment of external obligations at market-related terms—the ultimate country risk—have been rare occurrences (instances of which are Cuba and more recently Nicaragua). Up to the present, the main country risk facing international lenders has been the inability of countries to generate hard currencies for the timely repayment of external debt. This has led to a restructuring of the debt coming due, but at prices that have at least preserved the present value of the restructured obligations. The 1982 and early 1983 experiences with external debt servicing difficulties in Latin America, however, suggest that the probability of outright unwillingness to repay external obligations could increase in the mid-1980s and beyond. Thus, greater attention should be given to political risk assessment at international-oriented banks, as these evaluations in the past have been too heavily weighted towards economic (ability to repay) factors. There are two main reasons that suggest the need for increased attention to political risk variables:

- The external debt servicing issue has become publicized in Latin America. Countries such as Mexico, Chile, and Argentina have become much more assertive in exercising their significant leverage as large borrowers. For example, according to a recent Federal Reserve survey, U.S. banks had $81 billion in claims outstanding in Latin America as of June 30, 1982, of which $64 billion was owed to the top 24 banks in the U.S.

- The economic and social costs of servicing external obligations in a disinflationary environment have sharply increased for Latin American borrowers. Thus, from a country perspective the calculus of benefits and costs of repudiating external obligations cannot be simply assumed to be weighted heavily against such an event.

In addition to political risk assessment, recent experiences with the external debt servicing problems of most Latin American countries suggest that greater attention should be given to:

- The U.S. policy mix, and the impact of such a mix on the international economic environment. To a significant extent, the degree of severity of Latin American debt servicing problems can be traced to the so-called "monetarist" revolutions of the Federal Reserve on October 6, 1979. Federal Reserve policy led to the overshooting of the dollar exchange rate, and to a much diminished worldwide dollar liquidity. At present, the mismatch between U.S. monetary and fiscal policies is threatening to abort an incipient world economic recovery, which in turn will have very serious and adverse consequences on the external debt servicing capacity of Latin America.

- Internal policies that would shift domestic income shares in favor of the export sector of Latin American countries. Exports relative to GNP are, for example, less than 10 percent in most major Latin American countries, versus 32 percent in Korea nd 47 percent in Taiwan. Therefore, an export-led growth strategy will be required not only to service the present stock of external obligations, but to also regain the confidence of international lenders that future additions to this stock can be serviced. A necessary, but not sufficient, condition of this structural shift in the relative composition of GNP is more appropriate exchange rate management. In my view, the present external debt servicing difficulties of Mexico, Venezuela, Chile, Ecuador and Argentina can be traced, in part, to relatively poor exchange rate management.

ISSUES IN COUNTRY RISK ASSESSMENT

Donald E. Baer

Country risk assessment from a banker's viewpoint entails the evaluation of economic, social and political factors, which may exogenously impair a borrower's ability to service, in an orderly fashion, external debt commitments. Country risk assessment is part science, part art, and a recognition and blending of these two facets is essential to yield successful results. Most important, and at times most difficult, is integrating the input obtained from country risk assessment, which may run contrary to a bank's current marketing goals, into the bank's decision-making process. The current era of disrupted external lending strategies is accelerating efforts to make country risk assessment both more accurate and more integrated into a bank's management decision-making process.

In part, country risk assessment is dependent on utilizing historical data to evaluate trends in a country which may indicate, in an early warning fashion, countries where debt service problems appear on the horizon. Models can be utilized to assess significant deviations from past or normal trends by evaluating a series of significant economic variables which may affect debt servicing capacity. Meaningful country risk assessment also calls for projecting such key variables into the future. This latter aspect is at times more art than science.

Variables typically incorporated in country risk assessment include a series on the country's balance of payments, and such other information as its current account balance, its dependence on primary commodities, the openness of the economy, the differential between exchange rates and inflation, and the like. Additionally, a series of variables evaluating the internal economy, such as investment, domestic savings capacity, its public sector deficit, its per capita GDP performance, and the structure of its GDP, need to be included. Moreover, much attention is to be placed on external debt and its composition, external servicing, arrears accumulations, as well as direct investment inflows.

On top of these economic variables, country risk analysis must include meaningful assessment of political and social risk factors. Such evaluation calls for input from non-economists from external specialists as well as from those of the country in question. Such political and social risk input must then be blended into the bank's full country risk assessment process.

Successful projections in times where linear trends cannot be anticipated, and where historic business cycles are not applicable, make the qualitative input by the analyst particularly important. Most of all, it calls for serious assessment of the underlying assumptions being utilized. For instance, one well regarded economic model in 1981 forecast Brazilian economic performance in the 1982-85 period, with current account deficits in 1982 of $12.6 billion, in 1983 of $12.9 billion, in 1984 of $14.5 billion and in 1985 of $15.8 billion. Real GDP in Brazil, according to these projections, was to once again grow from the 0.4 percent level achieved in 1981, to 3.1 percent in 1982, 4.5 percent in 1983, 5.0 percent in 1984, and 5.3 percent in 1985. These are linear type projections based on past experience. However, none of these forecasts approached reality. What happened was that the model assumed the external capital inflows would continue to support such current account deficits in a continuing fashion. But this assumption was unrealistic. Rather than chronic $13-$16 billion current account deficits in the 1983-85 period, Brazil now projects deficits of $6.9 billion in 1983, $5.1 billion in 1984 and $4 billion in 1985. Whether these new targets are achievable can also be questioned, but the trend change is clear. These changes resulted, in large part, from the alteration of a key assumption: that banks would continue to support such high chronic current account deficits.

Therefore, country risk analysis calls for viable underlying assumptions. On top of these assumptions, there are other key factors such as industrial-country recovery, commodity prices, interest rates, petroleum prices and many others that should be taken into consideration. Obviously, this area of significant volatility and non-linear price and rate changes makes the country risk analyst's job unenviable. Projecting too far into the future in this current environment may prove to be more of a disservice than an attribute—since it undertakes more than can be reasonably delivered. The use of alternative scenarios under different assumptions can be of some value and these are in fact utilized by economists and econometricians in country risk analysis. But in the end, for integration into a bank's final decision-making process, a best-guess scenario is required. On the one hand, this kind of answer tends to frustrate rather than impress management trying to incorporate country risk into decision-making. More acceptable to management would be periodic revisions of analysis as conditions change. This calls for continuous, rather than periodic, input and makes country risk analysis more than a once or twice a year exercise, which in the past decade has tended to be the norm.

SOUTH FLORIDA AS A GATEWAY TO U.S. TRADE WITH LATIN AMERICA

J.Kenneth Lipner and Amitava Dutt

Introduction

By 1980, of the $220 billion of total U.S. exports, $37 billion was exported to Latin America and the Caribbean; $15 billion of these exports were sent to Mexico, primarily across the land border from California to Texas, $7 billion were shipped from South Florida* alone and the remaining $15 billion were exported from ports all over the U.S. The figures from 1980 show that 40.3 percent of all U.S. exports to the Caribbean and 20.7 percent of all U.S. exports to South America were shipped through South Florida.[1]

These figures document the importance of the South Florida region in the trade between the U.S. and the Latin American and Caribbean regions (which we shall call, for reasons of brevity for the purposes of this paper, the Latin American region). The object of this paper is to examine how South Florida has assumed this preferential position to assess how this posture is likely to evolve in the future and, finally, to comment on its implications for the South Florida economy.

To understand the importance of South Florida in U.S./Latin American trade, we first need to examine the nature of the role it plays. This is done in section two, in which we characterize South Florida as a central place where U.S. exports are routed to the Latin American economies. Some implications of this characterization are then spelled out. In section three, we present some econometric evidence confirming that our characterization conforms to the actual pattern of South Florida exports. In section four we examine how, assuming that our portrayal of the situation is correct, South Florida's role in U.S.-Latin American trade may be expected to evolve in the future. In the fifth section, we briefly comment on the implications of these tendencies for the local economy.

South Florida as a Central Place

One of the first facts that is noticed about the exports from South Florida is that most of them are not produced in the region, but are products from other parts of the U.S. What this immediately implies is that the South Florida region is only a link in a chain connecting the U.S. and the countries importing its products. The obvious question that arises is, are there any economic reasons why Miami has on its own emerged as an important link in the chain, or is it just that it happens to be along the way? The answers to this have obvious implications for the question as to how the importance of the nexus will change in the future.

To understand this question one can draw on the literature of central places in the economic theory of location, which tries to explain the clustering of firms, and also studies the conglomeration of retail stores in shopping centers.[2] The query posed is the following. Suppose there are a group of buyers and a group of sellers in a region. Why will there then be a tendency for the sellers to cluster geographically in a single area? The literature usually refers to the indivisibilities from the buyer's side—in finding goods, purchasing and transporting them. But there could also be indivisibilities on the sellers' side, starting from such simple ideas as the joint use of walls which economizes expenses, to the complex sharing of infrastructure and institutions. This analysis can also be

---

*Throughout this paper the terms South Florida Region, Miami Region, and the Region are used interchangeably.

applied to the reasons for the growth of trading centers. Producers and consumers will obviously be located at different points—producers, presumably because of some production advantages those points must bestow upon them, and consumers, for reasons such as choice or history. However, the trade between these buyers and sellers can be expected to be routed through a few trading centers, where buyers and sellers can reap the advantages of sharing financial institutions, insurance companies, warehouse facilities, freight forwarders, customs brokers, consular offices, and the like. The importance of such trading centers is increased in the case of trade between buyers and sellers separated by cultural and linguistic barriers, since in theses situations, knowledge of foreign markets and the ability to set up foreign trading contacts would be scarce resources, and need to be shared in a single central area. Historical examples of trading centers, especially those linking two different cultures, abound. There are also contemporary centers in the U.S. itself: San Francisco for Asian trade and New York for European trade.

This analysis implies that in trade between two economies, even if initially these are several trade links, given the passage of time a more limited number of trading areas will emerge. One may visualize a process by which those with some specific advantages will become increasingly important and compete the other centers away. Once these centers with some initial advantages begin to grow in importance, there will be a tendency for the kinds of institutions and infrastructure previously mentioned to develop in those areas. The other trading centers will then begin to lose their importance. The process may be thought of as a cumulative one, in which, given some initial advantages, these centers are likely to keep increasing in relative importance through the interaction of trade and infrastructure-institutions growth. It also seems to us that there are increasing returns to this process, since the growth of such institutions and infrastructure leads to lower average (implicit) costs of trading. Economic theory tells us that increasing returns usually results in complete specialization. What this suggests is that unless there are some specific bottle necks to the growth of the central area, in the form of capacity constraints, the fastest expanding area (on the basis of its initial advantages) will have a tendency to draw trade away from its less advantaged peers.

It is our contention that South Florida has emerged as "the" trading center between sellers in the U.S. and buyers in the Latin American region. It is not difficult to explain why this has happened. A mere look at a map of the Western Hemisphere shows that the South Florida region juts out like a dagger (a friendly one, of course) into Latin America. This proximity implies that routing exports through the South Florida region economizes on distance. Also, because of this nearness, the more frequent availability of services of both ships and planes from this region to the Latin American countries, as well as the fact that domestic insurance rates are lower than those found abroad, helps the area become the natural point of exit for goods destined to Latin America. Finally, due to this proximity, the Miami region has been the point of entry for immigrants from the Latin American regions, causing Miami to have a concentration of the scarce resources that make it easier to bridge the cultural and ethnic barriers preciously mentioned. Given these initial advantages, the growth of the Miami region as a central place is easily understood. The discussion of the possibilities of its growth is postponed until section four.

Determinants of Exports from South Florida to Different Countries

In this section, we propose to examine whether the available data confirm that our characterization is correct. We have argued above that the South Florida region has developed as a central place because of the advantages it has in terms of the distance to markets and its ethnic composition. If this hypothesis were correct, we would expect to observe that, other things being equal, South Florida's exports should be greater to countries which are closer to it, and to those which are Spanish-speaking and Latin ethnic composition. On the other hand, if the region was not developing as a central place, one does not necessarily expect to find such a correlation.

To examine the data, we have used the approach of the social physics school, which has tried to explain differences in the levels of one country's exports to another by focusing on different variables, and using regression analysis to see how important the different variables are.[3] Following this approach we may expect the exports from South Florida to a particular economy to depend positively on its level of GNP (with a larger market size), inversely on its population size (which increases the size of domestic markets and therefore reduces dependence on trade), inversely on distance from South Florida (since greater distance increases trade resistance by raising transport costs and breeding unfamiliarity which reduces interaction). Also, since Latin and Spanish-speaking countries are ethnically and linguistically closer to the South Florida region, one would expect such countries to have greater imports from the region, assuming that such factors give any advantage to the South Florida region at all, as we have argued above. We have estimated the equation in log linear form,[4] as follows:

$$\log X_j = a_o \log Y_j + a_2 \log P^j + a_3 \log D^j + a_4 \, ECD_j + a_5 \, OD_{j\ x} + u_j$$

where the a_i are the constants to be estimated, X_j the exports from South Florida to country j, Y_j the GNP for country j, P_j the population of country kj, D_j the distance of country j from South Florida. ECE_j is a dummy variable measuring ethnic composition of country j: it takes a value of 1 if the country had a majority of Spanish speakers, or Spanish and/or Mestizo populations, and 0 otherwise.[5] OD_j is another dummy variable which reflects the existence of other U.S. ports closest to country j: if there was some other port such as Los Angeles, New York, Tampa, New Orleans, Houston, among others, closer to the main city in country j, the variable takes a value of 1, and O otherwise. It is clear from our discussion that a_1 and a_4 may be expected to be positive, and a_2, a_3 and a_5 to be negative.

We have used the method of ordinary least squares to estimate the above equation using a sample of 47 countries which had the highest levels of imports from the South Florida region. This included all the Caribbean and Latin American economies for which data were available for all the variables used, several European, Canada, and some Asian and African countries. The data on GNP and population were obtained from the World Bank Development Reports and refer to midyear estimates for 1979.[6] Data for the value of exports to each country were taken from the Miami World Trade Report (MWTR) and refer to values for 1980. The ECD dummy series was constructed from the Appendix of the MWTR, while the distance variable—we had to have separate air and sea distances--was obtained by measuring the usual shipping route to the main port in each country and the air route to the largest city in each country.

We ran two separate equations, one for value of exports by air and the other for the value of exports by sea, using different distance and OD variables for each. While the detailed results and interpretations of these equations need not concern us here, and will be examined on another occasion, we should note that despite several limitations of our analysis, we obtain generally plausible estimates. What is important for the present context is that the distance variables and the ethnic composition dummy have coefficients of the expected sign (see Appendix I).

One serious deficiency of our approach has been the failure to consider trade policies in the importing countries, for which no simple explanatory variable could be constructed. To rectify that problem we took the ratio of South Florida exports to total U.S. exports to each country, and estimated a function of the form

$$\log R_j = a_o + a_1 \log D_j + a_2 \, ECD_j + a_3 \, OD_j + u_j$$

where R_j is the ratio mentioned above. Notice that we have not included the GNP and population variables, since both should affect total and South Florida exports in the same way, since South Florida exports are primarily goods produced in the U.S. and sent through South Florida. Given South Florida's unique ethnic composition, the variable capturing this characterization has been kept to examine the importance of that factor, and the other dummy variable has been maintained since the existence of other closer ports can be expected to reduce South Florida's share. The distance variable has also been retained. The form in which we keep it can be justified in the following way: if a country is further away from the South Florida region, the latter's export share will fall, even if it implies that other U.S. ports are also further away, since greater distance weakens the relative advantage of the region.

Our regressions have a fair amount of explanatory power, and all the signs turn out to be as expected. In particular, countries with Latin-Spanish ethnic composition tend to import relatively more from South Florida, and so do the countries closer to it (see Appendix I).

The econometric evidence presented in this section can be interpreted as showing that distance and ethnic composition are important determinants of the magnitude of trade. And with South Florida having geographical proximity to, and ethnic similarity with, much of the Latin American region, the region has important advantages, making it a natural central place in U.S.-Latin American trade.

South Florida's Future Role

We have argued in the above sections that the South Florida region has emerged as a central trading place between the U.S. and the Latin American economies. We now examine the future outlook.

If our analysis is correct, then it would seem that the importance of the South Florida region should grow, and further, that there may in fact be tendencies for complete specialization of this region, assuming there are no capacity constraints for the growth of the area as a trading center. The cumulative process, resulting in more Latin American trade being routed through South Florida, can then be expected to continue.

South Florida's institutions and infrastructure seem to be growing rapidly, and no capacity bottlenecks appear to be emerging. Ambitious expansion plans are currently under way at Miami International airport, already the world's fifth largest air cargo facility (ranking behind New York (JFK), Los Angeles, Frankfurt, and Chicago) and the world's ninth busiest passenger airport. The seaport of Miami is currently improving operating efficiency by adding two modern state-of-the-art gantry cranes, which will speed the loading process and decrease demurrage costs. Since 1976 through 1981, the Miami seaport has experienced an average increase in tonnage of 13.5 percent over the preceding year (see Appendix II). To the north of Miami, the underutilized Port Everglades in Ft. Lauderdale is available for overflow or expansion. In addition to the physical facilities, the financial infrastructure includes 44 international foreign banks, 41 Edge Act banks, a 37-member consular corps representing virtually every nation in Latin America and the Caribbean, and direct airline service by the national airline of these countries and territories to and from Miami.

Without capacity bottlenecks, we find no reason for the cumulative process not to operate. That the process is making some headway is seen from the way Miami seems to be capturing a larger share of the Latin American trade away from New York. Given the low volume of Latin American trade prior to 1974, the development of a new central place for that trade was not previously warranted, and it could be handled through the previously established center of New York, a center which had developed because of the European trade. With the growth of Latin American trade, however (more of this later), and with the development of the Miami region as a market area, one can expect the South Florida region to continue to capture a larger part of the market away from New York. Increased shares in the southern cone of South America and Brazil (although

Portuguese speaking), and perhaps even indirectly in Mexico through the development of a Caribbean sea link for manufactured and transhipped goods, are strong possibilities.[7] There also do not appear to be major competitors in the South, which could enjoy some geographical advantage in the Latin American trade. Examination of the Gulf ports of Tampa, Mobile, New Orleans and Houston shows that the trade from these regions does not resemble trade from South Florida, and hence are not competing with it.

Implications for the South Florida Economy

We have argued in the above sections that the South Florida region has emerged as the central trading link between the U.S. and Latin America as far as exports are concerned, and that its importance in this area is likely to grow. Thus this region can be characterized as a gateway to U.S. trade with Latin America. We examine briefly the implications of all this for the local economy of South Florida. The implication will depend on two factors: (1) the growth of total exports from South Florida, and (2) the relationship between the growth of exports and local economic performance. We discuss these in turn.

The growth of total exports can be seen to depend on three factors: (i) the growth of total imports, especially by the Latin American region; (ii) the share of the U.S. in Latin American imports; and (iii) the share of South Florida in U.S. exports to Latin America. We have up to now focused only on the third of these factors. The second factor is beyond our present scope, depending, as it does, on the competitiveness of U.S. industries vis-a-vis their exporting rivals, and also on the commodity composition of Latin American demands. The first factor clearly depends on the growth prospects of the Latin American economies (something which other papers have looked at), on the trade bias of such growth, and on the trade policies pursued in these countries. Our analysis of these factors led us to believe that despite the current recession, the long-term prospects of increased total trade of the U.S. with the Latin American region are good, provided U.S. competitiveness is not too sharply eroded in commodities in which the U.S. now enjoys a comparative advantage. This implies that total exports from the South Florida to the Latin American region may be expected to grow.[8]

We now turn to the other factor, the implications of a growth in exports for the South Florida economy. Since most of the exports are not produced in the region, the value-added (in South Florida) components of exports from the region can be expected to be small. However, a casual look at the data on export growth and regional performance seems to suggest that the implications of export growth on the local economy—together with the associated growth of infrastructural facilities and tourism, etc.—may not be negligible.

Conclusion

In this paper we have shown that the South Florida region has become an important point of exit for U.S. goods destined for the Latin American region. We have argued that the role of the region in this trade can be approximately characterized as a central place, to borrow a term from the theory of location. We have further argued that as such a central place, the role of this region in the trade between the U.S. and Latin America is likely to increase, and such developments can be expected to have a favorable impact on the local economy of the region.

ACKNOWLEDGEMENTS

This paper addresses some of the issues we have been concerned with in an examination of export data made available in the Miami World Trade Report. We would like to thank Robert Cruz, Raul Moncarz and Jorge Salazar-Carrillo for discussions, and George Depaolis and Robert Schwarzreich for research assistance.

FOOTNOTES

1 See Miami World Trade Report.

2 See Losch (1954), which is the pioneering work. See also Eaton and Lipsey (1982) for a recent presentation.

3 For a survey of the literature on the economic applications of Social Physics in general, see the paper by Isard and Bramaball in Isard (1960). For a survey of applications to international trade, see Olsen (1971).

4 Apart from tradition, there seems to be no overwhelming reason to use this form; we experimented with several other forms, but chose to adhere to this one on account of its relatively good fit.

5 Some countries, such as Bolivia, which did not have an absolute majority of these elements, were given a value of 1 if it was clear that the economy was dominated by these elements.

6 For those economies for which no data were available, we used data from the Appendix to the Miami World Trade Report.

7 In 1980 only 1 percent of exports to Argentina, 7 percent to Brazil and .6 percent to Mexico, were shipped through South Florida. Given these low shares, the possibilities of increasing them, especially at the expense of New York, seem high. Given probable increases in transport and communications cost relative to distance, this seems to be a likely development.

8 We should comment on the importance of factor (i). Not only is it important to the extent that if total trade with Latin America fell and South Florida's share of that falling trade increased, that would not necessarily imply greater exports from the region, but falling Latin American trade may even spark off a cumulative process away from Miami. The importance of such an eventuality is based on the significance of Latin American trade, so that factor (i) has a direct bearing even on the share of the South Florida region on U.S. exports to Latin American economies.

REFERENCES

Eaton, B. C. and R. G. Lipsey, "An Economic Theory of Central Places," Economic Journal, March 1982.

Isard, Walter, Methods of Regional Analysis, MIT Press and Wiley, New York and London, 1960.

Lipner, J. Kenneth, Miami World Trade Report, Downtown Development Authority and Florida International University, 1981, 1982.

Losch, August, The Economics of Location, Yale University Press, New Haven, 1956.

Olsen, Erling, International Trade Theory and Regional Income Differences, North Holland, Amsterdam and London, 1971.

World Bank, World Development Report, 1981.

APPENDIX I

This appendix reports the fitted equations referred to in the text, section 3. The notation of the text is used here, with X,R,D and OD replaced by XA, RA, DA, ODA and XS, RS, DS, ODS, depending on whether the relevant variables refer to air or sea variables.

For the value of exports, the fitted equations are:

$$\log XA = \underset{(4.92243)}{12.5096} + \underset{(1.56)}{.39472} \log Y + \underset{(.65)}{.179423} \log P - \underset{(-2.89203)}{.76144} \log DA + \underset{(1.4064)}{.662425} ECD \underset{(-3.19)}{-2.15835} ODA$$

$R^2 = .63$
F = 13.342

$$\log XS = \underset{(5.93)}{14.2059} - \underset{(-.92)}{.261576} \log Y + \underset{(.69)}{.241151} \log P - \underset{(-1.54)}{.230731} \log DS + \underset{(1.98)}{1.10796} EDC \underset{(-2.34)}{-1.10796} ODS$$

$R^2 = .46$
F = 6.811210

The figures in parenthesis are the t-statistics

For the ratio of exports, the fitted equations are:

$$\log RA = \underset{(4.56)}{6.01865} - \underset{(-1.83)}{.327170} \log DA + \underset{(2.84)}{.77986} ECD - \underset{(-8.62)}{3.10726} ODA$$

$R^2 = .88$
F = 98.92292

$$\log RS = \underset{(3.22)}{4.21606} - \underset{(-1.88)}{.294479} \log DS + \underset{(3.10)}{1.53672} - \underset{(-5.04)}{2.46829} ODS$$

$R^2 = .57$
F = 18,48847

CARGO SHIPMENTS FROM THE PORT OF MIAMI

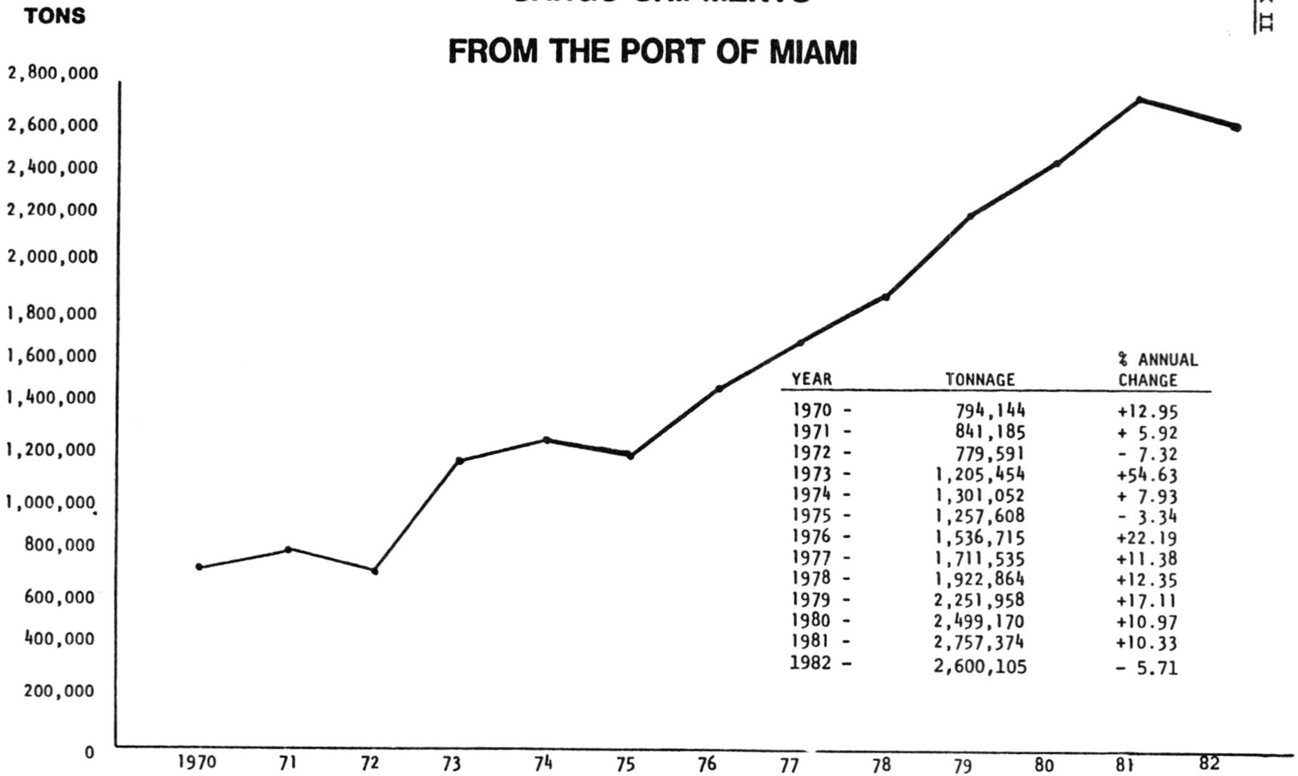

YEAR	TONNAGE	% ANNUAL CHANGE
1970 -	794,144	+12.95
1971 -	841,185	+ 5.92
1972 -	779,591	- 7.32
1973 -	1,205,454	+54.63
1974 -	1,301,052	+ 7.93
1975 -	1,257,608	- 3.34
1976 -	1,536,715	+22.19
1977 -	1,711,535	+11.38
1978 -	1,922,864	+12.35
1979 -	2,251,958	+17.11
1980 -	2,499,170	+10.97
1981 -	2,757,374	+10.33
1982 -	2,600,105	- 5.71

Source: Metro Dade County, Seaport Division

SOUTH FLORIDA AS A GATEWAY TO U.S TRADE WITH LATIN AMERICA

Edward K. Smith

In their paper on U.S. trade with Latin America, Professors Lipner and Dutt have taken central place theory from regional economics and applied it to South Florida's role in international trade. As international trade is only a special instance of the more general case of inter-regional trade, their application is an apt one.

The results obtained are fruitful. They document the importance of the South Florida region in trade between the U.S., Latin America, and the Caribbean. They also show why South Florida has attained dominance in Latin American and Caribbean trade and speculate about its future. In addition, the authors comment on the importance of this connection to the South Florida economy. Their paper, especially if it is read in conjunction with Robert Cruz's analysis of the impact of foreign trade on the economy of South Florida, which was derived from the FIU South Florida econometric model, reveals the increasing role of exports in the South Florida economy, as opposed to imports from Latin America, which were dominant in the early 1960s.

Miami has emerged as a geographic center for Latin American trade and will, in all probability, continue to grow in that direction. As this growth proceeds, economies of scale will increase the economic (cost) advantages of Miami over other ports. Moreover, specialized services are arising which are complementing and increasing these economic advantages. The growth of international banking in the Miami area is an example of this sort of complementarity. As the agglomerative forces proceed over time, specialization leads to further efficiences and the region's competitive advantages are strengthened.

The Lipner-Dutt model shows that the South Florida location and its ethnic composition, among other variables, do indeed have the expected effects on trade growth. The model is a log-linear regression and does not tell us how important each of the variables are, an exercise which must come from a more sophisticated explanatory model which we would hope to see in the future. It does, however, show that the variables of population, distance and ethnic composition have the expected signs. One can infer from the results that the Miami area fits central place description.

It is important to note that the model oversimplifies, but does not distort, the "real world" of South Florida trade. The data employed were drawn from an earlier study of Miami world trade done by Professor Lipner for the Downtown Development Authority of Miami. These data included over 1.5 million pieces of trade information from U.S. Department of Commerce trade data tapes. Within these data are answers to a host of questions which should be of interest both to students of economic development and South Florida business developers, especially the Miami port authorities. Professors Lipner and Dutt, who were constrained by the usual time limits of conference proceedings were unable to discuss many issues at length. I would hope that the authors continue their work and shed more light on the phenomena of an expanding Miami in order to enhance the opportunities for business planning and its more effective support by the public sector.

We need to know more of the sources of growth and identify the best ways in which to increase Florida's income and employment. Now that the FIU staff has made the investment in the models and software necessary to manage and manipulate the data, business and government should support their efforts by funding the yearly update and analysis of the data base. In doing so, time series analysis will be possible as well as the cross-sectional approach of the present study, thus vastly enhancing the analytical capabilities of, and output from, data-based economic analysis. In the process some of the more outlandish guesses on the importance of trade in South Florida may fail to meet statistical verification, but a body of new insights to possible trade opportunities will likely be revealed.

THE IMPACT OF FOREIGN TRADE ON THE ECONOMY OF SOUTH FLORIDA: AN ECONOMETRIC MODEL FORECAST

Robert D. Cruz

Background

The character of South Florida's economy changed significantly during the decade of the seventies with the emergence of a discernible set of business activities which are dependent upon the Latin American demand for U.S. goods and services. The massive Cuban immigration of the late sixties had already made its imprint on the socio-cultural character of the region by the mid to late seventies, with the obvious emergence of business ties between area enterprises and "Latinization" of South Florida.[1] A brief look at transportation and banking data will serve to illustrate the strengthening commercial ties between the region's economy and the economies of Latin America and the Caribbean.

In 1960, approximately 411,000 tons of cargo were handled through the Port of Miami, with incoming cargo exceeding outgoing cargo by a ratio of just over a three-to-one.[2] In the early sixties, then, Miami was primarily a point of entry for Latin American goods into the U.S. market. By the mid 1960s, however, exports were growing at a much faster pace than imports, and during the 1970-72 period it became evident that exports now surpassed imports. During the period, the Port of Miami handled just over 800,000 tons of cargo per year, while Miami International Airport registered about 175,000 tons of foreign cargo shipped through its facilities. Approximately 55 percent of this combined cargo activity resulted from exports. The largest increases in foreign cargo activity were experienced in the latter half of the seventies, and by 1981 Miami's airports and seaports were servicing 1.8 million tons of exports, while imports had grown to 976,000 tons. So within two decades, the international commercial role of the region had changed from one of a point of entry for U.S. imports from Latin America to one of a gateway for U.S. exports to Latin America.

A similar dramatic expansion was also experienced in the number of international air passengers using Miami's airport facility. During the sixties, the airports' number of international passengers grew at a trendline rate of 14.4 percent, while in the seventies the pace of expansion decelerated to 7.5 percent. The region has become a transportation center for cargo and air passengers in transit between the U.S. and most of the countries of Latin America and the Caribbean. Along with the growth in air passengers and air and waterborne cargo serviced through the region's ports, there has also been a rapid growth in foreign tourists.[3]

One of course cannot mention the growth of international commerce in South Florida without noting either the growth of Latin American headquarters of multinational corporations (MNCs) or of the growth of foreign banking operations in the area. By 1980, over 100 MNCs had offices in the region, whereas a decade earlier there were virtually none. Edge Act and foreign banks located in the area have also grown at a fast pace. In 1975 there were nine Edge Act banks,[4] but by 1982 this number had grown to 44 and offices of foreign banks, moreover, numbered 36.[5] Federal Reserve Bank data also show significant growth in international lending and deposit activity within the region.

Unfortunately, the data on international banking are presented at a highly aggregated level with only loans to banks in foreign countries and deposits of foreign government central banks and private foreign banks being reported. Table 1 compares this financial data for the Miami and New York SMSAs and for the State of Florida, and also illustrates its growth since 1975 through 1979. From this table we can see that international banking in the area has grown rapidly, that area banks dominate international banking in Florida, and that international banking in the area has gained in size relative to New York, although it is still very small by comparison.

A question often asked by local observers and yet to the adequately addressed is, what is the impact of foreign trade and commercial activity on the local economy? Before we turn to this question, however, we must clearly identify what we define as "foreign trade and commercial activity." For the purposes of the following discussion we will consider three types of activities as being associated with the "foreign sector" of the local economy: the volume of exports and imports shipped via the Port of Miami and Miami International Airport, foreign tourists and international air passengers.

While much attention has been given to real estate purchases (particularly commercial properties) by Latin American investors, the bulk of these transactions been asset transactions and do not represent demands for new construction. The effect of these transactions on local construction activity is not perceived to be appreciable. While there is usually a service activity involved with any asset transaction, particularly a real estate transaction, the direct employment effects of these transactions are not likely to be significant relative either to total employment or to the employment impacts resulting from cargo, international tourism, and international air passenger activity. Hence, our definition of foreign trade and commercial activity excludes real estate transactions.

Table 1
International Banking Statistics: Commercial Banks
($ millions)

	1976	1977	1978	1979	1980
Loans to Banks in Foreign Countries					
Miami, SMSA	67.9	99.2	126.8	166.5	250.9
% of (net) loans	2.3	3.0	3.3	3.9	5.3
New York, SMSA	n.a.	3481	4917	3963	5528
% of (net) loans	n.a.	4.4	5.7	4.0	5.0
Florida	77.8	105.3	137.6	172.4	272.6
Deposits of Foreign Public and Private Banks					
Miami, SMSA	55.3	55.2	61.4	85.7	83.8
% of all deposits	0.9	0.9	0.9	1.1	0.9
New York, SMSA	n.a.	13715	12942	12343	13439
% of all deposits	n.a.	11.2	9.8	9.1	8.8
Florida					

Source: Federal Reserve Board, special tables
n.a. = not available for this year.

The Importance of Foreign Activity on the Recent Economic Growth of South Florida

To examine the role of foreign activity on the local economy, one must have an explicit view of how the local macroeconomy behaves and how the demand pressures in one industry, which lead to direct changes in the industry's level of employment and payroll, give rise to demand pressures in other local industries. That is, any phenomena which directly lead to an expansion of employment in one industry, should also lead to an indirect expasion of employment in other industries. Our view of how the local economy functions is given in the South Florida Econometric Model.

A complete description of the model is beyond the scope of this essay and is fully described in a forthcoming monograph. We may say, nonetheless, that the model is similar to national econometric models in general, and other metropolitan econometric models in particular. There are two important differences, however, between the South Florida Model and other metropolitan models. The first is that the South Florida Model explicitly considers differences in average production costs between the region and the nation, as well as the size of the local economy, as important determinants of local manufacturing activity. The second unique feature of the model is its emphasis on population growth as a source of economic expansion. Special attention, moreover, has also been given to the local impact of international commercial activity.

In the model, air and seaport cargo activity and international air passengers are important direct determinants of employment in the transportation industry, while the level of foreign tourists directly affects employment in private services. Since international banking has been primarily focused on trade financing, international trade activity through area ports is also a direct determinant of employment in the finance/insurance/real estate industry.

In the model we also recognize that import activity through area ports is related to export activity, given that ships and cargo planes returning to the area would find it profitable to return with cargo rather than return empty. Moreover, the relationship between international tourism and international air passengers has been explicitly considered in specifying the model. We have also structured our equations which determine air and sea cargo to reflect the differential importance of U.S. exports to various regions of Latin America. The data from the United Nation's International Trade Statistics allowed us to analyze the local impact of U.S. exports to three regions: Venezuela and Colombia, the Central American Common Market Countries (CACM),[6] and the remaining developing market economies of the Western Hemisphere. The exact specifications of the equations in the "foreign activity sector" of the model appear in the appendix to this essay.

This specification of the model, therefore, allows us to simulate the historical economic growth of the region under alternative assumptions regarding the pattern of development of the area's foreign sector. That is, to examine the historical importance of foreign activity in the area's economic growth, we have simulated the model under the assumption that international air and seaport cargo, international tourism and international air passengers remained at their 1963 levels throughout the 1963-79 period. In reality waterborne cargo increased three fold, international aier cargo increased five fold, international air passengers increased seven fold and international tourism increased four fold during this period. We then compare the simulated values, given by the model under the alternative assumptions, with the results using the actual historical values for these four data series.

Although the model allows us to examine the impact of this difference in foreign activity on many different economic variables, ranging from retail sales and residential construction to total wage earning and the unemployment rate, we have chosen to characterize the historical impact of foreign activity by examining three key variables: total wage and salary employment, total personal income and personal income per capita. The first two variables characterize the aggregate economic performance of the region, while the latter can be viewed as a crude measure of economic welfare. Figures 1-3 illustrate the impact on these three variables.

Each of these figures shows a growing importance of foreign commercial activity in the local economy over time. By 1979 a stagnant foreign sector implies a decline in employment of 96,000 persons, or 9.2 percent below that year's simulated workforce when the actual values of the foreign activity variables are considered. When we note that in 1979 five of the nine major non-farm industries[7]each had actual total employment of less than 85,000 the importance of foreign activity in total employment is quite impressive. Nevertheless, the results indicate that the common perception that foreign commercial activity accounts for as much as 25-30 percent of total employment is quite exaggerated.

The effect of the stagnant foreign activity sector on local area personal income is illustrated in Figure 2, where one may discern an impact similar to the one we've noted for employment. By 1979, the personal income gap resulting from zero growth in foreign commercial activity reaches $1.4 billion, or 5.8 percent below the value simulated under the actual historical circumstances. We should note, however, that the burden of nearly all of this decline in income falls on wage earning. Given that the lower income groups depend very heavily on wage earning, a lack of growth in foreign commercial activity would have led to a deterioration in the degree of equality in local income distribution.

Figure 3 illustrates the two patterns of growth in per capita income under the alternative assumptions. In this figure, a widening gap is also discernible. By 1979, under the assumption of stagnant foreign commercial activity, per capita personal income is etimated to be $580 less than the historical simulation under actual foreign activity conditions.

Figures 1-3 illustrate that foreign commercial activity has indeed played a key role in the area's overall economic expansion. Since most of the area's trader flows are with Latin America,[8]it is, therefore, important to consider the local impact of changes in U.S. exports to this region.

Table 2 presents the impact multiplier effects from changes in U.S. exports to different regions in Latin America and the Caribbean. In the upper half of this table we present the impact on employment and real personal income (in 1979 dollars) resulting from an approximate decline of 30 percent[9] in U.S. exports to Venezuela, Venezuela and Colombia, CACM countries and the countries of the Latin American Integration Association[10] (excluding Venezuela and Colombia), respectively. When the model is simulated with a $1.35 billion decline (at 1979 prices) in U.S. exports to Venezuela, local employment declines by 137,00 and regional personal income falls by $178.4 million.[11] A decline in exports of nearly $1.9 billion to both Venezuela and Colombia leads to an employment decline of just over 19,000 and a loss of $251 million in the region's personal income. By contrast a decline of $9.6 billion in U.S. exports to ALADI countries, excluding Venezuela and Colombia, leads to a loss of 6,3000 employment positions, and a $83 million loss in personal income. A proportionately similar decline of $600 million in U.S. exports to the CACM countries leads to a loss of about 800 jobs and a loss of $11.5 million in personal income. The implicit (one-period) multiplier effects of these changes in U.S. exports, which are calculated in the lower half of Table 2, suggest that changes in trade with Venezuela and Colombia have appreciably larger repercussions for the local economy, than U.S. exports to either of the other two defined regions of Latin America.

We can suggest two primary reasons for this large differential impact. The first is that Venezuela and Colombia are by far the two largest markets for exports via South Florida Customs District 52, while South Florida's exports to the remaining members of ALADI combined account for less than Venezuela's share alone. South Florida's exports to Venezuela and Colombia accounted for 33 percent of all exports, even though they accounted for only 13 percent of all U.S. exports to Latin America and the Caribbean (1980).[12] In sharp contrast, we find that South Florida's exports to the ALADI countries, excluding Venezuela and Colombia, account for less than 18 percent, while U.S. exports

Table 2
Local Impact of a 30 percent Decline in U.S. Exports to Latin America

Total Wage & Salary Employ. U.S. Exports to:	Gross Personal Income (thousand)	(1979 $ Million)
Venezuela[1]	-13.7	-178.4
Venezuela and Colombia[2]	-19.1	-259.6
Central American Common Market[3]	-0.8	-11.5
ALADI (exc. Venezuela and Colombia)[4]	-6.3	-82.6
"Export" Multipliers (per $100 million at 1979 prices)		
Venezuela	1.01	13.2
Colombia	1.01	13.2
CACM	0.13	1.9
ALADI	0.07	0.9

Notes: [1]Based upon a $1350 million decline in U.S. exports (1979 prices) or roughly 30 percent of U.S. exports to Venezuela in 1980.

[2]Based upon a $1870 million decline in exports to both countries or nearly 30 percent of U.S. exports to both countries in 1980.

[3]Based upon a $600 million decline in exports to these countries or nearly 30 percent of exports in 1980.

[4]Based upon a $9600 million decline in exports to these countries or 30 percent of exports in 1980.

The Importance of U.S./Latin America Trade Prospects in the Short-run Growth of the Local Economy

For most of the 1970s the economies of Latin America, particularly those of Venezuela and Colombia, grew at exceptionally fast rates, and the U.S. experienced a concomitant increase in its exports to this region. But during the opening years of this decade, world wide recession, declining export earnings and unrealistic exchange rate policies (combined with financial market deregulation in some countries) led to sharp decelerations in the rate of economic growth of most countries and significant declines in some economies. With the recent apparent collapse of the OPEC cartel and anticipated sharp reductions in oil prices, significant declines in the Venezuelan and Mexican economies and their imports from the U.S. are virtually certain. For countries with large oil import bills, such as Brazil and the small countries of Central America and the Caribbean, a decline in world oil prices will stimulate their economies. But the greatest economic stimulus to these countries may result from an increase in demand for their commodity exports, deriving from a larger than expected recovery in the industrial economies which itself would be precipitated by a significant decline in petroleum prices.

To illustrate the importance of economic activity in Latin America on the local economic performance, we have simulated the South Florida Model for the 1983-85 period under three distinct assumptions regarding the future path of U.S. exports to these countries. In all simulations, however, we have maintained the same pattern of growth in the U.S. national economy. Let us first describe our assumptions regarding the future path of national economic performance.

For purposes of this essay it is not essential to state our assumptions regarding the rate of change in each of the national economic variables which appear in the South Florida Model; instead we will focus on the key national variables which affect the model and note that our assumptions regarding the remaining variables are consistent in that they are the result of a national macro model.[13] Local manufacturing output and employment critically depend upon national manufacturing industry performance and we have anticipated that national value-added output in manufacturing will increase in real terms by 3.2, 7.1 and 5.4 percent in 1983, 1984 and 1985, respectively. National residential housing starts, which characterize the general economic environment in which local residential construction activity takes place, is expected to grow at rates of 30, 21, and 14 percent, respectively, during the 1983-85 period. The last key variable which we need to consider is the inflation rate as measured by the rate of change in the GNP implicit price deflator. Our simulations are based on a national inflation rate of 5.2, 5.4 and 6.3 percent, respectively, over the forecast horizon.

Table 3 illustrates three alternative scenarios for the growth of U.S. exports to Venezuela, Colombia and the rest of the developing market economies of the Wester Hemisphere. These alternative growth paths are referred to as the optimistic, baseline and pessimistic export scenarios. The optimistic scenario assumes that speculative pressures on the Venezuelan currency do not persist in 1983, and that a major collapse of world oil prices is averted, allowing sufficient export earnings which permit a 5 percent increase in the nominal value of U.S. exports to Venezuela in 1983. With a recovery of world energy prices in 1984 and 1985, Venezuela's export earnings are assumed to be sufficient to allow a growth of 12-25 percent, respectively, in its imports from the U.S. Under the optimistic scenario, U.S. exports to Colombia increase by 10 percent in 1983, followed by gains of 12 percent in 1984 and 25 percent in 1985. This same growth path for U.S. exports to the remaining developing countries of the hemisphere is assumed under the optimistic scenario.

In contrast, the pessimistic scenario is based on a sharp drop in Venezuela's imports from the U.S. this year, with only a partial recovery in 1984 and a moderate expansion in 1985 (see Table 3). Similarly, this scenario envisions an appreciable decline in U.S. exports to Colombia and the other LDCs of the hemisphere in 1983, only a partial recovery in 1984 and moderate expansion in 1985.

The more "reasonable" scenario is that of the baseline forecast, which anticipates a moderate decline of 10 percent in U.S. exports to Venezuela in 1983. This is followed by a complete recovery in 1984 and moderate expansion in 1985. An increase of 5 percent in the value of U.S. exports to Colombia in 1983 is assumed under this scenario, with gains of 10 and 15 percent following in 1984 and 1985, respectively. The other LDCs are expected to experience gains of zero, 5 or 15 percent in their demands for U.S. exports over the forecast horizon. The implications of each of these three scenarios are presneted in Table 4.

Table 3
U.S. Exports to Latin America: Alternative Scenarios

Exports To:	Annual Rates of Growth in Nominal Exports (%)		
	1983	1984	1985
Venezuela			
Optimistic	5.0	12.0	25.0
Baseline	-10.0	10.0	15.0
Pessimistic	-30.0	20.0	20.0
Colombia			
Optimistic	10.0	12.0	25.0
Baseline	5.0	10.0	15.0
Pessimistic	-10.0	12.0	20.0
Rest of Developing Countries:			
Optimistic	10.0	12.0	15.0
Baseline	0.0	5.0	15.0
Pessimistic	-15.0	12.0	20.0

Table 4
Forecast Simulations: South Florida

	1982*	1983	1984	1985
Wage & Salary Employment (000)				
Baseline	1260	1298	1364	1427
Pessimistic	-	1281	1348	1414
Optimistic	-	1309	1381	1456
Rate of Growth in Employment (%)				
Baseline	1.9	3.0	5.1	4.6
Pessimistic	-	1.7	5.2	4.9
Optimistic	-	3.9	5.5	5.4
Unemployment Rate (%)				
Baseline	8.1	9.3	7.9	7.1
Pessimistic	-	9.3	8.4	7.3
Optimistic	-	9.3	7.8	6.9
Gross Personal Income (million $)				
Baseline	38028	41936	47002	52843
Pessimistic	-	41617	46588	52548
Optimistic	-	42137	47352	53493

Note: *Historical estimates.

This table illustrates the importance of foreign commercial activity on the future dynamic path of the economy. The level of employment in 1983 is reduced by 17,000 in the case of a serious decline in U.S. exports to Latin America and the Caribbean, while the rate of employment growth is reduced to 1.7 percent form 3.0 percent anticipated under the baseline scenario. We should note that while the negative impact of a severe drop in exports on employment and income is significant, the effects are not large enough to offset the positive influence of a recovery (albeit a weak recovery) in the national economy. In the "worst case" scenario, major economic difficulties in Latin America, particularly in Venezuela, lead to a rate of growth in employment similar to that witnessed in 1982. Part of the loss in employment and income is regained during 1984 and 1985, but these variables remain below their levels in the baseline scenario.

The primary conclusion we wish to draw from this table is that while the local economy is sensitive to the economic performance of its southern neighbors, the economic ties are not so strong as to reslut in a major disruption in the local economy when the Latin American economies are experiencing severe difficulties. The experience of the late seventies and early eighties, moreover, suggests that cyclical fluctuations in the U.S. economy and the Latin American economies do not necessarily coincide. Consequently, one may view the emergence of Miami as a center for U.S./Latin American trade and commerce as a source of economic stability in the region, as well as an important factor in the long-run growth of the South Florida economy.

FIGURE 1

EMPLOYMENT: SIMULATION

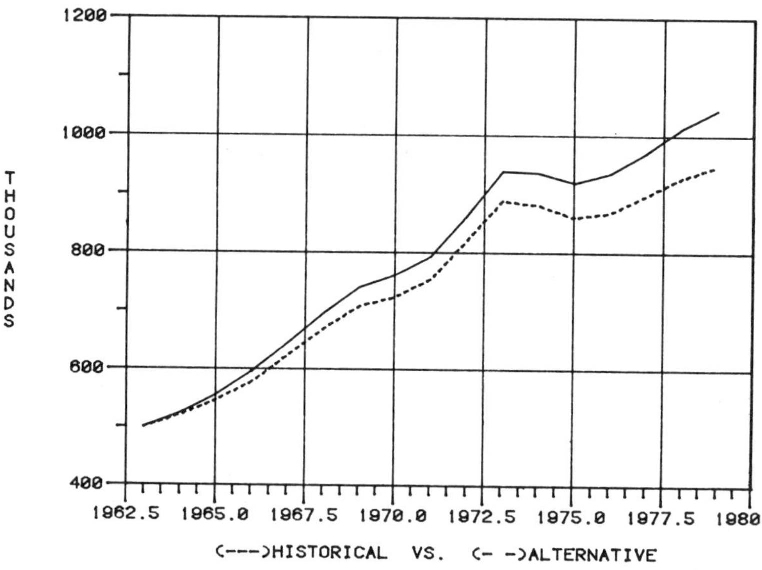

FIGURE 2

GROSS PERSONAL INCOME: SIMULATION

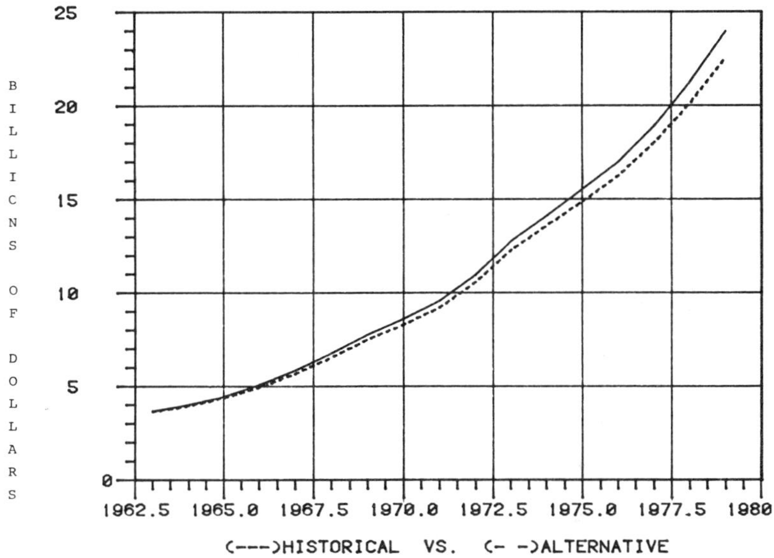

FIGURE 3

PER CAPITA PERSONAL INCOME: SIMULATION

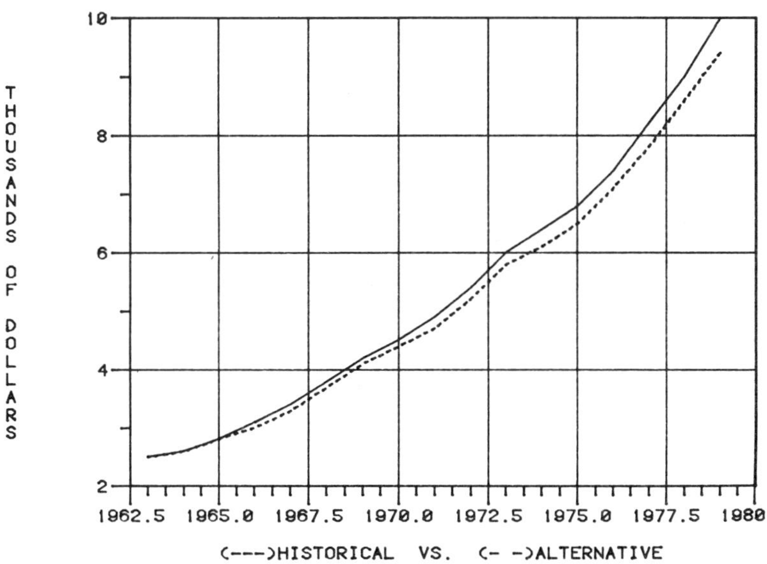

Appendix

The Foreign Activity Sector Equations
of the South Florida Model

*Tons of Export Cargo from Port of Miami: R2 = .96

$$PMXCAR = \underset{(-4.5)}{-331.609} + \underset{(4.2)}{0.689117}\,(UXVNTR + UXCOTR) + \underset{(0.3)}{0.72824}\,(UXCACMR) + \underset{(0.8)}{0.0229242}\,(UXOTHR)$$

Tons of Export Cargo from Miami International Airport: R2 = .97

$$MAXFCA = \underset{(-4.7)}{-64.37} + \underset{(3.8)}{0.119142}\,(UXVNTR + UXCOTR) + \underset{(0.9)}{0.0937102}\,(UXCACMR) + \underset{(1.2)}{0.00683852}\,(UXOTHR)$$

Tons of Import Cargo via Port of Miami: R2 = .86

$$PMMCAR = \underset{(0.9)}{111.358} + \underset{(2.3)}{0.313846}\,(PMXCAR) + \underset{(1.0)}{0.319031}\,(UMAMDR)$$

Tons of Import Cargo via Miami International Airport: R2 = .94

$$MAMFCA = \underset{(1.0)}{12.6843} + \underset{(2.4)}{0.305451}\,(MAXFCA) + \underset{(0.6)}{0.0021962}\,(UMAMDR) + \underset{(1.2)}{0.0250496}\,(MAXFCA-1)$$

Foreign Tourism Index: R2 = .96

$$STURFI = \underset{(-0.1)}{-0.2043} + \underset{(4.5)}{0.053621}\,(UXVNTR + UXCOTR) + \underset{(0.8)}{0.00352876}\,(UXCACMR + UXOTHR) + \underset{(1.4)}{0.120509}\,(SPOPSL3MA)$$

International Air Passengers: R2 = .97

$$MAPINT = \underset{(-1.8)}{-444.657} + \underset{(2.7)}{25.6217}\,(STURFI) + \underset{(1.6)}{0.43286}\,(MAPINT-1)$$

---

*Note: t-statistics appear in parentheses below estimated coefficients

UXVNTR == U.S. total eports to Venezuela, deflated by a unit value index for all U.S. exports

UXCOTR == U.S. total exports to Colombia, deflated by a unit value index for all U.S. exports

UXCACMR == U.S. exports to CACM countries, deflated by a unit value index for all U.S. exports.

UXOTHR == U.S. exports to other market developing countries in Western Hemisphere, deflated by a unit value index for all U.S. exports.

UMAMDR == U.S. imports from market developing countries in Western Hemisphere, deflated by a unit value index for all U.S. imports.

SPOPSL3MA ==Three-year moving average of South Florida's population of foreign origin: Hispanic.

ACKNOWLEDGEMENTS

I would like to thank F. Gerard Adams, Raul Moncarz, Antonio Jorge, and Jorge Salazar for helpful discussions. Also the FIU Foundation and International Banking Center, which provided support leading to the development of the South Florida Econometric Model. Research assistance was provided by George Depaolis and Marjorie Rodriguez.

FOOTNOTES

[1]See A. Jorge and R. Moncarz, "Latin-Anglo Cross Cultural Influence and the Political Economy of Change." Mimeo, Florida International University, March 1982.

[2]Source of seaport data: Port Authority, Port of Miami.

[3]Dade County's Division of Tourism estimates that in 1982 foreign tourists accounted for 22.1 percent of all tourists, while this category represented only 6.4 percent in 1970.

[4]Jan Luytjes, Raul Moncarz, Emmanuel Roussakis, et al. "Foreign Banking Operations in Florida: Its Economic Impact and Future Potential," mimeo. F.I.U., 1979.

[5]J. Kenneth Lipner, "Miami World Trade Report," mimeo. F.I.U. and Downtown Development Authority, June 1982.

[6]This includes Honduras, El Salvador, Costa Rica and Guatemala.

[7]The five are agricultural services/fishing/forestry/mining, construction, transportation and utilities, wholesale trade, and finance/insurance/real estate. The remaining four are retail trade, private services, government and manufacturing.

[8]See J. Kenneth Lipner, "Miami Trade Report."

[9]From 1980 levels.

[10]ALADI's members are Venezuela, Colombia, Argentina, Bolivia, Chile, Mexico, Peru, Paraguay, Uruguay, Ecuador and Brazil.

[11]All export and personal income figures used in Table 2 are at constant 1979 prices.

[12]Export data is from J.K. Lipner, Miami World Trade Report, 1982.

[13]Our national forecast assumptions are drawn from the "Wharton Long-term Model: Short-term Update," Wharton Econometric Forecasting Associates, Inc., January 1983.

THE IMPACT OF FOREIGN TRADE ON THE ECONOMY OF SOUTH FLORIDA: AN ECONOMETRIC MODEL FORECAST

Mickey D. Levy

Professor Cruz's paper reports on his findings and methodology in an important topic of economic research that has received far too little systematic analysis. Accordingly, I wholeheartedly encourage his continuing effort in this field. Since the paper reports on the results of an empirical model, my comments are necessarily limited until he publishes his monograph that includes specifications of the equations in the model.

The paper provides an overview of foreign trade in Miami, and then reports on simulations of local economic activity from 1962 to 1967 in which four parameters (waterborne cargo, international air cargo, international air passenger, and international tourism) of the model are varied to measure their impact on three economic variables of the same model: (1) total wage and salary income, (2) personal income, and (3) personal income per capita. These simulated results are then compared to actual data: an important finding being that foreign trade activity has a significant influence on the South Florida economy, but an impact not as large as the 25 percent-30 percent employment figure that has been casually mentioned on several occasions. The paper then measures the effect of the U.S. foreign trade with Venezuela, Colombia and Central American Common Market Countries (CACM). Again, the measured impacts are substantial. Finally, simulations for the period 1983 to 1985 are conducted based on the estimated parameters.

The general conclusion of the paper is that the Miami economy is sensitive to foreign trade, and its stability is enhanced by the large foreign trade sector. However, it concludes that the effects of foreign trade on Miami are outweighed by the reverberations of the U.S. economy on the local economy.

I do have several comments on the paper. First, the analysis seems to be limited to the impact on the South Florida economy of only merchandise trade. This category includes foreign tourism, but excludes real estate transactions. Since real estate transactions are not merely redistributions of assets but also generate other economic activities, I would recommend either strictly limiting the analysis to foreign trade, or expanding the category to include real estate. Second, I believe the study underestimates the full impact of foreign trade by neglecting some of its indirect impacts, particularly on raising the demand for banking and other white collar service industries. It is noteworthy that banking follows commerce, and more international commerce generates demand for lawyers, accountants, and other professionals who on average earn above-average wages and also generate the demand for other service industries. In this regard, the effects on total employment, income, and income per capita may be underestimated.

Third, there may be some problems with portions of the model although, as stated earlier, any comments must be considered preliminary until the full set of equations can be analyzed. The equations for exports from the Port of Miami and the International Airport are too mechanical, with the right-hand variables merely being the component exporting companies. As structured, there is no room to measure the sensitivity of imports and exports to relative exchange values or changes in gross national product or gross domestic product, or to consider other structural variables that also may influence foreign trade. Fourth, on a more technical note, each time-series equation should show Durbin-Watson statistics to validate its results. In the equations displayed, the R^2s are high and the t-statistics low, which suggest that autocorrelation may be present. Adding a lagged dependent variable may improve the forecasting ability of the model, but on the other hand, may diminish the significance of the other right-hand variables.

Fifth, in general, I believe this paper attempts to cover too much ground. Instead, it should emphasize one direction of causality and go into more detail.

In conclusion, despite the reservations I have about the empirical work and my suggestions, I applaud Professor Cruz's effort in this admittedly difficult topic of research and, moreover, I find the results to be quite plausible. Clearly, further research in this area would be fruitful and should be pursued.

CLOSING STATEMENT

Lionel H. Olmer

Most of the attention given to the international debt problem has centered on the question of debits and credits, something for the banks and the countries in the developing world to work out with the support of international assistance agencies. But this is not merely a financial problem, it is also a trade problem of growing seriousness. Reaching a comprehensive understanding of the trade, economic and financial aspects of this complex issue is crucial to finding long-term solutions to the debt situation. I would like to illustrate the interrelated nature of this issue, focusing in detail on the pressures building on the trading system.

Finance

The borrowing of LDCs, which has grown dramatically since the first oil shock over nine years ago, was for a time offset by increasing economic growth and expanding exports. It allowed for a rapid rise in U.S. exports to these countries, and strong growth in the LDC and OECD economies. However, this borrowing was also a way for some countries to postpone adjustment to the first oil shock as a combination of increasing export earnings, low interest rates and high inflation kept real debt burdens manageable.

After the second oil shock of 1979 and the beginning of the current world recession, the situation in many LDCs took a dramatic turn for the worse. Interest rates rose worldwide, yet most LDCs attempted to avoid adjustment by increasing short-term borrowing. A declining demand for exports and an outright drop in export prices (primarily commodities) left LDC exports earning in 1982 unchanged from 1980 levels. With rising real interest rates, short-term debt growing rapidly and export earnings flat or declining, banks became unwilling or unable to maintain the pace of lending required to sustain the debt service of key LDCs.

Many LDCs which have accumulated large amounts of debt are currently unable to attract capital inflows or run the current account surpluses necessary to service this debt. At their present stage of development many LDCs cannot be expected to be net exporters. The U.S. was in a similar stage of development in the 1800s. U.S. current account deficits averaged close to 25 percent of total exports. External debt averaged over 300 percent of exports between 1885 and 1890 and interest costs ranged between 10 and 15 percent of exports. These ratios were well above those recorded by most LDCs over the last two decades. If our creditors had gotten cold feet during that period, then the U.S. economy might not have developed as rapidly as it did and, consequently, decisions made in the U.S. banking community today might not have been so crucial to the world economy.

These decisions are crucial, however, and we should recognize the global implications of the policies we choose in addressing the current problems. Many banks are heavily exposed to developing LDCs and some would like to reduce exposure to these countries by reducing new lending. However, if this is done before LDCs can trim their financing needs, the countries will have to make further deep import cuts, even cuts into essential imports, or fall behind in debt repayments. The extent of our financial and trade relations with these countries means that the business community and/or the banking community would be adversely affected.

Trade

The trade area is probably experiencing the most immediate effects of the problems in the financial and economic systems. We have witnessed sharp drops in U.S.

exports in the last 18 months. U.S. trade with Mexico dropped 36 percent in 1982, with the decline accelerating in the latter part of the year. Sales to Argentina were down 40 percent, to Peru 25 percent and Chile 36 percent.

These developments stand in sharp contrast with the rest over the last 10 years, when these countries were part of the fastest growing U.S. export market. Between 1970 and 1980, LDCs share of U.S. manufactured exports grew from 29 percent to 39 percent. Key U.S. exporters had made major inroads into LDC markets during the period. Now these same exporters are experiencing rapid declines (See Tables 1 and 2). Let me briefly cover the situation in Mexico, our third largest trading partner.

- Cereal and preparation exports had increased by more than 200 percent between 1978-81 and were down 71 percent last year.

- Transportation equipment (except road vehicles), up over 600 percent between 1978-81, was down 71 percent last year.

- Iron and steel, up over 200 percent in these three years, were down 58 percent last year.

- Manufactures of metals, up 354 percent from 1978-81, were down 52 percent last year.

The overall decline in exports to Mexico alone was $6.3 billion.

If financial constraints increase this year, LDC imports will have to be cut even further; thus, trade problems and the jobs they represent for American workers are likely to become even more worrisome.

In the area of trade-related financing we are getting reports of further disruptions. While it is difficult to collect precise data on trade financing activities, we have recent reports from bankers and trading companies along the following lines:

- The so-called "balance of payments" or "general purpose" credits, which LDCs often use to buy commodities and other consumables, have been curtailed. Medium-term lending to support capital goods exports to high-debt LDCs has also been reduced, but at this stage it is impossible to determine exactly to what degree.

- Most major international banks in the U.S., Europe and Asia appear to be maintaining short-term trade credit facilities to problem LDCs, but the overall volume of this type of credit appears to be down sharply from last July's level (i.e., prior to the Mexican crisis). Banks appear to be confining short-term export credit to deals which benefit long-standing domestic corporate clients, or to key customers in LDCs, and for products which are essential for the functioning of LDC economies. New exporters or traders who now want bank financing for their sales are suffering most.

- In conducting business with some countries, many exporters are seeking bank cover for sales that have traditionally been concluded without the need for credit. This has placed added pressure on the financing of U.S. and international trade, since banks are unwilling or unable to increase lending to accommodate the influx of new requests for credit. As a result, a trade financing gap has developed which could produce an unplanned constraint on OECD-LDC trade for some time to come and make the availability of finance the major limiting factor in export sales.

Because of the convergence of growing debt, worldwide recession, and resulting liquidity problems, a substantial global upsurge in countertrade is occurring. Saddled with inadequate export marketing networks, with protection growing in some markets, with lagging demand for exports and a shortage of hard currency, non-market economies and developing countries have turned to countertrade practices as a means of restoring their trade balances, to redress external debts, to maintain employment levels and hopefully to find markets for their exports.

Major trading companies faced with the contraction in trade finance report that they are inevitably moving towards barter as a means of maintaining trade relations. But barter is a voluntary arrangement and should be distinguished from countertrade. In essence, countertrade is a form of reciprocal, conditional or linked trade, involving a requirement to purchase as a condition for sales to a particular country.

Estimates of the total amount of countertrade and barter are rough at best. However, a recent assessment by the Chase Manhattan Bank's Trade Information Corporation asserts that between one-fourth to one-fifth of total world trade is under some form of barter and, further, that the proportion is rapidly growing.

While countertrade, particularly in this time of world recession, could be viewed as having the advantage of creating trade which might otherwise not exist, or at least mitigating the impact of shrinking trade flows amid the debt crisis, it poses significant problems with respect to our multilateral trading system. Foremost among the problems is the tendency for countertrade to reinforce bilateralism, and this runs counter to progress achieved in trade liberalization since 1945.

One other factor influencing the interrelationship between trade and finance is exchange rates and capital flows. In the past, the trade component of the current account had a large direct influence on exchange rates. If a country's trade account was in deficit, its currency tended to depreciate, eventually making its exports competitive, improving its trade account and later the exchange rate. More recently other factors have, for a time, offset the effects of trade flows on exchange rates. The dollar continued to appreciate the yen and most other OECD currencies over the last two years as we registered surpluses in our current account, despite continued large trade deficits. This changing relationship between trade and exchange rates is explained by growing international capital movements, which vastly exceeded trade-related currency movements which benefited our capital account, as high interest rates caused demand for dollar assets and for the dollar itself to rise. The result is exchange rates that are not as directly linked to trade as before.

This appreciation has hurt U.S. exports. Since 1980, the strength of the dollar has raised trade prices of U.S. manufactured goods by 30 percent relative to our industrialized competitors. A 30 percent differential is a difficult marketing obstacle to overcome. American companies that have worked for years to establish export marketing and distribution networks overseas are, in many instances, finding their efforts wiped out by a sudden inability to compete because of the strength of the dollar.

Exchange rates have not only affected trade, they have also affected the international financial situation. Latin American countries that had initially pegged their currencies to the dollar found their competitiveness deteriorate as the dollar climbed, just when the opposite result was required. Many substituted protectionist policies and subsidies to protect their trade balance. Eventually, most have had to devalue, raising the domestic currency cost of their debt repayments and their imports, while increasing domestic inflation.

Economic

The trade implications of the financial problem have further implications on economic activity. The economic growth in LDCs and in the OECD in the period between 1974-80 was to some extent fueled by the ability of banks (flush with OPEC deposits) to provide the liquidity needed for a rapid growth in trade with LDCs.

In the recent recession, the decline in the U.S. external account has been a contributing factor to a decline in GNP. In fact, 46 percent of the 2.6 percent drop in

U.S. GNP through the fourth quarter of 1982 can be explained by the deterioration in the U.S. external account. Had our exports of goods and services merely stagnated in the second half of last year, rather than falling sharply as they did, U.S. real GNP would have risen at an annual rate of 1.8 percent in the second half of the year--rather than the decline of 0.9 percent per annum that actually occurred.

A solid U.S. recovery will be needed to yield a revival in trade. However, high-debt LDCs will need to reduce their imports and expand their exports further, if they are to meet their debt service payments. The extent to which the trade account will be affected depends on the availability of bank and IMF lending. Estimates vary but sharp reductions in bank lending to LDCs could reduce their imports to the extent that OECD and U.S. GNP would be lower by as much as 0.5-1.0 percent relative to what it otherwise would have been.

This presents us with an economic double-bind. LDCs' ability to recover and service debt will ultimately depend on an increase in exports, after an initial decrease in imports. This will come predominately as the result of recovery in major markets in the OECD. Pressures in the OECD are building to restrict imports and to increase our exports. Since LDCs have been a major market for OECD export growth, we face a clear contradiction. There is no way we all can increase exports without imports also increasing, and without initial export expansion there can be no long-term global recovery. Unfortunately, the recession, unemployment and debt burdens are leading governments to look to self-defeating policies of import reductions and export expansion as a solution to their problems.

Political

The dilemmas facing us in finance, economics and trade will be difficult to resolve because they are backed by significant political pressures. Political pressures in the 1970s led to inflationary policies and slowed the needed adjustments in LDC economies. The steps that need to be taken now will be all the more difficult because those decisions were not taken earlier. However, the options now are fewer and the pressures greater. Both in developed countries and in LDCs there will be strong resistance to take the actions that are necessary if we are to extract ourselves from this situation and move on a path toward long-term growth.

In many LDCs, the adjustments that are required will be costly in terms of political and economic sacrifice. Where population growth exceeds economic growth, political pressures will build. OECD creditors may become the scapegoats for those who choose to blame the banks for their troubles, as well as for those who are unprepared to implement necessary adjustment policies. Pressures in the OECD will build to stop lending to these countries and to prevent an influx of LDC imports. With 32 million people unemployed in the industrial world, using less than abundant financial resources to buy LDC imports or to finance their debt will not be popular. The political double-bind will come as pressures build in the OECD to stop lending to LDCs and to slow importing, while in the LDCs, leaders may be pushed to further extend their debt and to move to new markets for trade.

Conclusions

I hope that this review of the financial, trade, economic and political situation illustrates the complexity of the problem we face. If, on the one hand, the necessary adjustments in LDC trade accounts are allowed to take place, this may retard OECD economic recovery, increasing in turn domestic political pressures in key LDCs and heightening trade tensions. On the other hand, expanding financial flows will increase bank exposure, add to LDC debt burden, and may delay the adjustment in LDC economies needed to resolve the debt dilemma. In addressing this problem, it is obvious that decisions taken on financial policies will have trade and economic policy implications.

I believe the following elements should be taken into consideration in approaches to the current problems.

Finance

On the financial side, the increase in IMF resources is the minimum necessary to meet the current liquidity problems. The IMF is the only institution that can ensure prudent adjustment in the LDCs and adequate lending by private banks. Just the fact that this money is available to avert future crises will assist in stabilizing international markets and should produce essential lending by international banks, including restoring confidence to normal trade credit facilities.

This new lending, it should be noted, will come from both U.S. and foreign banks, since U.S. banks account for a little over one-third of total banks' claims in LDCs. In considering the extent of U.S. bank participation in international lending, it will be necessary to recognize the multilateral commitments needed to maintain adequate credit lines. While I certainly do not think the banks are faultless in the current situation, their continued involvement is necessary for long-term solutions.

As I have pointed out, the trade area is probably the first to react to negative signals in the financial systems. The ensuing trade contractions affect U.S. economic activity and the credit available to domestic exporters. If we are to move toward long-term stability in the financial markets, then the increase in IMF resources must be the first step.

Trade

In the trade area, we need to assure that the financial problems do not cause unnecessary disruptions in the free market for goods. Multilateral and bilateral meetings have been taking place to discuss ways to maintain the openness of markets. The GATT balance of payments committee reviews the measures taken by countries to meet IMF trade-adjustment goals, and seeks to phase out trade-restrictive measures as quickly as possible. We need to seek greater coordination between the IMF and the GATT to ensure that the adjustments that take place do not add to protectionist pressures, but rather provide some opportunities for trade expansion. As economic recovery takes place, we must move to dismantle the destructive trade barriers built up over the past decade.

In the area of trade finance, it has been made certain that the financial packages put together for a number of countries include export credits, thus ensuring the U.S. loans assist U.S. exporters. Given the growing problem in trade finance, it is also being proposed that $10 billion in EXIM bank guarantees be part of this year's EXIM bank authorization. Given the inability for normal channels of trade finance to operate smoothly in this climate, the EXIM bank, FCIA and some private insurers will undoubtedly be crucial in preventing an even greater decline in U.S. exports to high-debt LDCs.

On the issue of countertrade, there has been response on two fronts. First, this matter is being discussed in bilateral consultation with several countries (Mexico, Korea and Indonesia) who support countertrade.

This question has also being raised in the OECD, the UN and the GATT. It has been requested that these organizations study and then set up a mechanism for consultations, so members can present their case and obtain satisfaction, if appropriate.

While this practice should not be encouraged, it has been necessary to provide practical advice to U.S. firms, lest they lose their export markets. An idealized view of a multilateral trading system should not interfere with the pragmatic need to assist U.S. exporters in the real world they confront.

Consequently, the Commerce Department has begun seriously to examine the implications of countertrade and barter, and to initiate educational seminars for American companies. Last month in Miami, a seminar was held for U.S. foreign commercial officers stationed in Latin America. That seminar also provided information on the export trading company legislation, signed into law by the President last year. Fortunately, that law will put U.S. companies in a much stronger position to protect and expand U.S. market shares in situations where countertrade practices most often take place.

It will be necessary for the Commerce Department to continue to consider what practical changes in U.S. policies and laws could help avoid unnecessary export losses. It will also be helpful to examine ways in which countertrade can be made more visible among exporting nations, so as to develop maximum conformity with accepted international trade rules, and also to reduce the chances for buyers to play one supplier against another.

Economic

The third side of the triangle of problems is the economic one. Fortunately, the U.S. economy is beginning the long awaited recovery. However, the U.S. alone cannot fuel a global recovery, but it must work to assure that contractions in financial flows do not throw LDC economies into reverse by halting the essential imports necessary for their economic progress. LDC imports are an important element in OECD GNP, and furthermore almost all analysts agree that global non inflationary growth is essential, if the debt and trade problems are to be overcome.

In order to again emphasize how closely related these problems are, I would like to summarize the most recent annual report of GATT.

The words "trade war" now appear almost daily in the headlines. This danger should not be over-dramatized. Memories of the 1930s, and the enormous stake which most countries have in a continued flow of goods and services, should rule out a sudden, large-scale breakdown in trade relations. The gradual but continuing accumulation of restrictions on international trade of course poses a threat to the multilateral trading system which we must not underestimate, but the more immediate danger may be that it will trigger a severe disturbance in the already troubled international financial system.

This danger was demonstrated in the decade of the Great Depression. Not even today can full agreement be said to exist on all points of the economic history of that unhappy period. The standard explanation has emphasized the central role of the absolute decline (by one-third) in the U.S. money supply. However, at that stage the collapse of confidence was already far advanced. More recent discussion has identified two factors which can explain how the process started. First, there had been, in the 1920s, a sudden large increase in international indebtedness, most of which was "dead weight debt" (inter-Allied war debt and German reparations). Second, diplomatic efforts of the decade had not succeeded in establishing an institutionalized international order capable of preventing a rapid deterioration in the conditions of international trade.

These more recent explanations emphasized that the international financial crisis occurred after the U.S. Congress passed the highly restrictive Smoot-Hawley Tariff Act in June 1930. The long congressional deliberations on the Act were followed anxiously by other governments, and when it was signed into law, commercial retaliation by a number of countries followed promptly. As trade declined, a growing proportion of the debts of business depending on export trade, and of foreign debts, became uncollectable. Thus it is not surprising that the U.S. banking crisis began with runs on banks in the agricultural exporting districts in the Southeast and Midwest of the country.

It is often argued that a shortage of international liquidity leads to protectionism. This brief review of recent history suggests, however, that the danger inherent in the present situation is just the reverse--that protectionism could cause an international liquidity shortage, one severe enough to produce a series of insolvencies.

In short, trade protectionism has to be resisted, not just for the usual reasons associated with free trade, but for the viability of the international financial and economic systems so painfully constructed since 1945. If we are to escape this danger, financial, trade and economic problems must be viewed in an integrated fashion.

Table 1
U.S. Trade With Selected Countries in Latin America, 1981–82
(Data in million of dollars except where noted)

	U.S. Exports				U.S. Imports				Balance		
			Change				Change				Change
	1981	1982	$	%	1981	1982	$	%	1981	1982	$
Argentina	2128	1268	-860	-40	1123	1065	-58	-5	1005	202	-803
Brazil	3742	3369	-373	-10	4333	4171	-162	-4	-591	-802	-211
Chile	1436	917	-519	-36	543	669	126	23	893	249	-644
Mexico	17353	11026	-6327	-36	13704	15488	1784	13	3649	-4462	-8111
Peru	1467	1103	-364	-25	1147	1072	-75	-7	320	31	-289
Venezuela	5347	5061	-286	-5	5575	4757	-818	-71	-228	304	532
Total for above 6	31473	22744	-8729	-28	26425	27222	797	3	5048	-4478	-9526
Latin America	40987	32092	-8895	-22	38548	37558	-990	-3	2439	-5466	-7905
All LDCs (incl OPEC)	84758	76026	-8732	-10	115288	98373	-16715	-15	-300530	-22347	8183
World	228870	207158	-21712	-9	259012	242340	-16672	-6	-30142	-5040	

Notes: Exports are Census basis, domestic exports, fas value.
Imports are Census basis, imports for consumption, customs value.

Table 2
U.S. Domestic Exports of Selected Product Groups to Six Countries in Latin America and the World, 1979-81 and 1981-82

Product Groups		Percentage Change 1981-1982		Average Annual Growth 1978-1981	
SITC Code	Product Description	Six Latin American Countries	World	Six Latin American Countries	World
79	Trans. Equip. except road moteor vehicles	-50.25	-15.99	+39.82	+21.42
04	Cereals and cereal preparations	-43.71	-24.25	+29.22	+17.68
78	Road Motor Vehicles	-37.39	-14.72	+21.19	+5.35
74	Industrial Machinery and Equip. (nes)	-32.62	-14.52	+22.98	+15.33
71	Power Generating Mach. and Equip.	-23.21	+0.27	+24.17	+17.00
72	Machinery for Particular Industries	-21.59	-10.89	+24.00	+20.04
77	Electrical Machinery, Appliances & Parts	-17.93	-3.91	+22.51	+15.95

Notes: Data refer to aggregate for: Argentina, Brazil, Chile, Mexico, Peru and Venezuela. Average annual growth rates for 1978-81 are compound rates from natural log regressions of the form $\ln(x) = a+bt$, with 4 observations. Commodity Groups are those totalling (for the six countries) more than $1 billion at the 2-digit SITC level of disaggregation.